Growth poles and regional policies

European Coordination Centre for Research and
Documentation in Social Sciences

3

United Nations Research Institute for Social Development

Mouton

The Hague - Paris

Growth poles and regional policies

A seminar

edited by

A. KUKLINSKI and R. PETRELLA

Mouton

The Hague - Paris

Library of Congress Catalog Card Number: 73-184763

Jacket-design by Jurriaan Schrofer

Printed in the Netherlands

Preface

In 1969 the United Nations Research Institute for Social Development (UNRISD, Geneva) and the European Coordination Centre for Research and Documentation in Social Sciences (CEUCORS, Vienna), organised an international conference of experts on the problems of growth poles and regional policies. Scientists from developed and developing countries, as well as from Eastern and Western Europe, presented and discussed during five days a series of reports dealing with economic, sociological, geographical and institutional aspects of growth poles.

The present volume contains the up-dated results of the conference. We hope that this book will constitute a useful contribution to international discussion of regional policies and planning and will help in defining more concrete and practical ways of setting up a growth pole policy in both developed and developing countries.

Donald V. McGranahan
Director UNRISD

Adam Schaff
President CEUCORS

Descriptive note

The book is essentially based on the reports presented and discussed at the experts group meeting in Geneva. A detailed description of the scope, organisation and discussions of the meeting is given by T. Hermansen (Chapter 6). One of the basic reports with related comments and two other papers presented at that meeting have not been included in the present volume because they have already been published in French *(Pôles de développement et centres de croissance dans le développement régional,* Paris, Dunod, 1970*)*.

On the other hand, the reports by L. H. Klaassen, L. Frey, T. Di Tella and M. Penouil have been revised and supplemented by the authors, taking into account the results of the Geneva meeting.

Finally, the editors have introduced two new papers which reflect to some extent the continued and fruitful exchange of views between the various participants which took place in the course of 1970 and the beginning of 1971 on this particular problem.

Contents

LEO H. KLAASSEN

1A

Growth poles in economic theory and policy

I. INTRODUCTION

The existence and growth of large cities has become one of the most common phenomena in our industrialized world. Urbanization and industrialization are so closely linked with each other that it is hardly possible to think of the one without implicitly thinking of the other.

Recent shifts in employment from manufacturing to services have still further accelerated the process of urbanization. Large cities become still larger, and even for the largest in the world there seems to be no limit to their further growth. Each growth seems to produce new stimuli for fresh growth in new expanding sectors.

This picture of the world is so familiar to all of us that they are still very few who appreciate the unbelievable precision required for the operation of the immensely complicated organisms that constitute our cities. And those who are interested in cities are only able to increase their limited knowledge step by step, still far from understanding the whole mechanism, but just beginning to understand some of its main features.

Yet such knowledge is indispensable if we want to build new cities, if we want to create artificially something that has grown in other places so naturally. And creating new cities is exactly what growth policy wants. It tries to establish a better balance in our countries where, on the one hand, there seems to be no limit to the growth of the largest of our cities, and, on the other, whole regions remain depressed through lack of employment, low incomes and low growth rates for both employment and income. Such a balance could be attained by the creation of new cities in a concentrated effort to start an urbanization process that has brought so much prosperity elsewhere.

This idea, basically that of Professor Perroux, is a fascinating one. But it can hardly be denied that our knowledge is still insufficient to pursue such a policy successfully. And lack of knowledge is not the only obstacle; political interference has also often prevented the application of even the very limited knowledge we have of the functioning of cities.

In this paper the author endeavours to make a modest contribution to the understanding of the mechanism of urban areas, of the mutual linkages between human activities of different kinds and of the consequences of a policy planned to influence the prevailing tendencies in this field in growing economies. The paper leaves many questions unanswered but the author hopes that the views put forward will stimulate further discussion.

2. BASIC AND NON-BASIC ACTIVITIES

The study of the economic linkages between human activities of different kinds in urban centres has been partly focussed on the relations between basic and non-basic activities. Basic activities in a centre are those activities which do not necessarily have to be produced within the centre, and consequently non-basic activities are defined as activities which have to be produced within the centre. Examples of basic activities are an oil refinery or a steel mill, a university or an international airport; non-basic activities are primary education, local shops, service stations, etc.

Some writers have adopted a slightly different approach and have defined basic activities as export activities and consequently non-basic activities as those performed for the local market.

Clearly, these two definitions are not identical. A firm may be exporting its products to other markets and simultaneously sell a part of its production on the local market. If the second definition is accepted, we would have to divide the activities of such a firm between exports and sales on local market and consider the first as basic and the second as non-basic. According to the first definition, all the firm's activities would have to be considered basic because the fact that the firm is exporting, and thus other centres are importing, proves that its products do not necessarily have to be produced within the centre but could just as well be imported. It follows that this definition does not consider it important whether the firm *exports* or not but solely whether it is in principle *able to export* or not. If this is the case, and the fact that the firm actually exports its products is accepted as proof of this, all its activities should be considered basic.

It will be clear that the difference between the two approaches lies in whether we consider import substitution activities as basic or not.

A simple model may show the relations involved.

By definition

$$Y = C + I + X - M \tag{1.1}$$

in which Y = income of the region or of the centre
C = local consumption
I = local investments
X = exports from the region
M = imports into the region.

If $$C + I = \alpha Y \text{ and } M = \beta Y + M_A \tag{1.2}$$

in which $C + I =$ total local expenditure, and M_A stands for autonomous imports, it follows that

$$Y = \frac{X - M_A}{1 - \alpha + \beta} \tag{1.3}$$

In (1.3) $\frac{1}{1 - \alpha + \beta}$ is the local income multiplier.

It is clear from (1.3) that it is basically irrelevant how the firm discussed earlier divides its total production between local sales and exports. At each income level there is a given demand for the firm's products. At a given production level it can either sell a part of its production to the local market and export the rest or sell its total production elsewhere. In the second case, local consumption being given, imports will be increased by the same amount as exports, leaving the difference $X - M_A$ unaffected. Since the definition should be judged according to its relevance to the explanation of income formation in the urban area, import substitution activities should be considered basic.

The consequences of this choice for the statistical measurement of basic activities are, of course, considerable. Exports are easily measurable but import substitution is not, since a number of firms *might* sell only to the local market but not necessarily *have to* do so. A second difficulty in the application of this method is the form in which statistical data are usually available. This difficulty is basically the same as is encountered in preparing input-output tables, namely, the fact that activities of a completely different nature (in our case: basic as well as non-basic) are presented in one figure under the head of 'sector activities'. In order to meet this difficulty, the following method, which we call the minimum-requirement method,[1] is proposed.

This method draws a comparison between the economic structure of cities of similiar population size and income level and determines from this comparison what part of the cities' activities is basic and what non-basic. First, determine for a sufficiently large number of cities of similar size the percentage of the population working (or of total income produced) in the different sectors. Let the percentage working in city i in sector j be p_{ij}. Then, determine for each sector the minimum percentage found. Let this be p_j^{MIN}. This percentage represents the minimum requirement in sector j. The sum of all this percentages, $p^{\text{NB}} = \Sigma\, p_j^{\text{MIN}}$, gives the total of all non-basic activities. The difference between p_{ij} and p_j^{MIN} gives for each city i the level of basic activities in sector j. Evidently

$$p_i^{\text{B}} = \sum_j (p_{ij} - p_j^{\text{MIN}}) = 1 - \sum_j p_j^{\text{MIN}} = 1 - p^{\text{NB}} \qquad (1.4)$$

It appears that for medium-sized cities $p_i^{\text{B}} = p_i^{\text{NB}} = 0.5$ which means that the local employment multiplier for these centres equals 2, or one person employed in a basic activity needs one person employed in non-basic activities.

Although the foregoing analysis represents only a very modest beginning in the study of linkages between activities in centres, it none the less gives us a first insight into the nature of these linkages, showing us that the income earned in basic activities is partly spent locally, and that local activities satisfy this demand.

As we proceed with our analysis it will become clear that links between activities are among the most important elements in the explanation of the clustering of economic activities in what we call cities. However, in order to understand more fully the relations involved, we will have to go considerably deeper into the complexity of these relations in the real world. In the following section the endeavour will be made to clarify this problem, step by step.

3. INPUT-OUTPUT STUDIES

We will try in this section to remove one very important assumption made in the foregoing analysis.

This assumption was that basic sectors are independent of each other. An increase in basic activities was assumed to influence via an increase in local income the level of activities in non-basic activities, but influences on other basic sectors were disregarded. Yet it can hardly be denied that extremely important linkages between basic activities also exist. These linkages should be fully taken into account.

Evidently, if due allowance has to be made for such linkages the picture becomes considerably more complicated, since in principle we shall have to be informed about the linkages between all the sectors before we can proceed with our study. Although input-output data are usually available at the national level, this is seldom the case at the local level, although our knowledge in this fields is gradually increasing.

Let us suppose however that we are studying a given city and that a recent input-output table for this city is at our disposal. We could then proceed by assuming a given increase in the level of activities of a given sector corresponding to a given increase in final demand, and could go on to estimate the increase in the level of activities in all other sectors as initiated by the original increase in final demand.

If A denotes the matrix of input-output coefficients, Z the matrix of intermediate product flows and $\hat{g}$ the diagonal matrix of outputs in each sector, then

$$A = Z\hat{g}^{-1} \tag{2.1}$$

Furthermore,

$$g = Zi + e \tag{2.2}$$

In postmultiplying (2.1) by $\hat{g}$ we find

$$A\hat{g} = Z \tag{2.3}$$

Substitution of (2.3) in (2.2) gives

$$g = A\hat{g}i + e = Ag + e \tag{2.4}$$

$$g = Ag = e \text{ or } (I - A)\, g = e \tag{2.5}$$

in which I is the unit matrix.

From (2.5) it follows that

$$g = (I - A)^{-1}\, e \tag{2.6}$$

which gives the relationships between final demands and output in each sector.

Since, furthermore, the value added fractions are defined as

$$\frac{v}{g} = (I - A)'\, i \qquad (2.7)$$

total income y equals

$$Y = (\frac{v}{g})'\, g = i'\,(I - A)\,(I - A)^{-1}\, e = i'e = E \qquad (2.8)$$

in which E is total expenditure.

This means that the value added created by a final demand equals this increase.

In proceeding in this way we are taking the linkages between *all* the sectors into account but evidently not the influence of the primary income created on the activities in non-basic sectors, which we studied in section 2. There are thus considerable differences between the two approaches. The first and most important is that in the input-output analysis we may assume an increase in final demand of *any* sector and calculate the total effect in this sector plus all other sectors. In the basic – non-basic approach it would be very unrealistic to assume an increase in activities in a non-basic sector since such an increase could only result from an increase in the level of activities in a basic sector.

A second difference already mentioned is to be found in the fact that in the basic – non-basic approach the demand equations for the products of each sector as a function of income created in the basic sectors were introduced, while in the input-output analysis we are studying only the technical relations between production in different sectors and the inputs needed to realize a production increase in one sector. In this analysis, the secondary effects of the income increase resulting from the increase in activities in all sectors on the demand for goods and services, notably in the non-basic sectors, are left out of account; in order to introduce this aspect we should have to introduce demand functions for each sector which would then make it possible to calculate the final effect on the local economy of an increase in a given sector.

The procedure is simple. In the equation

$$g = (I - A)^{-1}\,(e + f) \qquad (2.9)$$

e are expenditures which are a function of income and f are exogenous expenditures (in the terminology of our first chapter exports minus exogenous imports).

Since

$$\left(\frac{v}{g}\right)' = i'(I - A), \text{ then } Y = \left(\frac{v}{g}\right)' g = i'(e + f) \qquad (2.10)$$

Now (2.10) may be written as

$$Y = E + F = \gamma\, Y + F$$

So

$$Y = \frac{F}{1 - \gamma} \qquad (2.11)$$

which result is basically comparable to (1.3). γ in (2.11) equals $(\alpha - \beta)$ in (1.3).

With the introduction of the demand equations in the input-output analysis, we have obtained a more refined instrument than the basic – non-basic approach gave us. We have clearly moved one step nearer to attaining insight into the mutal relationships that exist between firms.

However, we have to realize that we so far analyzed only the demand side of the problem. Our next step will therefore be the introduction of the supply side. We will dedicate a part of the next section to this problem which is closely related to locational analysis.

4. AN ATTRACTION MODEL

4.1 *Introduction*

The relations studied so far have been basically demand relations. Our analysis holds not only for the demand for local services and goods initiated by the increase in local income, but also for the technical relations. There, too, we have introduced the relation between the level of production in a given sector and this sector's demand for inputs from other sectors. Thus in both cases an increased activity in one sector only is created by an increased demand for its outputs by some other sector.

There are, however, many cases in which an increased output in one sector stimulates activities in the sector which uses these outputs as inputs. In this case the rise in production in the second sector results from increased local production of inputs. A weaving industry might be established in a place where a spinning industry is situated, a pharmaceutical industry might be set up in a region because oil refineries are located there, agricultural processing industries might be stimulated by an increase in local agricultural production, woodworking and paper industries will base their activities on proximity to forest resources, leather industries will lead to the launching of shoe industries, etc., etc.

Any number of activities are initiated in an economy by the presence of supplying industries. In all such cases it is not local demand that stimulates growth but the supply of inputs on which a new industry can be built.

In considering this aspect, we come to the conclusion that the introduction of a new industry or the expansion of an existing industry in a region has not only the demand effects we studied in the foregoing chapter, but also supply effects. Only the sum of the two effects gives us a complete picture of the consequences of the introduction of a new activity.

Admittedly, the demand effect seems to be in the main a short term effect and the supply effect in the main a long term effect. The increase in demand will be immediately felt, i.e. simultaneously with the production increase, while the supply influence will have its effect gradually over a period of time. However, since we are studying the linkages between firms in general, we do not need to worry very much about the short or the long term. The only essential fact is that sooner or later both influences will have had their full effect. It is this final situation that is of interest to us.

4.2 *The measurement of supply- and demand-effects*

So far we have considered the influence of demand and supply on the activities in a given sector in general, without indicating whether these effects will take place within the centre or region we are considering or somewhere outside the region. In discussing the demand-effect, using the normal input-output analysis, it is not unusual to consider the import quotas as constant. In other words, it is assumed that an increased demand for a given product will be satisfied by local production and imports in the same ratio as has been the case in the past. This ratio is then assumed to be equal to the average ratio observed in the input-output table. In a somewhat more refined analysis, if more input-output tables for different periodes are available the marginal quotas can be used.

However, this procedure is not very satisfactory. It is based on the assumption that the ratios used are more or less normative, although in reality only a few observations are available. It would therefore be much more realistic to compare, for example, the import quotas with those for regions of similar size and try to determine which factors are responsible for the differences, and thus what quotas may be expected in the future.

This comparison introduces an important new element into the analysis, viz. the degree to which demand and supply effects *usually* modify the size of local production and income in a centre or region.

Obviously, such an analysis can only be made if sufficient statistical data are available. In the Netherlands input-output tables for the eleven provinces recently became available and made the sort of analysis indicated above possible. However, in order to elucidate the procedure described in this study, more elements will have to be introduced.

Let us consider the following equation:[2]

$$\varphi_{kj} = \lambda_d \, \delta_{kj} + \Sigma \lambda_l \varphi_{lj} \qquad (3.1)$$

In this equation

φ_{kj} stands for the fraction of total domestic production in sector k ($k = 1,2,\ldots, n$) produced in region j ($j = 1,2,\ldots, m$) and consequently φ_{lj} stands for the fraction of total domestic production in sector l ($l = 1,2,\ldots, n$) produced in region j.

δ_{kj} is the fraction of total domestic demand (final plus intermediary) for k-products in region j.

λ_d and λ_l ($l = 1,2,\ldots, n$) are the so called attraction coefficients.

It can be shown that $\lambda_d + \Sigma \lambda_l = 1$ (3.2)

if these λ's are defined as the relative importance of communication costs (including transportation costs) between the demand of sector l on the one hand and that of sector k on the other.

If communication with the consumers (thus with demand) is extremely important compared to that with the l – sectors, then $\lambda_d = 1$ and, consequently, all $\lambda_l = 0$. The equation then becomes

$$\varphi_{kj} = \delta_{kj} \qquad (3.3)$$

We say that in this case the industry is completely demand-oriented. Production in the region equals demandin the region. Neither exports nor imports of product k take place. Sectors for which $\lambda_d = 1$ are thus closely related to the sectors called non-basie in the first chapter. Production in this case increases only as a consequence of an increase in demand. The case corresponds to the assumptions of input-output analysis.

Another special case is when one $\lambda_l = 1$, and consequently λ_d and all other λ_l's are zero. The equation then becomes

$$\varphi_{kj} = \varphi_{lj} \qquad (3.4)$$

In this case the industry is completely l-oriented. An increase in demand has no influence on local production, the latter being completely determined by the local supply of l-products serving as inputs for industry k.

The general case is represented in equation (3.1). In this equation the λ's represent the 'importance' of demand or the supply of other sectors for the level of local production in each sector.

The λ's are the unknows in the equation and can be estimated by regression analysis if data for a sufficiently large number of regions or centres are available. The estimates are the basis for a matrix in which the coefficients for all sectors are gathered, after having been transferred to value-added or employment coefficients. The inverse of this matrix gives for each sector the total regional multiplier including demand as well as supply-effects (see 3.6).

4.3 *The size of the centre (region)*

In considering (as an example) equation (3.3):

$$\varphi_{kj} = \delta_{kj}$$

this equation might hold good for centres or regions from a given minimum size onwards but not for small centres or regions. If δ_{kj} represents the local demand for higher technical education, the supply of this sort of education will not necessarily be found in the same centre if demand in this centre is too small to warrant the creation of a technical university. If neighbouring centres or regions are added together until total demand corresponds to the minimum size of such a university, we will find the university in this larger region and thus find a correspondance between demand and supply for the group of regions as a whole. We will call the region, in which demand equals supply, the *relevant* region.

A relevant region will be small for a local tobacconist or a kindergarten and very large for an electronic industry, an international airport or a refinery.

In the general case (3.1), the relevant region can be found if the following procedure is applied. We start with the smallest size areas for which data are available. If the correlation coefficient is low, we proceed by properly adding smaller to larger areas. If coefficient of correlation of satisfactory size is found, this size corresponds to that of the relevant region.

When cities are compared, the size of the relevant region can be found in a slightly different way. We can start by grouping the cities of similar size and carry out the regression analysis starting with the group of smallest sized cities. Sectors for which satisfactory results are obtained, can be left out of the analysis. The analysis can then be made for the remaining sectors for the next largest cities etc.

In practice these procedures are somewhat difficult to apply since usually only approximate data are available for cities. In the Netherlands, input-output tables are only available for the eleven provinces (and some parts of provinces) and thus any analysis will have to be made on this basis.

4.4 *Historical influences*

The attraction analysis treated in the foregoing sections has in fact a considerable advantage over the usual input-output analysis since it not only takes demand effects into account but covers supply effects as well. It is therefore much more general and if extended to include the indirect demand effects it gives a much more complete picture of the linkages between sectors than is assumed by input-output analysis.

However, if applied to a set of data relating to a given year our analysis might measure the linkages that existed in the past rather than those existing at present. This would render us liable to make considerable errors when using the results of our studies in making forecasts of the effects of the location of a given industry in a region. The reason for this is obvious. The siting of industries in the past might have been determined by different factors than those that would have to be taken into account at present.

A solution to this problem (leaving some complicating factors out of consideration) can be found by applying an analysis similar to the one described in connexion with the increase in production in a recent period. Indeed, this procedure is identical with the one proposed earlier for input-output analysis, namely, the use of marginal instead of average coefficients.

Clearly, if sufficient data are not yet available for the analysis of average coefficients, the analysis of marginal coefficients will be even less well served. This analysis will only be possible if we are willing to use approximate data.

However, even if we were in possession of a complete set of recent data our analysis would not enable us to make a long term forecast of the influence of the location of new firms since just as present linkages differ from past ones, future linkages will differ from present ones. It has to be admitted, moreover, that we are still so far from fully understanding present linkages that we can hardly be expected to say anything sensible about future ones.

4.5 *The distance factor*

In the foregoing paragraphs the influence of the distance factor has been implicitly taken into account. It is useful, however, to treat this factor somewhat more explicitly since it will be of crucial impotance for our analysis.

The λ's in formula (3.1) represent as stated before the *relative* importance of communication costs for the relevant factor. In other words λ_d represents the ratio of the communication costs (including transportation costs) with demand, i.e. with the market and total communication costs. It should be mentioned here, however, that these λ's were not measured directly but were treated as unknowns and estimated in an indirect way, namely by 'explaining' the level of activities in each sector by the level of activities in other sectors plus final demand. What is measured could perhaps be better called the relative importance of *communication* with the market or with a greater or lesser number of other sectors, instead of the relative importance of communication *costs*, although the two are identical for the purposes of the statistical analysis.

The *absolute* importance of communication is reflected in the size of the relevant region. If, for example, communication with the market is *very* important, then the relevant region will be small and consequently the size of the firms small too. If communication is of minor importance, then the relevant region will be large and the firms consequently large too. Within these regions the firm will be footloose. A small relevant region means an intensive contact with the market or, if the industry is supply-oriented, with the supplying firms. Therefore, the higher the communication costs, the smaller the relevant region, and also the smaller the distance between the firm and its market and/or supplyers.

Obviously, since communication costs increase with distance, the size of the firm also plays a role. If the relevant region is larger, the production will also be larger but communication costs will be higher since usually the average distance to the market or the supplyers will be greater. The size of the firm adjusted to these two factors will be optimal if the marginal communication costs arising out of an increase in the relevant region are just equal to the marginal decrease in production costs as a consequence of the increase in the size of the market (and/or supplies).

4.6 *Some statistical results*

Equation (3.1) can be written as

$$g_k = \lambda_{dk} \Sigma \beta_{lk} g_l + \Sigma \lambda_{lk} \frac{\alpha_{lk}}{\beta_{kl}} g_l + \lambda_{dk} e_k \tag{3.5}$$

in which

g_k and g_l represent gross production in sector k and l respectively.

e_k = final demand in sector k

β_{kl} = the fraction of gross production of industry k required from industry l

α_{lk} = the fraction of gross production of industry l sold to industry k.

In matrix notation

$$g = (\hat{l}B + A)\, g + \hat{l}e \tag{3.6}$$

in which $\hat{l}$ = diagonal matrix of demand attraction coefficients λ_{dk} $(k = 1,2,\ldots, n)$

B = matrix of β-coefficients (corresponding to the technical coefficients in the input-output table)

A = matrix of $\lambda\frac{\alpha}{\beta}$-coefficients (the supply-effect coefficients)

e = column vector of final demand.

From (3.6) follows

$$g = [I - (\hat{l}B + A)]^{-1}\, \hat{l}e \tag{3.7}$$

which gives the relationships between final demand and gross production.

The value added can be found by pre-multiplying (3.7) with the diagonal matrix of value added fractions. From this result the value added or income multipliers per sector can be determined.

In a study made in the Netherlands[4], the value added multipliers were calculated on the basis of input-output data for the eleven provinces of the country. The results are shown in Table 1.

'The location effect of a given industry in this matrix has been estimated by increasing final demand to such an extent that local production (value added) increases by one unit. This means that if the demand coefficient is say ½ the corresponding v element becomes half the increase in final demand. It is clear that the location-effect is a value added effect.

*Table 1. Partial regional multipliers for 15 industries**

		20	19	14	9	4	5	6	10	8	7	12	11	17	16	15
services	20	1.00	0.05	0.12	0.15	0.23	0.23	0.04	0.40	0.16	0.27	0.53	0.19	0.27	0.15	0.20
public utilities	19	0.02	1.00	0.05	0.02	0.03	0.04	—	0.06	0.02	0.08	0.09	0.02	0.05	0.03	0.04
pottery, glass and stone	14			1.00												
wood and furniture	9				1.00		0.02								0.02	
foodstuffs (animal pr.)	4					1.00						0.02		0.02	0.04	0.24
foodstuffs (other pr.)	5	0.07				0.02	1.00		0.03		0.02	0.04		0.02		0.02
beverages and tobaccos	6	0.07				0.02	1.03	1.00	0.03		0.02	0.04		0.02		0.02
paper-mills	10						0.02		1.00		0.02	0.02	0.06			
footwear and clothing	8									1.00	0.02	2.51			0.04	
textiles	7									0.08	1.00	0.16				
leather and rubber	12									0.03		1.00				
printing and publishing	11												1.00			
other metal industry	17											0.05		1.00	0.06	0.10
means of transport	16														1.00	
metal products and machinery	15				0.03	0.09			0.02		0.02	0.07		0.06	0.15	1.00
(partial) regional multiplier		1.16	1.07	1.17	1.20	1.39	2.34	1.04	1.54	1.29	1.45	4.53	1.27	1.44	1.49	1.62

* Values of 0.01 or smaller omitted.

'Similarly, employment effects can be calculated by using labour-intensity coefficients instead of value added fraction. The corresponding multipliers are employment multipliers. It should be stressed that the multipliers calculated according to our method are *not total* regional multipliers but indicate the multiplicative effect only for those sectors that have been included in the analysis.

'The industries shown in Table 1 have been grouped in a way which requires further explanation. Since an industry will be more non-basic the fuller its row and the emptier its column, two industries, services and public utilities, obviously appear as completely non-basic.

These industries both have low regional multipliers. But this conclusion holds only at the provincial level. If smaller regions were considered, many activities in both sectors would become non-basic at that level. The remaining industries[5] have been grouped in three categories. The first consist of 'primary manufacturing' consisting of agricultural and forestry products and pottery, glass and stone. The production processes in this category are simple. With the exception of the relation between the drinks and tobacco industry and the foodstuff industry (non-animal products) the interrelations between the industries in this category are negligible. The industries are thus footloose and the entire category is footloose. The category represents the first stage of industrialization. Apart from services and public utilities no other industries are needed at the provincial level to make the industries in this category operate. An exception to this rule is the metal products industry which is needed by many other industries and itself creates activities in a number of other sectors. This industry thus is of a mixed basic – non-basic character. The regional multipliers in this category are considerably higher than those of the non-basic industries.

'The second category contains "secondary" manufacturing activities and consists of the tightly interrelated activities, footwear and clothes, textiles and leather and rubber. Production processes in this category are somewhat more complex than in primary manufacturing but are still related to agricultural production. Moreover, it appears that these industries create activities not only in the non-basic sectors but also in "primary manufacturing". Consequently, the regional multipliers again are higher than in the lower-ranked groups.'

'The final category consists of the inorganic and more complicated processes associated with a higher degree of industrialization. Included are printing and publishing, metal products and machinery, means of transport and other metal industry. These activities will be called "tertiary manufacturing". Multipliers in this category are high, and the creation of activities in other branches (especially primary manufacturing) are considerable.'

'The metal products and machinery industry, mentioned before, are somewhat "outside" the categories. The double character of this industry implies, on the one hand, that its nature is non-basic since its activities are required by most other industries but, on the other hand, its production creates a great number of additional activities in other industries. The position of this industry in industrialization policy thus seems to be of utmost importance.'

'The sequence of the categories indicated the evolutionary process in industrialization. Many countries and regions are still in the first phase, that is, the processing of agriculture and forestry products. As industrialization proceeds, secondary manufacturing activities are introduced and an initial start in the metal products and machinery industry will be made. The final stage of industrialization consists of tertiary manufacturing with more complicated production processes in which metal industries play a dominant role.'[6]

The foregoing example shows clearly the increasing complexity of inter-industry relations for 'higher level' industries and the considerable sizes the regional multipliers may reach. This last point holds even more when we realize that these multipliers are not the total demand multipliers since demand effects via the consumers have not yet been taken into account.

The example may also show the strong tendency in several industries to 'cluster' with other industries. To put it the other way around, it shows how important it is to give these industries *opportunities* to concentrate. Active growth pole policy should use these relationships as a starting point.

5. BUNDLES OF INDUSTRIES

In the preceding sections we considered the linkages existing between activities of different kinds and the extent to which these linkages influence the spatial distribution of activities.

We stated that an increase in activities in a given sector has the following effects:

a) *Direct effects*

i) a demand effect. This effect is the result of the increase in demand of inputs.

ii) a supply effect, resulting from the increase in the supply of inputs.

b) *Indirect effects*

The indirect effects have their origin in local income created by the direct effects, part of which income will be spent locally. Through these increases the level of activities in most sectors will be influenced.

We will call all the activities that are created by an initial increase in production in a given sector the *sector-bundle*. If the sector-bundle is large, the regional multiplier is high, and vice versa.

Clearly, the larger the region of the centre we are considering, the larger will be the fraction of all effects that falls within the region (or centre), and the larger therefore the bundles as well.

The fact that we consider bundles of industries instead of individual industries is just another way of saying that human activities tend to concentrate, grouping together activities that are closely linked with each other. This concentration takes place as a consequence of the need for communication (including transportation) and the fact that communication costs increase rapidly with distance. Communication costs in this context are defined as the cost of communication itself plus the cost of stagnation in communication, which will be particularly large in cases of production. These costs increase especially rapidly with distance. A necessary repair that has to be postponed, a stagnation in production lasting until the new spare part arrives from some far away place, etc., all these factors may cause considerable damage to the firm.

Good communication also has its influence on the revenue side. The firm is kept informed of changes in consumer tastes, activities of competing firms, etc., giving it the chance to react faster than others who receive this information later or not at all.

All these services can be found in the larger cities; the sectors that depend on them will therefore tend to concentrate in urban areas, contributing further by their presence to the attractiveness of the city.

This is even more true of modern industry than it is of the conventional older industries. In modern industries, except in a few cases, transportation is of little practical importance. Communication in the narrower sense of the word tends to become more and more important, and this fact explains to a large extent the tendency for cities to grow even faster than they have grown already in the past.

Urbanization is in fact nothing more than a rational process for the creation of activity bundles that can only operate efficiently as bundles at a small distance from each other. This process, already roughly described above, runs as fullows: a firm, looking for a site considers possible locations from two angles, namely, the supply of inputs and the size of the market. If the industry is not a specific supply *l*-oriented industry, but is dependent on a range of supplies, it will look for a place where all or most of these supplies will be available. The larger the city, the broader this range of supplies will be and also the larger the size of the local market.

The location of the new firm in this city causing the twofold effects described earlier will create an even broader range of supplies as well as a larger market. This will again increase the attractiveness of the area. New firms will be attracted there and further increase both the supply of inputs as well as the size of the market. This process, which in principle has no end, is the basic force behind the urbanization we observe so clearly in our present world.

A possible statistical approach to the 'understanding' of this process would be the following:

a) The attraction model defines for a given increase in production in sector *i* an economic complex created by this increase. Call this complex *i*. There are obviously as many complexes as sectors.

b) The speed and 'easiness' with which the new complex will be created in area *j* will depend on the degree to which each of the sectors belonging to the complex is already represented in the area. The more developed the sector is, the faster and easier a further increase will be. In other words, if $\Delta\, g^i_{lj}$ is the production in sector *l* as part of the new complex *i* in region *j*, this production increase will be realized faster and easier the higher g_{lj} is. If we call this speed and easiness (adaptability or) flexibility (f^i_{lj}) of the economy of the region j for sector *i*, we may write (for example)

$$f^i_{lj} = \frac{100}{100 + p^i_{lj}} \qquad (4.1)$$

in which

p^i_{lj} stands for $\dfrac{\Delta g^i_{lj}}{g_{lj}} 100$

c) The flexibility of the region for the whole complex i may then be dcfined as

$$F_j^i = \frac{1}{n} \Sigma \frac{100}{100 + p_{ij}^i} \tag{4.2}$$

if $i = 1,2,\ldots, n$.
This index varies between zero and unity.

d) The flexibility index can be calculated for each region for each complex.

e) Since each economic structure defines a given degree of flexibility, a development path (other things being equal) can be indicated as follows:

i) Introduce in the region the complex for which the region has the highest flexibility index. This introduction should be made on the basis of a reasonable production increase in sector i.
ii) Calculate for the extended structure of the region the new flexibility index for each sector. These new indices define the 'best' next choice for the complexes. Then again new flexibility indices can be calculated and again the then 'best' complex introduced, etc. The path found is that of minimum resistance.

However, even with the foregoing the process is not fully described. For this we shall have to study in somewhat greater detail the demand-oriented activities, particularly in the sector of service industries, perhaps better called amenities. These amenities, like education, recreation, medical care, etc., are of the utmost importance in the process of urbanization and their position in this process is worth studying for several reasons. In the following section we will dedicate more attention to them

6. AMENITIES

6.1 *Introduction*

It is usual to distinguish in economic theory between investments and consumption. Investments, it is said, increase the productive capacity of our economics and thus indirectly, their consumptive capacity. Consumption itself is unproductive in the sense that it does not increase the productive capacity of the economy as a whole. It is just the final goal of production.

Gradually some doubt arises concerning the validity and efficiency of this distinction.[7] If investments are considered as a contribution to the quantity as well as the quality of the capital stock, then why not consider education, vocational training, medical care, recreation, etc. as contribution to the quality of labour, the most important input in our whole economy. A better educated worker with good medical care having the opportunity to make good use of his leisure will not only be happier and healthier but certainly through this also a more productive worker. And a more productive worker will earn a higher income.

If we accept this line of thought, and it seems reasonable enough to do so, we might even take one more step and assume more generally that the consumption of each good or service will influence, positively or negatively, the income level, or rather, the total future income flow of the worker. Accepting also this generalization, it would be possible for the consumer to spend his income in such a way that this future income flow is maximized, instead of, as is usually assumed, his present level of satisfaction. The difference between the two approaches is to be found in the fact that the horizon of the consumer is different: if he spends his income to maximize his ophelimity or his present level of satisfaction, his horizon is near, if he maximizes his future income flow, his horizon is distant. The optimum choice he could make is the one that takes his subjective interest rate as well as his and his familiy's ages into account.

However, his choice between the two possibilities, which can hardly be called an objective one, is influenced by the set of prices confronting him. And the government can by subsidization on the one hand and taxation on the other, exert a considerable influence on the choice he finally will make. In all our societies education and medical care are subsidized or to a certain extent even compulsory and free, while alcohol, drugs, cigarettes, etc., are taxed or even to a certain extent forbidden.

What the motives behind this have been and whether all decisions taken in the field are rational or not are questions that need not be considered here. It can be safely assumed that major motives have been the protection of health and the promotion of knowledge, both contributing very considerably to the productivity of the worker. Whether or not the promotion of productivity itself has been one of the targets of government policy is of secondary importance. The important fact is that by this policy productivity has been increased since both health and happiness positively influence man's willingness and ability to work.

However effective government policies in this respect may have been, it hardly can be denied that the supply of amenities in some regions is considerably larger than in others or in other words, that some people live further away than others from the places where these amenities are to be found. This fact is of particular importance, since the propensity to consume services not only depends on the price for which they are supplied and on the consumers' income, but also on the distance the consumer lives from the place where they are supplied. Since for most services the places of production and consumption are identical, this distance is much more important for services than for goods.

6.2 *The influence of distance on the consumption of services*

Many studies have already been made on the influence of distance on the consumption of a variety of services. The afore-mentioned OECD study (see note 7, p. 40) cites a number of these studies. They concern *inter alia* education, recreation and medical care. In these studies it has been found, as has been said above, that with increasing distance the propensity to consume services decreases. Our knowledge is not yet complete enough to enable us to grade amenities definively according to their distance elasticity. The results obtained so far, however, indicate that, for example, in education the distance elasticity decreases with the level of education, being extremely high for kindergartens and relatively low for higher education. The use of hospitals decreases with distance also. As yet, however, not enough quantitative information is available. For recreation it has been found, for example, that, other things being equal, the visits of the Los Angelinos to State Parks in California decreases in quadruple proportion to the distance from Los Angeles.

In the present context the exact sizes of the distance elasticities are not important. Why should someone further away from the place where the amenities are supplied behave differently from some-one living closer to it? The answer to this question is in principle not very difficult to give. The bridging of the distance is both time- and money-consuming and since both available time and income are limited, the consumer has to spend both in an optimum way. The longer the distance, the more he will be inclined to sacrifice the consumption of the more time-consuming activities. Evidently, since the relationship between distance and time needed to bridge this distance is different for each means of transportation, motorization will have a considerable influence on the time needed per unit distance. It might therefore be better to speak of car-time instead of distance in cases where the car density is high. It is for this reason that in most American studies car-time is used instead of distance.

Whether or not this means that the influence of distance in more highly developed countries is smaller than that in less developed countries is difficult to say since a higher value is set on time as such in richer than in poorer countries.

It follows from the foregoing that a subsidy on the price of amenities is not the only way to stimulate their consumption. Also the distance (car-time) should be considered as an important instrument influencing the level of consumption of this kind of services. The distance (or rather travel time) can be influenced by:

a) improvement of the infra-structure.

b) improvement of the availability of the means of transportation (e.g. school buses, public transportation for special performances in theatres, mobile medical units, etc).

c) decreasing the distance of the consumer by concentrating the population in centres where the amenities are provided.

Although we will take up point three in more detail later, two remarks should be made here. First, as stated above, there is already a natural tendency for the population to concentrate in urban areas where amenities are provided. Thus, a deliberate policy only has to stimulate existing tendencies. The first point mentioned (improvement of the infra-structure) is one possible way of attracting activities and with them, indirectly, population to centres.

Secondly, amenities themselves, of course, tend to be concentrated in population centres. In the next section we shall consider this tendency, and more particularly the ranking of centres and the ranking of amenities.

6.3 *The ranking of centres and amenities*

In this section we shall consider demand-oriented amenities in two respects, namely, the number of the different amenities and their minimum size. We shall see that, although there is some interrelation between these two aspects, it is useful to consider them separately first.

Let us consider a number of cities and centres together with the areas around the centre and let us call these urban areas. Clearly these areas can be ranked according to their population, total income, etc. In this context we will, however, take a different sort of ranking, which, although correlated with those already mentioned, is more useful for our purpose. Consider, therefore, the amenities provided in those cities. If these activities are ranked according to their frequency we might call the amenity with the lowest frequency the amenity with the highest rank. The city in which this amenity is located might consequently be called the highest ranking centre.

It should be clearly understood that the foregoing comments refer only to amenities located in the urban areas as a consequence of *local* demand in the urban area itself. If UNIDO is located in Vienna, this is *not* because of local demand but because of world demand.

If we were to rank all the amenities in the world we should perhaps get more ranks than if we were to consider only a limited range of cities. Here, however, we are not interested in the amenities of national or world rank but only in those that result from local demand. We have called these demand-oriented amenities, to which should be added, in the terminology used so far: with a relevant region not exceeding the size of the urban areas considered.

The question arises then immediately: why are all amenities not located in all cities because the demand is present everywhere regardless of the size of the city? The answer to this question is not difficult to give and is to be found in the minimum size of each separate amenity. This is elucidated by Figure 1.

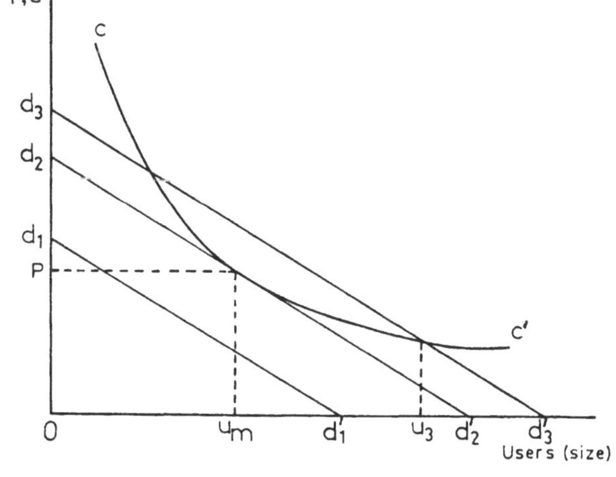

On the horizontal axis the size of 'production', called *users*, (number of students, visitors, etc.) is indicated; on the vertical axis, the price and the costs. cc' represents the costs per user as a function of the number of users. If demand in a city is represented by $d_1d'_1$, at no point of this demand function is there sufficient demand for the amenity in question. The minimum demand necessary for the amenity would be $d_2d'_2$ which enables an equilibrium to be established at (u_m, p). The equilibrium for demand d_3d_3' is found if the number of users is u_3. u_m is thus the minimum size of the amenity. Since each demand function corresponds to a given city size, the size corresponding to d_2d_2' will have the amenity studied as the amenity with the highest rank.

The important fact revealed by this simple analysis is that a city, if growing, does not just become larger, but at the same time enriches its structure. The growing demand will enable more and more new activities to develop and make the centre also more attractive for people and industries to settle in. The cumulative process we analyzed earlier, when considering industrial structure, also applies in the case of amenities. The link between the two is clearly twofold:

a) The larger the size of the city, the higher the supply of and thus the demand for amenities, and the higher therefore the productivity of the people living in the city.

b) The higher the supply of amenities, the more attractive the city is for new activities that not only need these amenities directly, but also indirectly as a result of the demand of the workers in these industries. Since new modern industries employ more highly trained personnel, earning higher incomes than those employed in conventional manufacturing activities, these new activities will be particularly attracted by larger cities.

One further point should be made in this connexion. We stated earlier that one characteristic of amenities is that the consumption of the services provided by them is a function of distance (car-time). This means that if the rank of a city is n, there will be a demand for amenity $n + 1$ but the size of this effective demand will depend on the distance from the city studied to the nearest city with a rank higher than n. This effective demand cannot therefore serve as an indication of the total demand that would exist in city n if the amenity were present there. The supply of amenity $n + 1$ would mean that the distance at which this amenity becomes available will be much smaller than before, which will considerably stimulate local demand.

The fact that local demand is stimulated by local supply is one of the most typical characteristics of amenities. To this phenomenon in general, economic theory has so far paid hardly any attention.

6.4 *Final comment*

To conclude this section, one final comment should be made. The foregoing considerations were only partly based upon quantitative research. In the field of amenities hardly any systematic research has been made. Only scattered quantitative studies for individual amenities are available. Better knowledge of these activities is extremely important, especially if regional policy is to be carried out as a growth pole policy.

If this were to be done, it might be worthwhile considering whether the level of amenities should be measured by the number of units only or whether a somewhat more precise instrument could be devised for comparing the level of amenities in different cities; such an instrument could perhaps be the total expenditure (private plus public) per amenity. In this way we could not only rank cities according to the level of the highest ranked amenity in them, but also indicate in more detail the level of production of each amenity in each centre. A more sensible and detailed ranking could thus be made.

7. SUMMARY OF NATURAL CONCENTRATION TENDENCIES

So far we have been concerned with natural tendencies in the development and growth of centres. Before turning to active policy directed to the creation of growth centres, a short summary of the main conclusions reached in the foregoing chapters may be useful.

These conclusions were:

a) The location of a new activity in a city will be the result of a confrontation of the needs of the new firm and the resources the city has to offer. The resources considered are:

i) the inputs produced in the city,
ii) the level of amenities in the city.

b) The consequences of the location of new activities in a city are:

i) more variation in input supplies,
ii) a higher level of amenities.

c) Points a) and b) together are the elements of a cumulative process which makes the city grow by itself. More activities create a larger and more varied production of inputs and a higher level of amenities. Both again increase the attractiveness of the city and induce activities in new sectors.

The fact that amenities are included in this process is of the utmost importance since it shows that cities not only have a more varied economic structure but are also able to produce considerably more and better social services than smaller nuclei. This holds not only for medical and educational services but also for the care of old people, physically and mentally handicapped persons, young mothers and babies, etc. Cities are better equipped than rural areas with facilities for indoor recreation and at least a considerable part of out-door recreational activities. It is a common mistake to think that people living in rural areas have more and better possibilities for recreation than city-dwellers. In reality, rural areas are badly off for many recreational facilities (especially for sport) since lack of demand hampers any initiative in this field.

We will deal later with the disadvantages of very large cities. For the present we are only interested in the advantages of cities over rural areas, without being too romantic about rural life or too pessimistic about the social problems created by very large cities. The problems of large cities will be treated in a wider context in a later section.

The cumulative process of the growth of cities influences the size distribution of nuclei simultaneously with the outflow of population from rural areas to larger regional centres and cities elsewhere in the country. This distribution changes gradually, as a consequence of these two forces, from a Pareto-shaped distribution to a skew, single humped distribution. The more agricultural production is mechanized and the higher the car density becomes in rural areas, the larger will rural centres grow and the greater will be the decrease in the number of the smaller villages in rural areas.

Apart from this general tendency, it is very difficult to indicate which cities will grow more than others. This is in a very large degree dependent upon the structure and geographical situation of the individual city and also particularly on the quality of the local government. If local authorities do not merely follow the growth of their cities but stimulate and anticipate it, the process of growth will develop both more smoothly and rapidly.

The role of the local authorities as far as the growth of areas is concerned is often overestimated and often underestimated. Sociologists and social geographers in many cases overestimate the importance of the quality of local government. Those guilty of underestimation are the economists. This factor cannot be truly appraised in the absence of any quantitative insight into the influence on local development of the whole decision-making process in local government. All we can say is that local government is only one factor in local development that is to a certain extent able to influence the growth of the area without, however, being able to change the general trend in urban development.

At one stage, however, local government has a very important task, namely, the preparation of the planning process which has to accompany development. This preparation consists in forecasting future developments and future structure as well as planning the services and personnel that will be needed in future situation. A study made in the Netherlands[8] has shown that the growth of a city not only requires more personnel in local government offices but also personnel of a higher average quality. The number of university graduates in city governments increases much more than proportionally with the size of the city. The planning of this structural change in the quality of the local government is one of the main tasks of the existing government, and it can hardly be denied that this requires considerable intellectual capacity as well as far-sightedness. In only a few cities do these requirements seem to be fulfilled. Physical planning particularly often leaves much to be desired in the imaginative appreciation of the consequences of expected growth and development. However, the physical design of present cities determines to a large extent the cost of future physical planning and thus the cost of further growth.

This subject brings us gradually from the study of natural growth tendencies into the more active sphere of growth pole policy and area development policy. In the following sections this side of the problem will be considered. It seemed desirable to discuss first some general aspects of regional policy and the development of cities before dealing with the various aspects of active growth pole policy, which is largely based, or rather should be based, on a profound knowledge of tendencies in existing cities.

8. GROWTH POLE POLICY

8.1 *Introduction. Regional policy*

Growth pole policy has become an integral part of regional policy, and for this reason it may be useful to give some attention to regional policy in general before embarking on the more special question of the role of growth pole policy.

In regional policy one of the main targets is to arrive at a better distribution of income over regions without too greatly endangering national economic growth.

This target of regional policy is not always formulated in terms of income. Often reference is made only to structural unemployment and the creation of jobs in regions with such unemployment. In this paper we prefer to use the income approach: first, because it is much more general than the employment approach, and secondly, because regions with high structural unemployment usually coincide with those with a low income and vice versa.

The reason that a proviso is made concerning national growth lies in the fact that the less developed regions in a country are usually not very easy to develop because their infra-structure is often defective, amenities are not well developed and housing is partly obsolete and partly of too low a standard to be attractive. As a result, considerable financial means from the more developed regions have to be used to bring the region up to date in these respects before any further investments can be expected to pay, or rather, before anybody becomes interested in investing in these areas.

One reason for income differences between the regions of a country are the differences in the structure of those regions. The average income being different for each sector of the economy, the total average income of a region will have a different level for each structure. Even if incomes per sector were equal for all regions, this difference in total average income would remain.

Equalization of incomes thus means in fact also a restructuration of the underdeveloped region in such a way that high income sectors will be better represented than in the existing situation.

The attainment of this target is usually, at least in European countries, accompanied by the addition of a further aim. It is stated that the growth of the largest urban areas will in the long run lead to such excessive costs that it should be limited as much as possible. These costs stem to a large extent from the need for substantial investment in the traffic infra-structure in in order to keep pace with rapid motorization. Other social costs, such as air and water pollution, are also adduced to prove that the larger cities are becoming too large and their growth should consequently be limited.

It may well be asked how is it possible for cities to grow far beyond their optimum size? The answer to this question can be found in the structure of our taxation systems, in which local governments get a large part of their income indirectly from the State or the federal government. If the areas themselves were responsible for their income, the situation would be quite different. Then, the inhabitants of each area would be confronted with the costs of the development of their own region, which, and about this fact there can be little doubt, are considerably higher in very large cities than they are, for example, in medium-sized cities. Local taxation, however, plays such a minor role in most economies, especially in most European countries, that there is hardly a direct or indirect link between local operating costs and taxation. Large cities get just what they think they need.

It should be remarked here that even the complete decentralization of taxes would not result in the optimum distribution of activities and population over areas and cities of different size. Any taxation system is based on the principle that people in the same circumstances pay an equal amount in taxes. In other words, if taxation were completely decentralized, average local taxation would reflect average local costs. For the optimum distribution of activities it would, however, be necessary for the level of taxation to reflect marginal costs. Only when the marginal costs of cities are equal can one speak of an optimum distribution of population.

However this may be, the important fact remains that governments think it desirable to encourage decentralization from large cities, or, at least, to prevent already very large cities from further unlimited growth. Given this attitude, this policy of decentralization should clearly be linked with development policy for backward areas by trying to divert activities (present or future) from the large cities directly to the backward areas. In this way not only are excessive social costs in urban areas avoided, but simultaneously, backward areas are assisted in their growth.

About the way underdeveloped areas should be developed there seems to be a *communis opinio*. It is held that it would be a mistake to try to develop the whole region at the same time, but since it is recognized that the concentration of activities has considerable advantages, assistance to the region should be focused at a few points, or nuclei, called growth poles, in order to create in the shortest possible time the basic requirements that make already developed cities so attractive to activities of all kinds.

The foregoing is a rough description of the line of thought usually followed in regional policy. It should perhaps be added that the limitation of the growth of large cities is hardly advocated and is certainly not a part of area development policy in the United States. It seems to be typically European.

The principles underlying this way of thinking in regional policy raise a number of questions. It seems desirable to mention at least a few of these.

8.2 *Development potentials*

A first doubt arises about whether it is really so evident that if a region is underdeveloped, measures to assist that region in its development should always be taken in the region itself. What we want to assist is not the region as such but the population in that region. If the population can be assisted best by creating employment possibilities for it in another region, a policy aiming at the creation of such possibilities might be more effective than the attempt to create employment possibilities in any and every region, however poor the development potentials of the region may be.

The point made here is that within the framework of regional policy a policy consistent with the target of maximum national growth could be designed if the measures taken were directed at the development of the regions with the best development potential, namely, the regions where investments could be expected to give the highest returns. These 'development-worthy' regions obviously do not necessarily coincide with the least developed regions nor with the most developed ones. The least developed are usually underdeveloped for very good reasons, while further development of the most developed might involve such high social costs that they also would not be the most attractive to be stimulated further.

In determining the 'development-worthiness' of a region elements to be taken into consideration might be, for example, the presence of one nucleus with at least 40,000 or 50,000 inhabitants, a favourable economic structure, a satisfactory level of amenities, sufficient local initiative and no excessive costs involved in future growth.

If positive criteria such as these were applied in the selection of regions to be developed, the regional policy of our countries might be considerably more effective than is now the case, and might contribute to the growth of national income instead of hampering it.

Our proposal assumes population mobility and it may be objected that, particularly in underdeveloped regions, people are not mobile at all and tend to remain with a low income in their own region rather than go and be-well-employed in another; for social reasons, therefore the proposed policy will never become effective.

This argument may to a certain extent be true, at least in the short run. In the long run, however, the present policy, even from a social point of view, does not seem very attractive. The very fact that cities exist proves that people have always moved from places with fewer to places with more and better employment possibilities. It is not difficult to find a city in which at least half the population has been born in another region. And migration statistics show us that annually large groups of the population move to other places. Statistical analysis shows that we do have in most of our countries considerable mobility.

If this mobility really exists, why not make use of it? Admittedly, the present generation may prefer employment in the home region; but will the next generation appreciate this as much if they realize that their income could be substantially increased by a move to more promising areas? It does not seem likely, and for this reason not even long term social arguments support the theoretical background of present-day regional policy.

8.3 *Costs and revenues of cities*

The second criticism points to the fact that usually only the operating costs of large cities are considered and the revenues are left out of account. But what we are interested in, from the economic point of view, are not the operating costs of a city but the difference between these costs and the income produced and earned in the city. From this viewpoint, the distribution of population over cities is optimum not if marginal operating costs are equal, but if marginal net incomes are equal.

It is a pity that so few quantitative studies have been made in this field. Some scattered information on city cost levels are available but we have hardly any systematic studies of net city incomes in relation to city size. The superficial impression one gets from the data available is that there are indeed differences in costs between cities of different size but that there are also differences in income which appear to be considerably larger than those in costs. In other words, although the costs of large cities are high, incomes earned there make it worthwhile from the financial point of view to live there, and would still make it worthwhile even if the inhabitants of the city had to pay the full amount of taxation needed to cover local costs.

If this could be proved the whole argument based on the high costs of large cities would break down. Whether or not it really is true only can be found out by careful quantitative research.

8.4 *The number of growth poles selected*

In the selection of growth poles political factors play a very important role, particularly in as far as the criteria for selection are concerned. According to economic arguments those nuclei should be selected which have the best growth potentials. Social arguments would point at nuclei that are (for the moment) in trouble and need short-term assistance. The final outcome is that a very large number of centres is selected to make everybody happy.

An objective choice of growth poles should be directly based on the principle that a city, from a given size onwards, has a tendency to develop itself further, in the way we described earlier. The growth pole policy thus requires that from among all possible muclei those centres be selected that are the most likely to react rapidly to stimulating measures. The greater the number of centres selected, the weaker the impact, because only a limited number of industries is in search of a location and because the financial assistance that can be given in the initial period is in inverse proportion to the number of centres selected.

Thus the larger the number of growth poles selected, the slower their development will be and the longer the period before the 'take off' size of each centre is reached.

8.5 *A rational regional policy*

It follows from the criticisms formulated in the preceding sections that the present regional policies cannot be expected to be very effective. The following changes are therefore proposed:

a) Regions should be selected on the basis of their development potential, which should include at least the presence of a medium-sized centre with a favourable economic structure and a satisfactory level of amenities.

b) Growth poles should be selected within these regions on the basis of the 'development-worthiness' of the existing centres.

c) A concentrated effort should be made to develop the growth poles selected and to adjust the national and regional infrastructure so as to focus the road and railroad system on these growth poles.

d) A time-pattern should be introduced for the development of growth poles, concentrating first on those with the best development potential.

These proposals do not mean that the criteria to be used should be completely independent of the typical problems of regions. In many cases structural unemployment results from the fact that a region with a onesided structure, be it coal mining or textile industry, experiences a structural fall in demand or heavy mechanization and consequently gets into difficulties. Not seldom, however, such regions have a reasonable infra-structure and an acceptable level of amenities. For these reasons they might at once, according to the foregoing criteria be selected as growth centres. The already existing traffic and social infra-structure might make it worth selecting them as growth poles, so that at least the capital invested in this infra-structure would be saved.

In other cases as well some deviations from the strict criteria given above might be desirable. The *basis*, however, should remain a rational decision-pattern aiming at long term maximum economic and social welfare.

9. THE MINIMUM SIZE OF NUCLEI

9.1 *Introduction*

We touched already in sections 8 on the subject of the impact of the size of cities on their level of operating costs. We indicated there that there seems to be a general tendency, even in quantitative research, to consider only the cost sides of the problem but that the really interesting problem is the net income earned by the average worker in the city, i.e. his income minus his share of the operating costs of the city.

Clearly, the solution to the problem of the differences in the price levels of cities is essential for the calculation of real net incomes in different cities. So far little work has been done in this field, although it is generally assumed that the level of the cost of living in larger cities is higher than in smaller ones. Nevertheless, it will be useful to consider this question further in this paper.

9.2 *Income differences between cities of different size*

The problem of the measurement of income differences among cities is a rather complicated one. The normal procedure would be to measure nominal incomes and reduce these in accordance with a price index calculated for the different cities in question.

For several reasons this procedure is inappropriate to the problem under consideration. The first reason is that in smaller cities a number of amenities is not available and for this reason substitutes are used. One could certainly proceed by taking as a price for the amenity in these cities, the actual price in the nearest city where the amenity is available, plus transportation costs to this city. This would, however, lead to overestimation of the price level in smaller cities, particularly if these are at a great distance from a larger city, since the possibility of substitution would be completely overlooked.

The second reason is that differences in size of cities cause considerable difference in the duration and price of the journey to work. Here also one could calculate a money-price for the use of a given means of transportation. But the price to be paid is a far less essential difference than the time involved in transportation. A proper treatment of the problem would require that the value of this time be estimated and added to the money price paid for transportation.

The third reason is that the difference in per capita local government expenditures not only result from different cost levels in the cities, but also from the fact that some amenities in larger cities are not found in smaller ones. Moreover, the quality of services might be better in the larger city. We should therefore make a correction for differences in quality as well well as for the range of services provided.

The problem is indeed so complicated that after only brief reflexion it becomes clear that any *a priori* statement that living in larger cities is much more expensive than living in smaller ones is nothing less than hazardous. The problem deserves careful consideration but we should realize that its solution is not as simple as it might appear at first sight. We should in fact need information on the price and income levels of cities in order to assess the marginal net income of different cities and thus judge which cities should be encouraged to grow and which not. There is, however, an alternative approach which enables us to get some idea of the direction in which the solution of the problem might be sought.

9.3 *Diversification and size*

In the section on amenities we indicated that the rank of a city (in reality the number of different sorts of amenities existing in a city) is a function of the size of the city: the larger the city, the higher its rank and thus the more diversified the supply of its amenities.

We now can ask how fast the rank of a city increases with the size of its population. *A priori* considerations suggest that the rank of a city will increase considerably with its size as long as the size of the city is small, but that this rate of increase will slow down in the larger size.

The study of this relation would be very helpful in the solution of our problems because it would enable us to judge from which level onwards a city could be considered to be 'gull grown' in the sense that not very much more variation in its activities could be expected to result from its further growth.

Colin Clark, as early as 1945, made a quantitative study in a number of American, Canadian, British and Australian cities, of the structural differences in cities of different size.[9] He came to the conclusion that, as far as services are concerned, an urban area with a population of about 200,000 provides practically every service of importance. To be 'full grown' in manufacturing, the area should have a population of about 500,000.

The study by Colin Clark has never been repeated in more recent periods. It would seem, however, extremely useful that this should be done, especially since modern industry might be completely different from the industry Colin Clark had in mind twenty-four years ago. It is not unlikely that modern industry comes much closer to service industry than to the manufacturing industry of the past and that, also through the higher income level of modern cities, a smaller population than 500,000 would suffice to create a full grown industrial pattern.

The importance of Colin Clark's study although some criticism on the analysis is possible, is considerable. It does not give any information on the real income level of the kind we should like to have, but it does inform us about the structural changes in the economy of a city as a function of its size which is also important for this problem. In particular, the conclusion that there is a city size, say 200,000 inhabitants, which offers practically all the necessary services is extremely important since it indicates that from that size onward a very important condition for further growth is already fulfilled. The minimum size of a city defined in this way might be much more interesting to our problem than the previously indicated size.

A study made at the Netherlands Economic Institute[10] is to a certain extent related to Colin Clark's study. In this study the growth rates of cities in Western Germany were considered as a function of the size of these cities. It became clear from this study that the growth rates of cities of more than 275,000 inhabitants are not only higher than those below this level but have a smaller variance, and furthermore keep on increasing with the size of the population. Needless to say, this study does not mean that the last word has been said about the minimum size a city has to reach before the 'take off' for more rapid development can be made. The results, however, fit in with the pattern outlined by Colin Clark, and both studies together give a picture that seems quite acceptable when compared with simple observation in the real world.

If studies of this kind could be made in greater depth, extended and brought up to date, they could provide us with a better basis for growth pole policy, i.e. with information about the size of cities that can offer the necessary range of services needed by both the population and industry in the city, as well as about the impact of size on the growth potentials of a city. The last point especially would be of considerable importance for regional policy, particularly with regard to the number of growth poles to be selected. Hitherto such decisions, even apart from political influences, have often been taken on the basis of vague feelings about the advantages of concentration and the possibilities for further growth created by concentration alone.

9.4 *The implications of minimum size for growth pole policy*

So far we have defined the minimum size of a city as a size that guarantees further growth without special assistance from outside.

Once this minimum is given, the problem for a government is to draw up a plan in which a time pattern is fixed for designating centres to growth poles. If this time pattern is built on economic arguments, the largest regional centres selected as growth poles (in the shorter or longer run) will be assisted first, since they are where the highest returns on investments can be obtained. Then, smaller centres will gradually be designated to growth poles until the investments that have to be made in accordance with this policy give returns that are too low to be attractive.

Admittedly, such a purely economic policy would hardly be acceptable from a political point of view, and the choice of a certain minimum number of growth poles in different parts of the country might therefore be more acceptable than the policy of establishing a sequence for the choice of growth poles one after the other. However, the principle could be maintained that centres closest to the minimum size should be selected first, and smaller centres be designated as growth poles only gradually, in the longer run.

There is yet another complication that makes our consideration only partly valid in the case of governments not as heavily centralized as is assumed in the foregoing. This is the fact that governments of provinces or *Länder* feel just as responsible for their region as the central government feels for the country as a whole. Consequently, the provincial governments may, as far as their authority allows, try to create growth poles additional to those designated by the central government in their region, but selected from the limited viewpoint of the region. The more a government is decentralized, which usually means also the more financially independent are the local or provincial governments, the more effective such a provincial policy and the less effective a central growth pole policy might be.

Indeed, provincial and local authorities are often much better informed about local development potentials than the central government is, and they are, moreover, heavily involved in the implementation of both central and local growth pole policy. The contribution they can make should not be underestimated.

Going a step further, local initiatives could be envisaged as being of such importance that, whatever the growth poles chosen by the central government, room should always be left within the framework of the growth pole theory for the incorporation of such initiatives in the general policy. In many regions in Europe and the United States local initiatives have proved extremely important in the process of regional development.

It seems that both interests can be united if the central government should decide to incorporate local initiative in its criteria for designating growth poles. It will not be very easy to quantify local initiative or even to compare the level of local initiative in different areas. A study in this field seems of great importance. In such a study the organizational aspects of the local society, willingness to co-operate, the attitude towards the introduction of 'foreign' intellect in the region, etc. should be considered and, as far as possible, quantified.

10. THE SOCIAL COSTS OF LARGE CITIES

We indicated earlier that many students of urban problems are of the opinion that large cities not only show large diseconomies of scale but also often suffer from so-called social costs that are not found in medium-sized cities. They point to the congestion in urban cores, the social problems in the obsolete parts of large cities and the ever mounting figures of crime and social unrest. Recent motorization has given rise to heavy air pollution and industries not only contribute to this, but are in addition the main source of water pollution. In short, the entire milieu of our larger cities tends to become so unattractive and unhealthy that everything should be done to limit their further growth.

If this were true, it would mean that there is also a maximum size of cities above which the city would become so 'costly' to operate that its existence would in fact be uneconomic. The per capita net 'welfare' of a city as a function of its size could then be represented by a rapidly increasing function up to a size of say 250.000, a more slowly increasing function until some large population, perhaps 5 million, and a decreasing function for still higher values.

The question might, however, be not so simple as that. There is hardly any doubt that there are congestion and air pollution and social unrest in large cities but the question is not whether there are problems or not in large cities, but whether the problems there are worse or not, *the larger scale taken into account*, and also whether or not *other* things are not much more favourable in large cities than in smaller cities or rural areas. And if there are problems like air pollution and water pollution, what then is the cost of solving them, and could not the large city pay for this solution? On this point also it is a pity that we have no systematic comprehensive study at our disposal. The problems involved in such a study would, of course, be tremendous but the problem itself is also a most important one. Why do not sociologists make more quantitative comparative studies of education, recreation, crime, social conflicts, slums, etc. in cities of different size and income? Perhaps there are many more than have come to the knowledge of the author. But it can hardly be denied that many sociologists are content to state that large problems exist without making any attempt to analyze the problems in depth or even to make an objective comparison with the intensity of these same problems in smaller cities and rural areas.

It would be better, moreover, not to speak so much of the problems of large cities but rather to concentrate on the cost of solving those problems. The air pollution problem can be solved by the compulsory use of appropriate devices on cars and factories, the congestion problem can be solved by adjusting the structures of our cities, housing problems can be removed by large scale low cost housing programmes, etc. And if the cost of solving all these problems were economically justified, then the disadvantages of large cities would be considerably less than they might seem at first sight.

A quantitative study of net income and operating costs in cities of different size would seem the only way out of the problem. And it is not unlikely that the result of this study would, in spite of what has been said above, be unfavourable to very large cities. This result may indeed be expected since gross per capita income as a function of size shows that the increase in income for a given increase in size is a decreasing function of the size. In other words, the curve of the per capita income flattens off for large sizes. Since the per capita operating costs may be expected to increase more rapidly, some diseconomies of scale may be expected. How large these are is still unknown, but *a priori* considerations would lead us to expect that very large cities are in a somewhat more unfavourable position than large cities.

If this should be the case, there would indeed be a second reason for growth pole policy. Then, this would have as its aim not only the creation of sufficiently large cities in the country instead of scattered activities in small uneconomic units, but also, indirectly, the prevention of the further growth of cities that are already too large as a goal in itself, served by the same policy. A better distribution of activities over cities of smaller and larger size would then be the result of growth pole policy.

It seems important to make it clear that the aim of growth pole policy should not be just to create cities of larger size. The aim should be to contribute by growth pole policy to the growth of those cities that have the best growth potentials and where, therefore, money invested will get the highest returns, and simultaneoulsy to prevent, by the same criteria, the further growth of over-large cites. This means that the *distribution of sizes of cities* will have to be changed. Fewer small, uneconomic units, more medium-sized cities and a careful slow-down policy concerning the largest cities.

NOTES

1. First published in L. H. Klaassen, D. H. van Dongen Torman and L. M. Koyck,

Hoofdlijnen van de sociaal economische ontwikkeling der gemeente Amersfoort 1900–1970, Leiden, 1949.

2. For the mathematical derivation of this equation see L. H. KLAASSEN, *Methods of Selecting Industries for Depressed Areas*, Paris, OECD, 1967.
3. *Op.cit.*, p. 118.
4. L. H. KLAASSEN and A. C. van WICKEREN, 'Interindustry Relations: An Attraction Model', in *Towards Balanced International Growth*, H. C. Bos (ed.), Amsterdam, North-Holland Publishing Co., 1969, pp. 245–268.
5. Results from the chemical industry are not presented in the table since they in many ways seem to be inconclusive. This probably results from the fact that non-basic activities in this sector (pharmacies) are included with the typical basic activities (refineries). Further studies of this industry are in progress.
6. *Op.cit.*, pp. 263 and 265–266.
7. See also L. H. KLAASSEN, *Social Amenities in Area Economic Growth*, Paris, OECD, 1968.
8. Netherlands Economic Institute, Internal Report.
9. Colin CLARK, 'The economic functions of a city in relation to its size', *Econometrica*, 13, (2), 1945, pp. 97–113.
10. *Eerste resultaten van het voor West-Duitsland verrichte agglomeratieonderzoek* [First results of an agglomeration study for Western Germany], Rotterdam, Juli 1961.

MRINAL DATTA-CHAUDHURI **1B**

Comments on Klaassen's report

Professor Klaassen's report, 'Growth poles in economic theory and policy' is an important contribution to the literature on growth poles. Professor Perroux's pioneering work brought out sharply the inadequacy of competitive equilibrium analysis to explain the process or growth and development of an economy, particularly in the context of its resource allocation over the geographical area covered by the economy. As one goes to smaller and smaller geographical units, problems of indivisibilities and externalities of various kinds assume greater and greater importance, leading to the familiar story of 'market failure'. The policy conclusion in such situations is clear: deliberate and purposeful intervention in the market process and, therefore, planning.

But effective intervention and planning require a clear understanding of the technological, behavioural and institutional forces at work. The work of the 'growth pole' theorists goes some way in identifying the nature of the linkages among modern industrial activities and in explaining the tendency towards concentrated growth; and, therefore, these theorists rightly emphasize the close link between the process of industrialization and urban growth. But here the trouble begins: Economists' understanding of the economics of urban growth is painfully inadequate. It is not easy even to pose the conceptual problem of the optimum pattern of urban development in an economy; getting quantitative answers is a far cry. But these are urgent social problems. Therefore, people tend to have strong views on the 'right' size for a city. These views are often backed by nothing more than one's immediate experiences and prejudices or at most, by some casual empericism. The net result is that even though one is often in sympathy with the concern of others, and one is in broad agreement about the need for certain remedial measures, one does not always find it easy to discuss these questions within a rational framework of analysis.

The importance of Klaassen's work lies in the lucidity and thoroughness with which he has attacked the problem. He has rightly extended this enquiry into its regional dimensions: industries are concentrated in cities, but cities are supported by wider geographical areas with diverse economic, social and cultural links. He has brought into his analysis a wide variety of conceptual and quantitative tools to establish meaningful relationships among economic activities of different categories. Professor Klaassen's work will remain a model of systematic study for any conscientious research worker trying to evolve rational economic policies for the regional development of an economy. In my discussion of his report, I shall not try to cover his entire ground. I shall not even try to comment on either the methodological or the statistical aspects of his study. I shall only concentrate on the question as to how far Professor Klaassen has given us the outline of an economic theory of 'growth poles'. It is possible that I am being unfair to his study, which is basically empirical; but this careful and comprehensive study presented in such a lucid manner, provides an extremely tempting base for asking certain important questions which always worry the readers of 'growth poles' literature. Besides, the title of Professor Klaassen's report leads the reader inevitably in that direction.

An important building-block in Klaassen's study is the distinction between 'basic' and 'non-basic' activities. 'Non-basic' activities respond to the local market, while the 'basic' activities come up in response to the national and international markets. The reasons behind this dichotomy may lie in prohibitive or nearly-prohibitive transport and communication costs. If all economic activities could be divided strictly into these two categories, then, for any region, given the exogenous variables (which in this case are the levels of basic activities), the requirements of non-basic activities could be ascertained. This line of analysis has been extended by Professor Klaassen to incorporate some of the clear-cut linkages on the supply side. If the location of an industry is completely dictated by the availability of some essentially non-transportable input, then the location of such an industry can also be endogenously determined like all the non-basic activities. But then the number of activities which are *strictly* non-basic or whose locations are *strictly* determined by the supply source of an input is very small indeed. Most activities are in the mixed category, where simple yes-no answers about the locational choice cannot be obtained from these linkages alone. Logically, one would like to identify other factors which affect the locational choice for such industries. But in our present state of imperfect knowledge, it is, indeed, difficult to formulate a complete analytical model of this sort. Therefore, Professor Klaassen took recourse to statistical estimation. He proposes to estimate 'attraction coefficients' for different activities 'by regression analysis if data for a sufficiently large number of regions or centres are available'. Important things to note here are that these 'attraction coefficients' are specific only to the nature of industry. Usual location theoretical considerations arising out of the facts of economic geography (resource endowments etc.) are not supposed to influence the locational decisions of these industries.

The next question is the determination of the location of 'basic' activities. It is true that the existence of 'non-basic' activities makes the solution of the regional allocation of resources somewhat easier, particularly if some kinds of resources are *only* used for the production of commodities, which are *only* produced for local market. But to the extent that different regions and different activities complete for national resources and that the economic future of a region depends on its competitive power in the national and international economy, Professor Klaassen's study does not provide much analytical insights. In order to get analytical insights of this sort, one will need to go deeper into the constituents of this 'competitive power'. In a market economy this would mean an analysis of how profitability calculations are made at enterprise level, how expectations are formed, how the market transmits information etc. * This is why, to most readers, an enquiry into the economic theory of resource-use in a market economy – because this is what Professor Klaassen is essentially concerned with – without any reference to the market forces will appear somewhat baffling. Professor Klaassen may be right: economic agents in a market economy possibly do not actually make profitability calculations in a text-book manner. But then how do they behave? So long as one does not know the answer, following Professor Klaassen, one may have to depend on purely statistical relationships at aggregative levels (macro-economic or inter-industry levels) for making rough predictions. But then, one would continue to feel extremely diffident about generalising such statistical relationships observed in a specific economic, geographical and social context.

* In a planning context, this would mean a comparison of the social costs of alternative regional allocation schemes. A planning model of this kind has to be a multiregional resource allocation model.

LUIGI FREY

2A

Growth poles and employment policy

I. INTRODUCTION

It is well known, as J.R. Meyer reminds us, that there are three different ways of defining regions in the economist's sense: 'The first stresses *homogeneity* with respect to some one or other combination of physical economic social or other characteristics; the second emphasises so-called *nodality* or *polarization*, usually some central urban place; and the third is *programming* or *policy-oriented*, concerned mainly with administrative coherence or identity between the area being studied and available political institutions.'[1]

It is also widely known that such definitions 'are not mutually exclusive'. It will not therefore be our aim to show that the first criterium based on homogeneity agrees to a certain extent, with the second criterium to which the theory on growth poles is related. The object of this essay is to point out a particularly important aspect of any analysis of regional development aiming at succeeding in influencing political development projects in the world of today, dominated by the pursuit of technical progress.

The level and rythm of the increase of productivity in the various economic systems is ever more dominated by the level of the residual factor which is different from the capital and labour employed. Within the limits in which the concept of technical progress is identified with that 'third factor', one is no longer dealing with the change in techniques of production (that is technical innovations) on which classical and neo-classical production theory concentrated, but with technical progress which assumes a wider meaning, including the continuous introduction of organisational innovations, and the exploitation of economies of scale, external and internal to the production unit.

Included in such a concept of technical progress is a series of qualities or structural characteristics related to labour and capital. Particularly, the pursuit of technical progress over time (i.e. the accumulation over time of additional stocks from which the third factor has been subtracted) provokes changes in the qualitative structure of the labour force employed and in the structure of capital.

If, concentrating on productive development, this development appears ever more tied to technical progress – defined as above in a wide sense – one is drawn to infer that an economic policy aiming at intense productive development must take into consideration the qualitative structure changes in the labour force which accompany the necessary pursuit of technical progress. On the other hand some of the effects of technical progress on the system may appear undesirable from the point of view of other economic policy objectives: technical progress may, for instance, create structural unemployment or some effects on labour mobility and work-time.

A policy of regional development aimed at avoiding the incidence of notable regional disparities within a national or international system, does not only pursue an intensive local productive development, but must absorb local manpower to a sufficient degree and solve the problems arising from labour mobility and work-time. Actually, in many systems, (particularly the most industrialised ones), employment policy has become an essential part of regional development policy in order to achieve a more balanced 'welfare' in local communities.

If production achievements are satisfactory and higher welfare objectives such as regional development are aimed at, the role played by technical progress in its wide sense leads to the abandonment of models too much tied to the take-off of single dominant units of production, (so-called growth industries), or to the development of industrial complexes interdependent technically one on the other. What has been said above leads us to look once more for a definition of a region and for some guides to regional policy based on the adoption of particular criteria of social homogeneity. This does not signify the abandonment of the idea of a regional development concentrated particularly in development or growth-pole areas, but rather the rehabilitation and clarification of the 'milieu vivant'[2] in which the growth-pole is placed.

2. GROWTH POLE AND 'MILIEU VIVANT'

Growth-pole theory[3] raises a series of problems: the choice of possible areas of intervention, the establishment fo a hierarchy among the areas of intervention, the choice of development measures likely to achieve polarization effects and at the same time to spread beneficial effects over the areas most proximate to the pole.[4]

If the traditional theory of growth industry is accepted the choice would fall upon areas where leading firms exist, or upon any place where a big investment is to be localized. The choice would pose problems only with regard to the interventions better able to magnify the effects of the leading firm upon local development.

Nevertheless it has been rightly pointed out that, when the dominant firm has not yet been localised and a decision must be taken, it is not enough to pay attention to the accumulative diffusion mechanisms put into action by the firm's presence, but it is necessary to take into account the opportunity costs (both private and social) of choosing a certain location rather than another. Such a point could lead some one to measure the opportunity costs in terms of the existence of technically integrated initiatives, allowing the leading firm or complex of firms to rely upon a series of supply points and outlets; however, one should note that in a world of rapid and intense means of communication, the technically necessary links among enterprises can be maintained even over large distances, that is inside 'macroregions'; beside, when one wishes to create from the start, a modern process of local industrialization, the problem of choice would turn from the large leading firm to the 'industrial complex', so that the question arises once again: shall we localize the complex of initiatives in the given area or in a different one?[5]

Another might refer to the experience in industrialized countries and suggest that leading firms and 'industrial complexes' be located near large urban centres – either previously existing or newly created – on the basis that a large urban centre tends to become a dominant entity in a polarized space enriched with many satellite urban centres and initiatives.[6] However, it has been rightly observed that 'The hierarchical relationships among urban centres, when observed from a dynamic point of view, show reversibilities and functional efficiencies to an extent which suggests that growth poles of intermediate size, far from being absorbed by larger centres, contribute, thanks to the complementarity and diversity of their functions, to rationalizing large agglomerations, while stimulating the development of their own areas'.[7]

Being confronted with the problems of choice to which we have made reference above together with the presence of technical progress, attention must be paid to the demand and supply of the labour structure.

Let us consider the problem of choosing the area in which to set the stage for a series of interventions able, in the light of regional development objectives, to speed-up productive growth and an additional demand for labour. A very high ratio between agricultural employment and total employment, between unskilled labour (and also the type of work done in the family business by relatives) and total employment, the high presence of aged workers in the total labour-force, either employed or unemployed and the low level of basic education, reveal that the location of large enterprises and also of industrial complexes meets a very unfavourable situation with regard to demand and supply of labour. Therefore, in the absence of 'ad hoc' interventions that will be mentioned later, productive initiatives are either exceedingly capital-intensive (with a very low contribution to the solution of local employment problems), or the realization of the 'industrial pole' becomes, in the short run, necessarily more expansive than the location of the same productive initiatives in a different area.

On the other hand, in the case that the above mentioned characteristics of the demand and supply for labour were accompanied by the lack of social infra-structures adapted to the indispensable structural changes, the opportunity cost problems would be complicated by the inability to obtain, medium or long run notable, automatic and cumulative attraction of complementary productive initiatives plus the spreading of socio-economic benefits over the area contiguous to the 'pole': the planned initiatives run the risk of being an isolated fact both at the productive structural level and also at a territorial level.

If one starts simply from given factual situations, it would result immediately convenient to choose as first growth areas those provided with notable social infra-structures, and possibly placed in territories with a high level of industrialization and a marked tertiarisation of a high-quality (as to skill, age, basic education) local labour force. It is then clear that the chosen areas will be those notably urbanised and already attracted by an urban centre of large size.

If instead, the aim of the regional development policy is to suggest relieving these same situations characterized by the above mentioned inferior conditions, in order to reach equi-distribution and dynamic equilibrium, in a wide sense, it would be necessary to choose the best ways for enacting the development policy.

In a situation characterized by a remarkable inferiority of the quality of the labour force employed, it would be utopic to think that a spatially concentrated location would allow a large firm or an industrial complex to give a decisive impulse to productive development and occupation in the area.

Taking into account the structure of the demand and supply of labour, it is necessary when planning growth poles, to vitalise the ambient in which such poles are going to be placed, through:

a) the rationalization of agriculture, the rapid reduction of under-employment and the absorption of the ousted manpower in activities related to the same process of rationalization (at least partially), and in services indispensable to the restructuring of the demand and supply of labour;

b) the reorganization of the local productive structure and the realization, either of an initial agglomeration of small industrial and tertiary units of production already existing, or the predisposition of services common to various productive initiatives of a not very relevant size;

c) the encouragement of immediate and medium-term reorganizations, even through the construction of physical infra-structures, in order to make units of production more interdependent and to connect the region to be developed with other areas undergoing transformation inside the national and international system in an organic way, (for instance rapid transport and communications connections would be extremely useful for this purpose);

d) the predisposition of social infrastructures which are deemed necessary in order to obtain prompt and continuos changes in the qualitative characteristics of the supply of labour.[8]

Among other things, the eventuality of tertiarization phenomena on a wide enough scale, the need for coordination of physical and social infrastructures, both claim a minimum territorial dimension in terms of population and labour force, and a minimum of demographic agglomeration in one or more urban centres (and therefore in an urban system), even, if not necessarily, in a very large urban centre. If the area to be developed lacked such an urban system, it would be necessary to create it in order not to make the spatially concentrated interventions a sheer palliative. In short if the purpose of a regional policy is to develop areas whose inferiority is very evident as far as the degree of productive development is concerned, the ability to pursue a higher level of technical progress in the future and to solve the problems of open and disguised unemployment, the isolated take-off of leading firms or even of industrial complexes is not enough to obtain appreciable results, unless those investments be anticipated by, or at least accompanied by, a well-articulated set of development policy interventions among which an active labour policy must be prominent.

3. SOME LESSONS FROM THE RECENT ITALIAN EXPERIENCE

Through the law number 634 passed in 1957, Italy has tried to get going a decisive industrialization policy in the 'Mezzogiorno', concentrated in areas or nucleii of industrial development, based on previous experience from diffused regional policies. Limited areas or nucleii of industrialization are foreseen with *consorzi* or trusts to direct their development with the 'Cassa del Mezzogiorno' responsible for infrastructural interventions and facilitations for industrial initiatives.[9]

The effects of such interventions on productive development and local employment have not proved very relevant. The indirect effects of investments made or facilitated in areas or nucleii of industrialization, whether in comparison with desired collateral initiatives or in comparison with wider surrounding areas, have proved much less significant than expected.

From 1959 to 1968 (see Table 1), that is during the ten years of interventions after the approval of the above mentioned law, income produced and income per head increased at a slightly higher level in the north-western part of Italy (the most developed area) in comparison with Mezzogiorno: in other words the policy followed over the last decade has not succeeded in narrowing the gap between the North and the South with regard to productivity per head. This signifies that the objective of creating a more generally balanced regional distribution of industry and the full employment objective is even further from being realized than that of reducing differences in income between North and South. Employment in industry in the Mezzogiorno has only increased by 3.9% during the last ten years, as opposed to an increase of 10.7% in the north-western region of Italy and an increase of 10.10% in the whole of Italy. Total employment shows a reduction of 8.2% in the Mezzogiorno as opposed to — 0.6% in north-western Italy and — 4.9% in the whole of Italy.

The failure to obtain a more equilibrated regional distribution of income and employment (the Mezzogiorno still has a high level of unemployment and underemployment, notwithstanding emigration on a vast scale to other regions or other countries) has been accompanied by a very relevant increase in investments. This increase in investments is natur-

Table 1. Variations in some characteristic data from 1959–1968 in the Mezzogiorno and in the north-western Italy

	1959	1968	variations from 1959 to 1968 absolute	percentual
net per capita income at factor costs (thousands of lire in 1963 prices)				
Mezzogiorno	256,7	379,1	+ 122,4	+ 47,7
north-western Italy	564,8	838,9	+ 274,1	+ 48,5
gross income at market prices (billions of lire in 1963 prices)				
Mezzogiorno	5.553,1	8.988,9	+ 3.435,8	+ 61,9
north-western Italy	9.083,9	15.406,7	+ 6.322,8	+ 69,7
gross total investments (billions of lire in 1963 prices)				
Mezzogiorno	1.201,1	2.179,4	+ 978,3	+ 81,4
north-western Italy	2.004,6	2.629,5	+ 624,9	+ 31,2
gross fixed investments in industrial activities (billions of lire in 1963 prices)				
Mezzogiorno	241,1	493,4	+ 252,3	+ 104,9
north-western Italy	814,0	878,1	+ 64,1	+ 7,9
employment in industry (thousands of units)				
Mezzogiorno	1.785	1.856	+ 71	+ 3,9
north-western Italy	2.805	3.106	+ 301	+ 10,7
Italy	7.176	7.890	+ 714	+ 10,0
total employment (thousands of units)				
Mezzogiorno	6.500	5.963	− 537	− 8,2
north-western Italy	5.726	5.692	− 34	− 0,6
Italy	20.169	19.069	− 1.100	− 4,9

Source: *Istituto Centrale di Statistica.*

ally higher in the Mezzogiorno than in the rest of the country, especially with regard to the machinery and fixed plants. At the same time there is an increase of 94% in the value added by industrial activities in the Mezzogiorno as against 86% in the north-west of Italy. Examining the data on the dynamics of production and industrial employment together it can be concluded that: 1) differences in the increase of investments have resulted in a greater increase in productivity per head in industry in the South of Italy than in the industries of the northwest Italy; 2) the increases in productivity per head have been scarcely sufficient to compensate for the effects of the lower rate of expansion in the Mezzogiorno in comparison with north-western Italy.

As a matter of fact the data available (see Tables 2 and 3) on industrial productivity, investments and employment according to sectors and branches clearly show that the distribution of the industry outside Mezzogiorno is still, in the second half of the 'sixties', much more equilibrated than industry in the south of Italy.

The industrial policy followed since 1957 has given much importance to very large investments aimed at creating basic motrice industries in certain strategic points in the Mezzogiorno, but the result of this has been the formation of a rather unequilibrated industrial structure. Statistics demonstrate that as late as 1968 the greater part of industrial investments in

Table 2. Distribution of investments and employment in industrial sectors and categories in the Mezzogiorno and northern central Italy in 1968

	MEZZOGIORNO		NORTHERN CENTRAL ITALY	
industrial sectors and categories	investments	employment	investments	employment
mining	3,1	3,6	1,9	1,5
manufacturing	67,2	56,5	65,1	72,1
food and related industries	5,9	24,1	6,2	9,8
tobacco	0,6	1,1	0,3	0,4
textile products	4,0	6,2	8,2	17,4
clothing, furs and leather	1,6	9,1	3,1	7,6
timber products and furniture	0,7	6,4	0,9	4,2
metallurgical	14,9	5,6	11,9	8,2
mechanical	15,5	17,4	32,4	28,1
building materials	5,1	8,0	4,3	5,3
chemicals	27,5	11,4	14,0	8,1
oil and coal derivatives	11,2	2,3	2,4	0,6
rubber	3,4	1,5	2,4	1,8
synthetic fibres	2,4	1,6	2,8	1,4
paper and printing	7,0	3,8	10,5	6,3
cinema and recordings	0,2	1,5	0,6	0,8
construction and fixed plant installation	7,1	35,5	10,5	23,6
electricity, gas and water	22,6	4,4	22,5	2,8
total	100,0	100,0	100,0	100,0

Source: *Confederazione Generale dell'Industria Italiana*, Rome.

the south was concentrated in the chemical and petrochemical sectors which gave rise to only a very modest increase in total industrial employment; the very extensive mechanical sector which occupies a key position in the rest of Italy both with regard to resulting effects on the formation of capital and on industrial employment was still in 1968 inadequate for the needs of Mezzogiorno.

The high level of investment in the above named sectors made the realisation of highly capital intensive initiatives possible, with relevant

Table 3. Annual average rates of variation in production, industrial employment and in elasticity of employment with respect to output in the Mezzogiorno and in northern central Italy in the second half of the 'sixties' (percentual annual rates of variation)

	MEZZOGIORNO			NORTHERN CENTRAL ITALY		
industrial sectors and categories	variation in industrial output	variation in industrial employment	elasticity of employment with respect to output	variation in industrial output	variation in industrial employment	elasticity of employment with respect to output
mining	+ 5,6	− 1,2	...	+ 7,3	− 0,7	...
manufacturing	+ 10,2	+ 3,7	0,36	+ 7,6	+ 1,4	0,18
food and related industries	+ 2,7	− 0,2	...	+ 2,4	− 0,9	...
tobacco	− 0,2	− 4,8	...	+ 1,0	− 3,3	...
textile products	+ 8,6	+ 3,6	0,42	+ 3,4	− 1,1	...
clothing, furs and leather	+ 12,7	+ 6,0	0,47	+ 11,5	+ 5,0	0,43
timber products and furniture	+ 9,8	+ 0,3	0,03	+ 8,9	+ 0,2	0,02
metallurgical	+ 11,8	+ 4,6	0,39	+ 7,8	+ 2,4	0,31
mechanical	+ 14,0	+ 7,6	0,54	+ 9,8	+ 3,3	0,34
building materials	+ 8,3	+ 3,1	0,37	+ 5,9	+ 5,9	0,19
chemicals	+ 15,2	+ 4,7	0,31	+ 5,9	+ 1,3	0,22
oil and coal derivatives	+ 13,6	+ 5,0	0,37	+ 3,6	+ 0,7	0,19
rubber	+ 26,5	+ 18,9	0,71	+ 6,7	+ 1,4	0,21
synthetic fibres	+ 16,2	+ 10,8	0,67	+ 9,7	+ 1,7	0,18
paper and printing	+ 17,7	+ 2,3	0,13	+ 5,6	+ 0,3	...
cinema and recordings	+ 14,6	+ 2,2	0,15	+ 3,9	+ 0,8	0,21
construction and fixed plant installation	+ 7,6	+ 3,8	0,50	+ 9,5	+ 4,1	0,43
electricity, gas and water	+ 8,7	+ 4,3	0,49	+ 7,1	+ 2,5	0,35
total	+ 9,0	+ 3,6	0,40	+ 8,0	+ 2,0	0,25

effects on output and employment which in the light of the more mature experiences of other regions will not be easily repeated to the same extent: it is enough to consider that output in the chemical and petrochemical industries of the south has increased from +13–15% a year with an increase in employment equal to +4.7–5% a year with an elasticity of employment in respect to output of above 0.3 Instead output in the chemical and petrol-chemical industries in areas not recently industrialised increased from +4–6% a year, as opposed to an increase in employment of approximately 1% a year and an elasticity index of employment in respect of output equal to about 0.2.

The concentration of investments in a single unit of production and in specific basic sectors, in the hope that this would result in a series of effects encouraging further industrial initiatives extending to other areas over not too long a period of time, has given rise to doubts about the possibility of such effects being verified within a reasonably short time. It is also feared that the industrial policy adopted may lead to the establishment of a territorial concentration of meridional industry with a lack of cohesion between the various specialised industrial areas which would remain insufficiently integrated in the total framework of economic growth.

It has been objected that more time must pass before the effects of the various stimuli to large scale industrialisation can be fully appreciated. The following data contradicts this objection: industrial policy concentrated on initiatives calling for high capital intensity has been accompied by a high 'mortality rate' among small and medium sized initiatives. This fact means that an increase in employment, which could have arisen in the Mezzogiorno as a result of the industrialization policy adopted, has not been realised because of the difficulties experienced by small and medium sized firms.

The failure of these small and medium sized units of production is worrying both for the immediate effects it has on employment and industrial productivity and because the theory of growth industries, which in its turn is dependent on the growth poles theory, rests on a 'blossoming' of small and medium sized inter-connected industrial initiatives.

Now the question of whether a different industrial policy could have been adopted will be examined, together with the problem of up to what point a new policy could have been realized for growth poles or growth areas.

In order to be able to answer these questions it is necessary to keep in mind the structural characteristics of the regions to be developed. At this point it could be useful to classify each area according to particular types[10] on the basis of various structural characteristics. Given the importance of technical progress on the effects of productive growth and of compatibility between the measures necessary to obtain growth and full employment objectives, given the relationship between the quality of the labour factor and 'stock' when technical progress understood in a wide sense has finally been arrived at, and given the importance of the phenomena of underemployment and unemployment when planning full employment objecttives, it is clearly necessary to concentrate on the structural characteristics of the demand and supply of labour.

The italian Mezzogiorno can be most realistically defined as an underdeveloped area with a labour supply that is still tied to agriculture: the relationship expressed in terms of percentages between employment in agriculture and total employment was very high in 1959 and is still much higher in the meridional regions than in Lombardy and higher than the national average. Labour employed in agriculture includes numerous workers not fully employed and a potential mass of unemployed: whatever efforts to obtain industrialisation are made, will end up by accelerating the already marked process out of the agricultural sector. The flow of emigrants towards other regions or out of Italy, if existing industry cannot absorb the agriculture outflow to a sufficient degree, will continue. Italian experience during the decade from 1959 – 68 demonstrates a very high reduction of labour employed in meridional agriculture (884 000 units). The possibility of re-employment in industry was (and is) very modest, as has already been said (only 71 000 units) which led to pressure on the tertiary sector and a further expansion of the migratory movement towards north and central Italy and towards other countries. The tertiary sector became 'swollen", with important consequences for actual and future productive growth and for the possibility of resolving future unemployment problems. Net emigration from the meridional area has involved at least 1 500 000 people during the decade. The emigrants have mostly been individuals whose average age tended to be young with a relatively high level of education, initiative and capacity to adapt to new situations. This has led to a very relevant deterioration in the structure of labour supply in the departure region. The projected future increase in production will require a larger scale retraining of the labour supply in the meridional area than in the rest of Italy.

During the years 1959–68 besides the high level of emigration out of the meridional area, internal movements of the population have also been reg-

Table 4. Industrial investment per employee in the Mezzogiorno (millions of lire, trimestrial average at current prices)

industrial sectors	1957–59	1960–62	1963–65	1966–68
mining	4,3	2,9	9,4	15,1
agriculture and food	3,4	5,7	7,1	9,0
tobacco	0,8	1,1	1,1	5,1
textiles	4,6	4,1	7,1	11,9
clothing	1,2	1,7	1,9	2,1
skins and leather	1,6	2,8	2,7	4,6
timber	2,4	3,5	4,5	6,8
metallurgical	3,2	5,8	10,6	39,9
mechanical	2,8	3,6	4,6	10,3
building materials	3,1	6,2	6,9	9,3
chemicals	14,7	26,4	36,5	63,4
rubber	3,3	11,3	11,6	10,0
cellulose for textiles, artificial and synthetic fibres and textiles	—	15,2	9,7	12,8
paper and related industries	3,8	16,3	14,4	29,1
printing	2,5	2,9	4,9	10,7
plastics	7,0	6,1	5,5	6,3
total	4,5	8,4	9,3	18,8

Source: *Cassa per il Mezzogiorno.*

istered. The territorial concentration of the limited new employment opportunities, and the inadequate transport connections between agricultural and urban zones has favoured rapid urbanisation not controlled by a rational planning policy. This phenomenon has given rise among other things to a natural limitation of the possible 'diffusion effects' of the benefits of production.

On the other hand it should be said that emigration and the creation of new jobs in industrial and tertiary enterprises directly or indirectly related to development policy has not solved all the outstanding problems related to unemployment. This is illustrated by the explicit rate of unemployment (5% of the total Mezzogiorno labour force unemployed in 1968, as opposed to 3.5% in all Italy and 2.2% in Lombardy) as well as the implicit unemployment calculable in terms of the striking reduction in the total population participating in the labour force (the 30–35% which has been demonstrated in Sardinia, Sicily, Campania, Apulia is without any doubt too low).

Therefore before the progressive realization of the principles approved by the 1957 law, the Mezzogiorno already had a high quota of employed individuals working in agriculture out of the total number in employment, pockets of unemployment much more relevant than in other parts of Italy, a much lower general level of education than the Italian average, numerous self-employed workers in respect of the total labour force. Emigration was already established as a means of resolving the problem of the access of the labour supply to demand situations (particularly as far as the young were concerned). There was a net division between the country and the city, with however, phenomena of progressive urbanisation. The new development policies based on an industrialization with an ever higher level of capital intensity have avoided a relevant increase in the differences between north and south in terms of income produced but have speeded-up both emigration from the meridional areas and phenomena of urbanisation within the area.

Today the structure of the demand and supply of labour in the Mezzogiorno presents: a) a very high level of employment in agriculture in comparison with the rest of the country; b) a high rate of explicite unemployment and above all a high level of implicite unemployment calculated in terms of the reduction of the total labour force; c) differences between the level of education and capacity to show initiative and adapt to new circumstances (due, as has already been noted, to the exodus of the young) at a higher level than in the past; d) a high number of self-employed workers out of the total number in employment; e) a heavy concentration of population and of the labour force in certain urban centres (for example Palermo and Naples) with consequent social costs similar to those found in larger metropolitan centres in articulated and developed industrial areas; f) a relatively higher level of employment in the tertiary sector in comparison with other areas of Italy giving rise to underemployment within the sector.

Past experience demonstrates that a different growth policy should be followed. The size of labour reserves existing in the agricultural sector constitutes a permanent risk of an excess labour supply in relation to the demand for labour outside the agricultural sector which can only be overcome to a small extent by the expansion of the service sectors unless radically new in the sphere of social infrastructures is realised.

The risk of an excess labour supply can become in its turn another incentive to emigrate leading to the results on the qualitative structure of the remaining labour supply which have already been described. In order to avoid this risk an emphasis should be put on reinforcing social infrastructures in order to 'create' new work opportunities so as to be able to count on an expansion of industrial employment in the Mezzogiorno at a higher level than has been experienced in the past without sacrificing the pursuit of a more intense level of local productivity.

The creation of new work opportunities signifies abandoning the policy of concentrating investments in basic industries requiring a high level of capital intensity (as has often been the case in the past, see Table 4) and aiming at a diversified industrial policy which would rationalise and modernise small and medium sized firms already existing in the area (thus reducing the 'mortality' rate already described in related fields of employment) and would also put into motion a series of new initiatives in sectors particularly open to technical progress, without however failing to reinforce already existing basic industries. Among sectors open to technical progress the electromechanical tools industries, telecommunications, the construction of means of transport, sections of the clothing industry and some branches of the food products industries are of proved importance.

The investment effort necessary to realize modern industrial initiatives capable of having a relevant effect on production and employment must be of very generous dimensions. The possibility of guaranteeing an industrial demand for labour large enough to absorb most of the unemployment deriving from a decreasing demand for labour in the agricultural sector may well depend on the dimensions of this effort as well as on the sectoral structure of investments. The problem of matching the qualitative characteristics of the labour supply to the need of the demand (that is the problem of training and retraining) arises at this point. As emigration has altered the structure of the labour force, and as new industrial sectors require more ability to adapt and keep abreast of technical progress, this problem is ever more serious. In the train of the proposed industrial growth the need for specific social infrastructures arises. Investment in these infrastructures may have a profound effect on the possibility of realising a dynamic equilibrium between the demand and supply of labour and on whether or not explicit unemployment persists (under the form of structural unemployment) notwithstanding an eventual expansion of large dimensions in labour demand.

The existence of many new work possibilities in industry is a necessary condition for the partial absorption of the reduced demand in agriculture, a reduction of explicit unemployment, an increase of the total proportion of subordinate labour employed and the limitation of implicit unemployment.

However the expansion of work possibilities in industry may not be adequate both from the point of view of a general qualitative plan (absorption of new members of the labour force and of the unemployed from the agricultural sector in non-agricultural activities) and in order to specifically guarantee the limitation and absorption of implicit unemployment that presents particular qualitative characteristics (mainly with regard to sex and age in the Mezzogiorno). It is also necessary to have an important expansion of employment in the production of services, particularly in the sector of personal and social services where the characteristics of a very high elasticity of employment with respect to the product, and of products which partly meet the already stated need for social infrastructures are united.

The problem of whether or not new work opportunities in industry and the service sectors should be territorially concentrated remains open. It is evident that in order to encourage already installed basic industry, investments which maintain the existing concentration are required. From this follows a further partial concentration of investments aimed at the production of the relevant services.

However the rationalisation and the modernisation of small and medium sized firms, the localisation of new industrial enterprises (mainly medium sized) and the localisation of an extensive number of new centres of production in the field of services need not necessarily be spatially concentrated near basic industries. On the contrary, the eventual presence of the phenomena related to congestion in the urban centres under consideration, or even the likelihood of these phenomena arising in the future, as well as the opportunity to organically adapt the restructuring and rationalisation of pre-existing firms to new developments, may well impose a high degree of decentralisation of new investment initiatives.

In the Mezzogiorno the necessity to follow a policy of decentralisation over extensive areas (global growth areas) is very pressing partly because of recent errors. The necessity for a policy of close co-ordination between old and new enterprises evidently remains, which can if necessary situate industrial concentrations in chosen areas as part of an accurate territorial development policy.

Some of the lessons which can be learnt from the experiences of the Italian Mezzogiorno which is composed of extensive underdeveloped areas have been proposed. They may lead us to the following general conclusion: the theory and policy of growth poles which is partly based on the past experience of the industrialised countries probably needs to be adapted to the reality of underdevelopment situations, while keeping in mind that certain fundamental characteristics of the demand and supply of labour suggest that specific investment policies should be based in a 'milieu vivant' sufficiently rich and articulated, closely protected, and developed in complex territorial plans.

It is in this light that the expediency of giving a position of primary importance to huge investment plans in the so-called basic or leading industries must be closely re-examined.

NOTES

1. J.R. MEYER, 'Regional Economics: a Survey', *American Economic Review*, 1963, p. 22.
2. See J. MILHAU, 'La théorie de la croissance et l'expansion régionale', *Economie Appliquée*, 1956, p. 353.
3. *Cf.* the essays included in J.R. BOUDEVILLE and others, *L'Espace et les pôles de croissance*, Paris, P.U.F., 1968.
4. *Cf.* F. VITO, 'Lo sviluppo economico delle zone arretrate, sottosviluppate con particolare riguardo alla industrializzazione ed al miglioramento dell'agricoltura', *Rassegna Economica*, 1961, pp. 1–85.
5. It would be a clear derivation from the 'industrial complex analysis'. *Cf.* W. ISARD, and others, *Industrial Complex Analysis and Regional Development*, New York, Wiley, 1959.
6. *Cf.* J.R. BOUDEVILLE, *Problems of Regional Economic Planning*, Edinburgh University Press, 1966.
7. A. CALOIA, 'Riesame della teoria dei poli di sviluppo alla luce degli studi sulla crescita urbana e metropolitana, e di alcune indagini empiriche', *Città e Società*, 1968, n. 6, p. 47.
8. L.H. KLAASSEN (*Social Amenities in Area Economic Growth*, Paris, OECD, 1968, p. 139) says that 'social infra-structures affect growth in two directions [...]: first there is the demand effect, the influence of better education, housing and medical facilities, etc. on welfare and thus on the productivity of workers in the area; secondly, there is the supply effect, the attraction of amenities to modern industries and, as a result, a more rapid redevelopment...'.
9. See R. DRAGON, *L'intervento sul territorio del Mezzogiorno*, *Ricerca e studi*, Formez, Roma, 1969, p. 71, for a clear synthesis of such interventions.
10. See for example the classification into depressed and underdeveloped areas done by F. VITO in various articles, one of which is cited in Note 4.

PETER R. ODELL

2 B

Comments on Frey's report

1. M. Frey's paper confronts us with one of the fundamental issues in regional development policy and planning. This is the likelihood – for political reasons if for no others – that such policy and planning will aim at development in areas other than those which would be chosen on strictly economic grounds either by individual firms seeking to maximise their profits, or by the state seeking to secure the highest possible rate of return on the investment of scarce resources from a national standpoint. The reality of regional development policies, in which employment considerations and, more-difficult-to-quantify-considerations like 'a more balanced welfare', is stressed. Most of us from European countries, at least, will recognise just how much validity this argument has. The question as to the appropriateness of such policies – rather than of policies which seek to ensure that the best (= most economic) opportunities are always followed up – will, I think, be dealt with in other sessions. Here we may take M. Frey's presentation of the 'reality' as the starting point for our discussions.

2. In looking at the first main theme, *technical progress and the structure of the demand and supply of labour*, the phenomenon described by M. Frey of a labour force in the underdeveloped regions unable to cope with the demands of technical progress (interpreted broadly in line with the author's argument) is readily recognisable, but one wonders if the model presented is sufficiently well structured to take note of the several types of problem areas in which development might be required to 'take care' of unemployment. Such types include:

a) areas of structural unemployment arising from the decline of industries which, at an earlier period had led to the areas' growth and development e.g. many of the traditional coal-mining areas of N.W. Europe;

b) relatively underdeveloped areas of traditional agriculture or other similar occupations in countries with strongly developing national economies and significant growth zones, e.g. Southern Italy, Brittany and other parts of Western France, S.E. Germany.

c) underdeveloped areas of traditional occupations in countries with weakly growing, or stagnant, economies in which the growth zone is limited to the small area of the capital city and its immediate surroundings with only a small percentage of the country's total population involved in the growth.

3. The *active labour policy* recommended by M. Frey could have radically different component parts depending on the type of area with which one is dealing. For example, whilst one could agree that the existence of a reasonable social infrastructure might indicate the possibilities of an area's ability to solve its problems in the case of types b) and c) above, it is not self-evident in the case of a), where the provision of a social infrastructure has been built up over a long period of time such that it may not be really seriously deficient in the main aspects required. The existence of such an infrastructure in itself, however, seems unlikely to enable such an area to be covered by the analysis in this paper, but it would appear desirable that we give some attention to them in light of their significance in regional development policies of most old-industrial nations.

4. Neither does the paper appear to be an altogether valid statement for the problems of type c) areas – i.e. for regional policy planning decisions in underdeveloped countries where the labour situation throughout most of the national territory reflects the deficiencies of the sort pointed out here. In those cases the scale of the problems appears to be altogether too grand for the introduction of an articulated set of development policy interventions and for the application of the concept of 'integral or global development areas'. The cost of planning the latter both in resources and in time, appears likely to be beyond the realms of possibility for all developing countries. Moreover, these countries also often lack the kind of well articulated urban hierarchy, on the basis of which in the case of Southern Italy it has been shown to be possible to pick out areas in which development efforts might be concentrated. In light of the very marked regional disparities which exist in all developing countries and in light of the large number of such countries, we could perhaps attempt to reformulate M. Frey's ideas and concepts such that they would also be helpful in analysing the regional problems of developing countries.

5. Italian experience is presented in evidence to confirm the deficiencies of traditional regional planning methods and practice for areas of type b). The arguments presented for the first need of revitalising the 'ambiente' are persuasive in theory, but one is inclined to speculate why, in principle, this should be any more successful than the hitherto employed methodology of locating single large projects or a complex as a means of initiating a local growth cycle. An interesting question which is not dealt with in the paper at length is why the usual approach has failed. In theory, all the measures that Frey visualises as necessary to revitalise the 'ambiente' should have been initiated in a feed-back process from the construction in a locality of a large project or complex. Traditionally, one has had intuitive arguments about the local multiplier effects of such developments and, more recently, there have been several[3] attempts to quantify such effect.

6. Is the Southern Italian experience in this respect a unique one – arising perhaps from a particular combination of social and other restraints – or does it mark the beginning of a fundamentally different trend from that observed in the past as a result of industrial location policy? This is obviously an important question to resolve in light of the numerous regions whose successful development could depend upon the answer – as could the most appropriate use of scarce resources of both capital and technical expertise/managerial abilities.

7. Finally, M. Frey's somewhat depressing presentation of the Italian experience may lead to conclusions other than the one he presents, i.e. the conclusion that there is a need to adjust the mechanisms and methodologies of regional development planning to fit the socio-political realities of such areas. If the technical organisation of modern industry has so changed as to eliminate local multiplier effects; and if the underdeveloped regions with their labour and associated problems are now so far removed from an ability to participate in modern economies, then it may be alternatively argued that they (i.e. the underdeveloped regions) should be written off as areas for development. Particularly so as the recommended integral or global development policy planning does sound very costly with no possibility of a positive return on the investment. The problem then becomes one of defining the socio-economic regions without a hope of expansion and of formulating policies (e.g. the financing of migration) which will have the effect of minimising the degree of human misery which has to be suffered in such regions.

Such policies, too, could surely also be described as *active labour policies* in that they remove the labour from the social, political, institutional and other restraints of the area in question to areas within which its potential is perhaps easier to develop. Generous benefits to those that cannot leave could still further reduce the misery of the underdeveloped regions – with such benefits being a decreasing charge on national resources through the continuing fall over time of the population involved. Perhaps, therefore, in light of this alternative argument, even this session of the seminar cannot avoid a discussion of this fundamental issue which, as noted above, one saw M. Frey's paper bringing out very clearly.

TORCUATO S. DI TELLA

3A

The concept of polarized development in regional planning
A sociological interpretation

I. THE PROBLEM STATED

Most processes of economic development have taken place in an extremely uneven fashion, booms and depressions following each other and causing gross maldistribution of income between social classes and geographical regions. There has always been a feeling that there was something wrong with this uneveness of development, although it has also had its defenders. Economic theory has often argued that in order to increase the overall product it was necessary to leave the factors of production free to combine in their own way, and let the remuneration of the social classes be determined by the scarcity of their talents or resources, regardless of the inequality that might result; the mobility of the factors of production could be relied upon to correct the worst features of the system. Today, particularly in connexion with unemployment or distribution between classes, this argument is seldom heard in its extreme form. It is now accepted that considerations of social equity as well as long term productivity compel the community to intervene in market mechanisms so as to ensure a steadier rate of growth and a better sharing of income. It is not the purpose of this paper to enlarge on this very well known fact. The aim is to analyse the situation with regard to the regional distribution of the benefits of economic development among different parts of the same country. Most of the time we shall have in mind a 'mixed' economy, with a sizeable private sector, although many of our generalizations are also applicable to a socialist economy. With due precautions, some conclusions derived from a study of regions within a country can be applied as well to different countries within an evolving supra-national economic community.

One of the main reasons for differences in prosperity among the various regions of a country is their inequality in natural resources in relation to the prevailing type of technology which makes these resources usable. Thus, the Argentine pampas were no great asset during most of the 18th century, but they became valuable under 19th century conditions, and increasingly so as the century advanced. A number of other historical considerations must, no doubt, be added to complete the picture, but it is obvious that regional inequalities have a component that is much more *natural* than the components of inequalities due to social class or to cyclical ups and downs. It can thus be argued that people should preferably set things right by voting with their feet, so to say, and move to the more prosperous zones, thereby making labour scarcer in the underdeveloped areas and initiating the whole series of compensatory mechanisms studied by economic theory. In ideal circumstances, with freely moving factors of production, the worst that could happen would be that some regions might become near-deserts, but prosperous deserts, something like the present state of Nevada or Utah in the United States. Of course, we know that factors of production are not so easily movable as that. We must, however, ask ourselves: is there really any reason for stopping people from leaving a poorly endowed area within their country as fast as they can? After all, if they are going to be more efficient in the place to which they migrate, the national product will be so much the larger and eventually a part of this larger product can be used to relieve the situation of those that have been left behind. This would give rise to a *welfare oriented* regional policy, based on considerations of social equity towards those who for one reason or another remain in the backward area. The welfare policy, by making things more tolerable would retard migration, slowing down general economic growth, but it would also reduce political tensions of a separatist or revolutionary nature.

This line of argument should not be peremptorily dismissed as unreconstructed Manchesterianism. Even with a national system of planning, why use up scarce resources in trying to revivify a dying zone, where they are less productive than elsewhere? Take, for example, the case of Brazil, where the national Government, through SUDENE (Superintendencia de Desenvolvimento do Nordeste) allows tax exemptions and other advantages to capitalists who invest in the north-east, and would not do so without them. As a result of these tax exemptions and other benefits, the capitalists make or expect to make more money then what they would by investing in prosperous Sao Paulo. The region where SUDENE operates (the backward north-east) benefits from the influx of capital. But what about the national economy? Doesn't it lose a lot by this expensive and 'unnatural' operation, which sacrifices valuable tax payers' money in order to divert funds from places where they would have a higher over-all productivity?

The answer depends on the relative values of a number of economic and sociological parameters, and on the time perspective adopted, as is shown by T. Hermansen in his model of the interregional allocation of investments.[1] If, as he points out, the parameters change over a period of time owing to sociological considerations, the results are bound to be different from those that would be obtained if the parameters remained constant. Given appropriate changes, the operation, which at the beginning may be a *wasteful* one, may end by being in the best interests not only of the given region, but of the whole country.

The fact remains, nevertheless, that it is necessary to channel into the region, for a number of years, large amounts of funds from other parts of the country (government subsidies or tax rebates, and private or public investments). The next problem is how to distribute these funds in the region. Should they be concentrated in one or two promising points, or should they be spread out evenly? To what extent can local initiative be harnessed in the process, so that it will not need continuing central prodding? And if funds are concentrated in a few promising points, how can we make sure that the benefits will somehow trickle through to the rest of the region so that this will not continue to lag behind? These are the main questions which a regional planner has to face. The theory of polarized development maintains that it is best for efforts to be concentrated at a few promising points, or growth centres, within the region, which will thus become a *polarized* one. In this paper some of the sociological problems raised by the theory will be analysed. *No attempt will be made* to determine the general sociological preconditions for economic growth, a subject too vast and unwieldy for treatment here. Only those sociological problems which are directly relevant to the problem of *concentrated versus diffuse strategies* of regional growth will be analyzed.

To begin with, a definition of regions will be attempted, making a distinction between *home communities* and *catchment regions*. The forces determining the attraction of populations between various regions will be dealt with in a following section. In the concept of 'population' a number of distinct components can be found: there are different social classes or sub-classes – 'actors' as they are referred to in the text – some of which are more strategic for economic growth than others. The differential behaviour of each social actor will be the subject of a separate section. Further on, a link is established with an economic model of regional growth by suggesting some sociological factors responsible for the attraction of investments to a given region. Finally, the changes in social stratification brought about by the new investments are considered. Throughout, the exposition is in the form of propositions easily translatable into formulae which lend themselves to the construction of simulation models of regional growth.

2. HOME AND REGION

Geographical space may be divided up in a number of arbitrary ways. It has no clearly determined 'cells', separable from each other by definite boundaries.[2] For the purposes of this paper, though, two levels of human clusterings will be defined. The most minute we will call the *home community*, encompassing people who are in daily contact; a broader one is the *region*, which includes several home communities solidary with each other through various types of interrelatedness. We can envisage a *home community* as an urban centre and the area round it, which is within daily commuting distance of the centre. This of course is vague, because everybody has a different tolerance for the length of his journey to work, but it may be more clearly determined through research on actual commuting. An average or maximum tolerable length may be determined, measured either in actual distance or in time or cost; it will probably vary with differing circumstances. In the case of London, for example, it would certainly include the whole of the Greater London area, plus parts of the neighbouring counties, but would exclude cities like Oxford or Cambridge. For smaller towns, the acceptable commuting distance may be shorter. If there are two or three medium-sized urban centres within commuting distance of each other, they will all be included in the same home community. The delimitation of these areas may need more precise criteria so as to rule out dubious cases where a town could be allocated either to one or to another powerful neighbour. It is not pertinent to this paper to give a more detailed description of appropriate methods, of which there may be a wide variety, all containing arbitrary elements, though all based on the common concept of the direct area of influence. In this way the whole area of a country could be divided up in a set of *home communities*, each of them having a given population and a centre of gravity or a communications cente. In purely rural zones in sparsely populated countries the problem may occasionally raise difficulties owing to the inapplicability of the concept of 'commuting to work', but it should not be too difficult to find an equivalent criterion.

It should be noted that for people living near the borders of a given home community it will be easier to go to work in some parts of the neighbouring community than in the centre of their own. It should be more difficult for them, though, to go to the centre of the neighbouring community than to the centre of their own, and this is what makes the boundary-line relevant. Members of the same community are more likely to know each other or to be affected by the same things than are those from outside. This is so even if the absolute level of interaction is not very high, as happens in large cities. It is also possible that a member near the border will have *more* in common with his immediate neighbours across the line than with most people in his own home community. But he will be much more of a stranger for the inhabitants of the rest of that nearby community than for those in his own, and this compensates for his friendliness across the border. When it comes to grouping home communities into regions, more serious problems arise. It is not very common that obvious geographic or economic criteria are present for boundary delimitation, and the usual situation is that each criterion gives a different regional boundary. It is possible to look for averages, or to apply gravitational models for dubious cases, eventually using some other *ad hoc* concepts, thus deriving a unique set of regions. The idea is that each one of them has a certain unity, either because of homogeneity or because of common dependency on a centre (this has given rise to the nomenclature of 'homogeneous' and 'polarized' regions, which is useful and descriptive enough). The interrelatedness between parts of a region is considerably less than that within a home community, but it still represents an important sociological fact. The assumption is that within a region the intensity of forward and backward linkages –to apply a concet from economics to a wider field – is greater than outside the region. This will make for solidarity among its inhabitants. They have a direct and rather visible stake in each other's well being, even if they are not in daily contact. It would seem that the key condition is the *accessibility* of the various parts of a region for any of its members. The individual member is interested in what happens in the region because the whole of it being easily accessible he can at any time make use of the existing facilities; he will therefore be prepared to make some effort or sacrifice in order to improve these facilities for purely selfish motives.

This basic economic calculus is likely to be implicit rather than explicit, and to take the more palatable form of regional patriotism or pride. This way of looking at things suggests one possible definition of a region, which may be particularly useful when studying problems of migration. A region can be thought of as that part of a country which is within easy reach from a given point, so that people living at that point may *use its resources* and therefore consider them to some extent *their own*. This definition raises immediately a number of questions. The first one is that there will be as many regions as 'points' in a country. Let's suppose that instead of 'point' we speak of *home community*. Then each home community will have its own region, and every region will overlap with several others. This implies that our concept of region – having no special 'reality' of its own – will be useful – mostly for analytical purposes – the more closely 'real' regions constructed with the aforementioned methods coincide with our analytical regions, probably those corresponding to the home communities which are the centre of the 'real' regions. But what is the use of our analytical concept? It helps us to understand the situation prevailing at its central home community. People at that community will be attached not only to the resources available to them at their own home, but also to those in the whole region, which because of this we will call the *catchment region*. The inhabitant of the community will be protected from the lures of the great metropolis not only by the more homely attractions in his immediate surroundings, but also by the diversified resources to be found in his catchment region.

It could be argued that it is better to look at things from the opposite point of view, and to define a region around a home community by including in it those areas *from which* certain important effects may reach the given community. The individual living in its centre would be concerned with the region because he could expect harm or benefit from what happens in it. This point of view is as justifiable as the other one, and in some senses more satisfying theoretically. But it is immensely more complicated to calculate the boundaries of a region in this fashion. So many things from outside a community can influence it, that the concept becomes extremely slippery. Without denying that it may be worth while exploring ways and means of measuring it, it seems for the moment more useful to look at things *from the community outwards*. Not that we advocate measuring influences of the community on other communities, which would pose similar problems. Our approach, as stated above, is to estimate the area to which the individual living in a given place has access, using existing means of transportation. To visualize this process, and as a first approximation, we may think that it includes those areas which are near enough to the home community under consideration, so that its inhabitants can go there regularly either for business or recreation without changing their home. Empirical research will be needed to determine the relevant distance, which will vary according to the economic status of the individual concerned, mainly according to whether he owns a car or not. Later on we will introduce this qualification in the size of regions, but for the moment we will limit ourselves to considering the average citizen, so that for every home community there is one and only one catchment region.

3. THE ATTRACTION OF POPULATIONS

Let us now take two masses of population, which may be two cities or, to make the case more general, two home communities, situated at a certain distance and exerting a set of influences over each other. We are particularly interested in the tendency of one to attract migration from the other. It sounds quite natural to assume that the larger community will attract population from the smaller one, because of the ampler resources of all kinds to be found in the larger city. Several gravitational models have been suggested to explain this force.[3] These have been derived from the formulae which represent the attraction between two physical masses or two electric charges. But another element should be taken into account, namely the average income level of each community. If the small community is richer than the large one, it may not feel much attraction towards the larger but poorer metropolis. On the contrary, the small but prosperous community may get its population from the city poor who in any case are not enjoying many of the benefits of living in a large town. The lure of money is, then, different from the lure of sheer numbers, but the latter also exists independently of income differentials: even with no differences in wages, one is always more likely to find a good opportunity in a large town than in a village.

The attraction which a population mass exerts over another has, therefore, two components: sheer numbers, and better standards of living. Let us begin with sheer numbers, which is the one more often analyzed. A force may be defined, on the gravitation analogy, as proportional to the product of both populations and inversely proportional to the square of the distance. The distance may be measured in kilometres, or in cost of transportation. To make the formula more general, we may allow both populations to have an exponent different from unity, and the distance also may have exponent different from 2. On the other hand, when we want to analyze the attraction operating in a given home community per unit of population (that is, the attraction on each person) we should drop its own population from the formula (assuming its exponent was unity). The result may be called the *migratory tension* which in its simplest expression, with all exponents equal to unity, will be:

$$M_{ij} = k_l \frac{P_j}{d_{ij}}$$

where M_{ij} is the migratory tension existing in i and originating in j, k_l a constant, P_j the population of the attracting j community, and d_{ij} the distance between the two places.

The above formula would apply even if there were no differences in income per capita. To take standards of living into consideration it has been proposed that the above formula should be altered, substituting the total income of the attracting community for its population. We would then have, including at the same time the population and the difference of income effect, the following formula:

$$M_{ij} = k_l \frac{P_j y_j}{d_{ij}} = k_l \frac{Y_j}{d_{ij}}$$

where y_j is the per capita income in community j and Y_j its total income.

There are other possible formulations, which may be more adaptable to special cases, but on the whole we can feel quite safe in working with this expression. It should be pointed out that following this formula strictly the attraction exerted by a population over its neighbours would be infinity at zero distance and would decline in a hyperbola, first sharply and then more moderately till beyond a certain distance it disappeared for all practical purposes. To make the values more realistic, we may decide that the maximum effect of attraction is reached at the border of the home community, that is, at the daily commuting distance which we will designate by c_i. Thus maximum attraction which a population centre i can exert over another, which would be very near to it, would be equal to $k_l \frac{Y_i}{c_i}$.

To complete the picture we should take into account a further factor.

We know that there are towns which do not suffer net outmigration to bigger urban centres in spite of being within their gravitational field. This can only be because there are forces retaining population where it is. These forces are not only due to the inertia of people shunning a change in their way of life, but may also arise from positive attraction to their own community. In a sense, the gravitational field which their own home community generates outside its boundaries may be thought of as operating within its own area. The individual would, thus, be exposed to tension from outside inducing him to migrate, but also to a retentive embrace from his own community. This latter magnitude might be calculated with the same gravitation formulae as above. The problem arises as to how to calculate the corresponding distance, because if it were zero then the retentive force would be infinity and nobody would ever move. The simplest solution is to assign to this force the maximum value that the gravitational field it creates may have, that is, the one existing at distance c_i (the commuting distance). If this is the greatest force the community can exert over others, when they are just on its borders, it may be assumed that it coincides with the one it exerts over itself. A different coefficient (k_2) might be considered to account for the different type of phenomenon, thus giving the following formula for the retentive home pull (H_i) in community i:

$$H_i = k_2 \frac{Y_i}{c_i}$$

Whether there is net migration or not depends on whether the *migratory tension* induced by the other population centre is larger than the *home pull* locally exerted. If the balance is negative there will simply be no outmigration while if the balance is positive migration will take place at a rate proportional to the difference, which we will call the *net migratory tension* (we will then use the name *gross* or *absolute* migratory tension for the term first defined). Thus we will have, in community i, as a result of influences from j, a net migratory tension (NM_{ij}) as follows:

$$NM_{ij} = k_1 \frac{Y_j}{d_{ij}} - k_2 \frac{Y_i}{c_i} \text{ (or zero if this expression is negative)}$$

A simplifying assumption, which we will follow from now on, would make $k_1 = k_2 = k$. A graphic representation of the gravitation fields around two home communities, a large and a small one, would appear as in Figure 1.

In Figure 1 it may be seen that the gross migratory tension induced in point *i* by population *j* (M_{ij}) is smaller than the home pull of population *i* (H_i), and therefore there is no migration. The population of *j* is assumed to be greater than that of *i* (though they are not directly represented in the figure). The commuting distance in *j* has been shown as slightly longer than in *i*, which is probably a correct assumption owing to the larger size of *j* (although commuting distance would not be linearly proportional to the size of the city). The lines representing the gross migratory tension created by each centre around it have been termed M_{ij} and M_{ji} in order to keep to the notation in the text, although strictly speaking in a graph of this type it would be more correct to designate them by M_{kj} and M_{ki}.

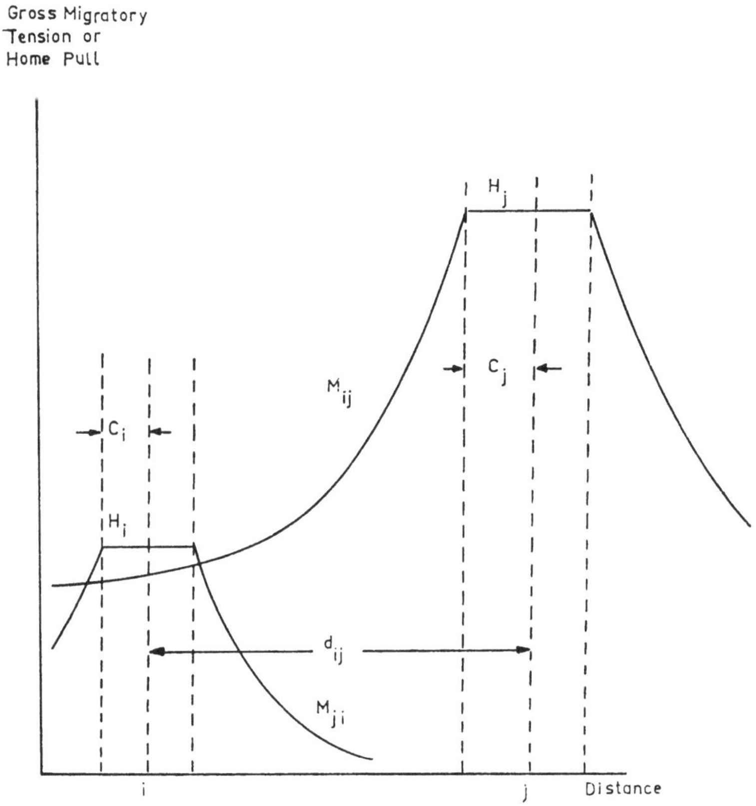

Figure 1. Migratory gravitational field between two population centres (home communities).

The simplest way to generalize this scheme and make it applicable to more cases would be to consider communities always in pairs. The home pull, then, would have to confront only one gross migratory tension at a time. Thus, if we assume a medium sized community exposed to migratory tension from a provincial capital which is not enough to overcome the local pull, no migration will ensue. If we assume, further, that there is also a migratory tension originating in the much more populous though distant national capital, this tension should be tested against the home pull, without being added to the tension derived from the provincial capital.

This extremely atomized way of looking at things is however in need of some corrections. It is true that most migration tensions are not additive, but in some instances there are groups of towns whose attractions may be combined. Thus, an Edinburgh professor considering migration to London will be attracted not only by the resources to be found in that city, but also by the knowledge that he will be within easy reach of Oxford and Cambridge, which happen to be within London's catchment region. Before he takes his decision to move he will of course put on the other side of the balance not only what he has in Edinburgh but also the resources of nearby Glasgow or even of the Highlands, all within *his* catchment region. We should then modify the extreme atomistic approach outlined above by allowing communities within a region to pull together. But the way this intervention takes place will differ according to whether we are analyzing the migratory tension or the home pull. The migratory tension acting on a community from another one will be due to the total mass of the population existing in the catchment region of the other community operating from the centre of gravity of its region (or its communications centre). To oppose this tension, the community under consideration can call on *its own home pull* and of the added 'migratory tension' produced in it by the other communities within its catchment region. It is as though those other communities were attracting the one under consideration towards themselves, and putting this force at the disposal of the home pull. Thus, in resisting the migratory tension from the big metropolis, the small community can use not only its own home pull, but also some extra strength derived from its region. This extra strength, of course, is considerably weaker, being located outside the community in question, than it would be if it were on the spot.

A typical situation is represented in Figure 2. For simplicity we suppose that the whole country consists of only three communities, *i*, *j*, and *m*. The one, *i*, is a small locality while *j* is the metropolis, and *m*, a provincial capital.

With each one operating on its own, that is with no regional bonds, the gravitational field is described by the full lines. It shows that both the small community and the provincial capital undergo a net migratory tension to the metropolis. Let us assume now that owing to the construction of a better road between *i* and *m*, both become part of the same catchment region (the province). They now benefit from each other's field of gravitation, adding its value to their home pull. Both become capable of resisting the gravitational pull to the metropolis. It could be argued that it is unfair to have allowed the two provincial towns to merge in a region, while the national metropolis stayed as it was. This is not too unrealistic, though, because a

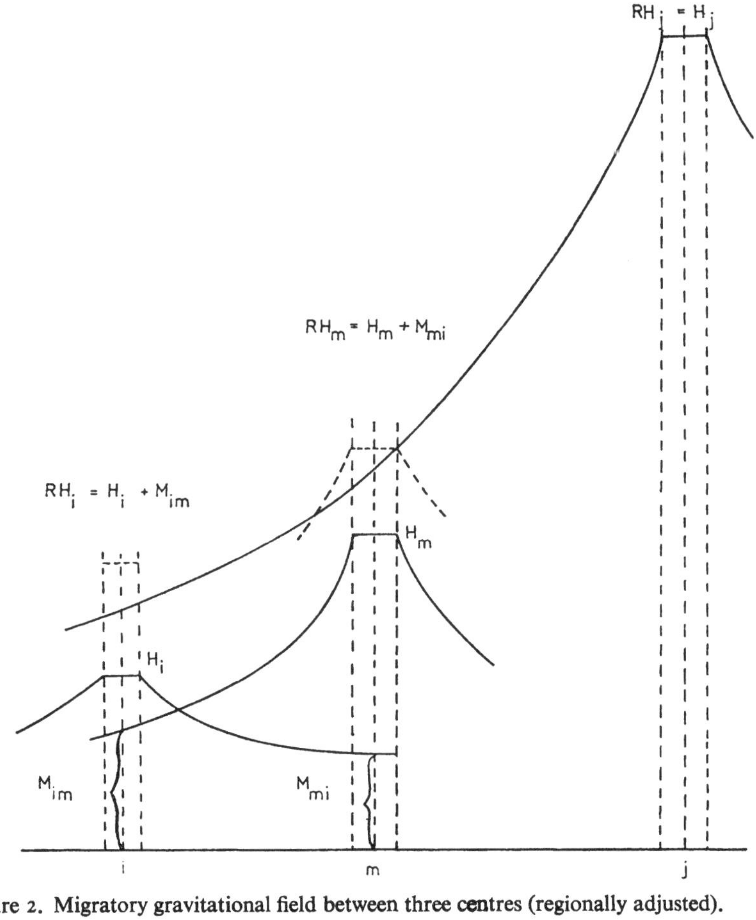

Figure 2. Migratory gravitational field between three centres (regionally adjusted).

national metropolis will often gain very little strength by the inclusion of its catchment region, while in the outlying parts of the country the inclusion of the region will make a lot of difference because proportionately it adds much more to the home community considered. It should be noted, also, in Figure 2, that the small community now *benefits* from the size of the provincial capital. The new home pull in the small community is

$$RH_i = H_i + M_{im}$$

(we write the adjusted tensions and pulls with a prefixed R to mark the fact that the regional situation has been taken into account).

RH_i is greater than RM_{ij} (the migration tension to the metropolis, which is the same regionally adjusted or unadjusted) because the local home pull has been backed up by the gravitational field of *m* at *i*, namely M_{im}. If the provincial capital were smaller, say equal to *i*, then its field would be represented by a curve as 'low' as that of *i*, then its field would be represented by a curve as 'low' as that of *i*, and would therefore have cut *i* at a much lower level. In that case M_{im}, the local gravitation created by the provincial capital in the small town, might have been so small that it would have been incapable of raising the local home pull to a sufficient level to prevent migration.

Regional adjustment adds not only to a community's home pull but also the migratory tension it creates elsewhere. This field takes into account the total population in the region, and it operates from its centre of gravity, or better from its communications centre. In Figure 2 it has been represented with dotted lines as spreading from *m*, which is assumed to be the communications centre of the province. There is no similar one spreading from the small community *i*, because this is not the centre of its own region, either from the point of view of the communications network or of population. As for the metropolitan field, it does not change with regional adjustments because in this case the metropolis coincides with its own region.

To complete the gravitational analysis with regions taken into account, we should see now what happens *within the region*. This should be done in a second stage. Having determined the capacity of each home community within the region to resist outside tensions, we should now focus our attention inside regional boundaries, using *only non-regionally adjusted values*. In the case of Figure 2 the small community can resist with its own home pull the migratory tension exercised from the provincial capital. Thus, in the case described, owing to regional integration (a good communications network), there is no net migration of any type. In other cases, it might be that though regional integration to the metropolis, this is only at the expense of increasing migration from the small localities to the provincial capital. Thus, let us assume that in Figure 2 community *i* were about half its size, and therefore covered by the gravitational field of the provincial capital. Having such a small field itself, it would not have been able to make much of a contribution to its capital, and there would have been migration from both cities to the metropolis and from the small community to the provincial capital. As a result of this latter migration, after some time the provincial capital might have gained more from its hinterland than it lost to the metropolis, thus developing a more powerful home pull, which might be check enough to further losses. It would continue, though, absorbing population from its hinterland, thereby growing even faster than before. At a given point its gravitational field would be strong enough to allow the small communities around it, like *i*, to increase their home pull (regionally adjusted) and so to resist the attraction of the metropolis, but they would continue to feed the provincial capital. This, however, will not necessarily happen; the outcome depends on the initial values and also on a number of other variables, as we shall see later.

A typical situation arises when there is a cluster of towns of about equal size, one of which is in a central position, so that it has access to all the others but the others are not linked adequately among themselves. This 'star' pattern is common enough. For example, historically Tucumán in the north of Argentina was in such a position, and it still is, although now it has a heavier preponderance in population over its neighbours than it used to have. Let us suppose that the central town is surrounded by five other towns, all with the same population (including the central one). Let the population (or income) of each one be 100, the distance separating the towns 100 km., and the commuting distance in all cases 25 km. The pattern will be as shown in Figure 3. The central town can incorporate all others within its catchment region. But for the other towns only the central one is included in their region (in other directions they are bounded by mountains, national frontiers, or desert areas). The situation may be such that most of these towns are being subjected to migratory tension from the metropolis superior to the regionally adjusted home pull. Let us take, for example, one of the peripheral towns, A_4. Its situation will be as follows, assuming constant k to be equal to unity:

Local home pull: 100/25 = 4
Gravitational influence of rest of region (only A_1): 100/100 = 1
Regionally adjusted home pull: 4 + 1 = 5

If the migratory tension from the metropolis is larger than this, say 5.2, migration will take place. A similar situation will arise at the other peripheral towns. At the central city (A_1) the situation may be different. Its regionally adjusted home pull is greater, because it benefits from the cooperation of all five other towns, and not just one, as was the case with the others. So we will have:

Local home pull: 100/25 = 4
Gravitational influence of rest of region (five cities of 100 population): 5 × 100/100 = 5
Regionally adjusted home pull: 4 + 5 = 9

The migratory tension from the metropolis might be larger in this central city than in the others, as it is likely to be nearer to it, but probably the difference will not be so great as to produce outmigration from it.

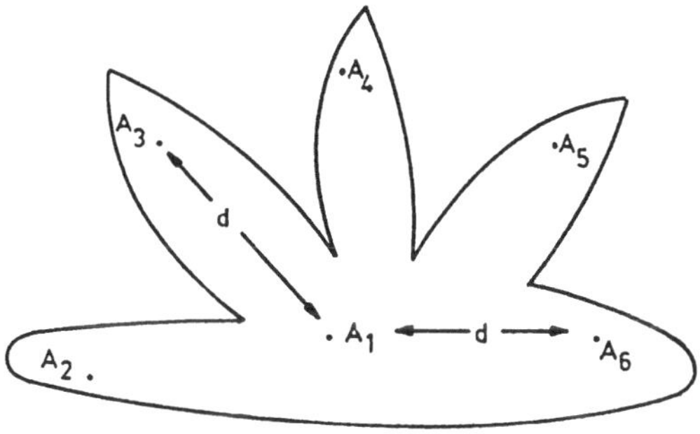

Figure 3. A star pattern of cities in a region. The boundary which has been drawn represents the limits of the catchment region of city A_1. For all other cities, catchment regions include only themselves and the star city.

Let us assume now that the country doubles its population. If this duplication is spread out evenly it will affect all places, including the metropolis, and the situation as far as the gravitational field is concerned will be unchanged. That is, migration will continue from the peripheral towns to the metropolis, thus slowly tilting the balance in favour of the latter, which will therefore grow more than proportionately, and in due course may start exerting its influence over the centrally located city also.

But let us assume that through some exogenous intervention, population increase in our region can be distributed in an uneven fashion, for example, all of it being concentrated in the central star city. Total population of the region would have doubled, that is, risen from 600 to 1200, and as the five peripheral towns remain with 100 each the population of the central place will be 700, that is, a sevenfold increase. The situation now, any of the peripheral towns will be as follows:

Local home pull (the same as before, because the population did not increase): 100/25 = 4
Gravitational influence from the rest of the region (only the enlarged central city A): 700/100 = 7
Regionally adjusted home pull: 4 + 7 = 11

As the metropolis has doubled its population, the migratory tension it exerts will have doubled also, that is, will be 2 × 5.2 = 10.4. This force is weaker than the regionally adjusted home pull, and there is therefore no migration away from the region. But if we look closer at our figures, we shall see that within the region the excessive growth of its centre will exert a dominating influence over the peripheral towns. Restricting ourselves to the within-region analysis, we shall see that a peripheral town will have a local home pull of 4, while it will be attracted to the regional centre with a force of 7, thus producing migration. The policy of stopping migration from the region to the metropolis has been successful, but at the price of depleting the peripheral towns to the benefit of the central town. This situation, which often occurs, explains why local rivalries between diverse aspirants to the status of provincial growth centre may wreck the entire regional policy. No locality wants to yield because it fears that if it does a snowball effect will get under way, benefiting some better placed rival.

The region will not be much better off with a policy of equally distributed growth, because in that case all the peripheral towns would continue to decline *vis à vis* the metropolis, having perhaps the sad compensation of seeing the centrally located star town also stagnate (though somewhat less than they). One possible solution would be the adoption of a more moderate version of the polarized development policy. Instead of concentrating all population growth in the star centre, the peripheral towns could be allowed to increase by 50 per cent (while the whole region increases by 100 per cent), the rest of the growth being concentrated in the star centre, which would then expand to reach a population of 450. In the periphery we would now have:

Local home pull: 150/25 = 6
Gravitational influence from the rest of the region (only from star centre A_1): 450/100 = 4.5
Regionally adjusted home pull: 6 + 4.5 = 10.5

As the migratory tension from the metropolis is 10.4, outmigration will have been stopped, as in the previous case. But the more moderate polarization policy has an important side effect: within the region there will not be migration from the periphery to the centre, because the local home pull will be greater than the migratory tension to the star centre (6 against 4.5). This solution is more likely to obtain support from the peripheral towns than the previous one, although they would still have to face the fact that their rival will outstrip them by a big margin.[4]

In our calculation it may seem that the population of a peripheral town would have reached 200 in the case of a 'homogeneous spread', while it would reach only 150 in that of the 'moderate polarization'. But this is not so, because from these figures we must subtract the effects of the outmigration that would take place to the metropolis in the first case. In accordance with the way we estimate this migration the end result of the first policy will leave the peripheral town with more or with less population than under polarized development.

To understand the real processes of regional development it is necessary to refine our analysis, dividing the population according to its social stratification and introducing certain factors significant of the dynamism of the area. We will now take a closer look at the social and economic forces that help to sustain the attractiveness of a given community.

The gravitational field of social actors

The various social groups existing in a community will react to the gravitational influence on the population in different ways. They will also make different contributions to the economic and social development of their home place. In this section we shall analyse their differential migratory behaviour, and in the following one their contributions to further development.

There are several ways in which a population can be divided into social strata or classes. For our purposes, we establish the following categories: urban working class, rural working class, urban middle class, rural middle class, urban executives, rural executives, government officials, cultura specialists and associationist leaders. There is some heterogeneity in this classification, as it includes some groups that are economically defined and others that are culturally determined, but it is adequate for our purposes. We will call these groups *social actors*, which suggests that each of them tends to act in individual and characteristic ways. The classification approximates to a three-tier hierarchy. In the upper tier we would have the urban and rural executives, the government officials, and some cultural specialists; the middle level would include the urban and rural middle classes and most of the cultural specialists, while the lower rung would be occupied by the working class, urban or ural. The associationist leaders could appear at any part of the stratification gamut, but they will mostly be found in the upper and middle tiers, or get to these if they come from anywhere else.

By executives we mean persons occupying important administrative positions responsible for the supervision of quite a number of people, and their equivalent in the professions. They may be the owners of private enterprises or senior managers or professional experts of a similar status. Those with a lower standing would be classed in the residual category of middle class, where people are not normally expected to make very strategic decisions in their jobs. Government officials are those who are at a level of responsibility similar to that of the executives, and they could include members of the armed forces. Their lower ranks would be in the middle class. In the rural sector (which may be part of the same home community) the situation is similar. The dividing line between middle and working class poses the usual problems, a possible criterion being the one that assigns to the middle class anyone having either a white collar job or who owns or manages a means of production of more than negligible value. The cultural specialists would be the teachers, journalists, intellectuals, priests, students and artists. In their case the nature of their work has made us include all of them in the group, without dropping the lower components into the residual middle class. The associationist leaders are a very special category, often with few members and with only transitory membership in the group. They are one of the more strategic elements in the social dynamism of a given region, so we may be justified in considering them in more detail.

An associationist leader is anybody who takes active part in representative or 'voluntary' associations or civic activities outside the requirements of his job. A union activist would qualify; a public relations officer probably not. There are some borderline cases, especially full-time, paid representatives (generally elected), such as union officials or members of Parliament or of local councils: we would include these owing to the nature of their work. Apart from associationist leaders who are professionals, others would have to qualify for inclusion in the category by the interest they take in such activities, the determination they show in carrying them out and the time they give to them. This suggests that the group will fluctuate more than others, and that it may have a high mortality ratio, for many people become disinterested in associationist activities after a certain time. The rate of disillusionment may be higher or lower depending on a number of social and cultural factors. On the other hand, since the people who make a living out of being associationist leaders are few, especially at local levels, most of those who engage in such activities will maintain close links with the group they come from. In a sense, it may be said that each group puts a number of associationist leaders in the field, either by paying them or simply by creating the conditions that induce some of its members to take a keen interest in the public weal. If we wished to go into greater detail we might subdivide associationist leaders according to the stratificational group with which they maintain organic ties. Alternately, we might lump together the various social actors in two or three broad categories (right and left, rich and poor, urban and rural) and assign the leaders to one of these camps. This is not necessary for the purposes of the present paper, though it might be useful if we wished to add a dimension of social conflict to our study.

As was suggested before, each of the social actors will react to population gravitation in a different way. For a community it is important not only to keep its population but also to have a good proportion of each component, otherwise, however large it may be, it will lack the necessary dynamism. The case is particularly serious for decaying areas, which often lose first their more dynamic elements, thus becoming increasingly incapacitated for recovery. In the rest of the present section we shall see what hypotheses can be stated about the behaviour in the gravitation field of each of the social actors. In the next section we will analyze the contribution that each group can make, directly or indirectly, to development, mostly by attracting new investments. Finally, in a further section, we will describe the process through which new investments alter the size of social groups in a community, or give more prosperity to some and promote the lower groups to the upper positions. The interlocking of these various processes can be built into a model which should simulate the actual path of regional development. We will only outline the main characteristics of this model in the present paper, so as not to overtax the non-mathematical reader. A grasp of the essentials of the model should make it easier to appreciate the advantages (and some of the dangers) of the polarized development of a region.

To begin with, the simplest way to analyze the migratory behaviour of a social actor is to suppose that it follows exactly the same laws that we have observed hitherto, with the proviso that it takes into account only the population masses (and incomes) of actors of the same type. For example, the cultural specialists would have a given population and per capita income in each home community, and these values would be the ones affecting them. They would ignore the rest of the population. This is not as implausible as it may seem because that 'rest of the population' is in point of fact indirectly taken into account, since it is generally responsible for the size of the social actor within its borders. Thus, if we take a hypothetical small city in the interior of a backward area, which has a tenth of the population of a nearby central city, the small city would suffer an attraction from the central city and develop a home pull, the strength of which would depend on the ratio of their populations (and on the distance and commuting length), following the gravitation model applied in the previous section. Let us assume a situation of equilibrium so that there is no migration. But let us assume further that the small city has a smaller percentage of cultural specialists than the central city (a very likely possibility). Then, if we use the formula for social actors suggested above, the cultural specialists would suffer a migratory tension from those in the central city greater than the home pull they can exert on thermselves; they would therefore migrate. This is what common sense would make us expect: for the cultural specialists the larger city is more 'valuable' than for some of the other groups, because it has more of the resources they are interested in represented by the number of their colleagues living there (we have assumed equality of per capita income). A similar situation might occur with the associationist leaders, though probably the opposite would be the case with government officials: it is not uncommon for the proportion of government officials to total population to be greater in a small town than in a larger city, though this might not be so if the latteris a provincial capital.

We may therefore provisionally accept this method of calculating the gravitational field for social actors together with all the regional adjustments we introduced before. We might, however, have to make allowance for the fact that the relative importance of the attraction of numbers and of money may be different for different actors. We took this double attraction into account in the general case by making the migratory tension proportional not simply to the population of the attracting centre but also to its per capita income (the product of both being the total income Y_i which was used in the formulae in the previous section). Now, we may want to give different weights to each variable. One way to do this is by letting the variables be affected by an exponent, which may vary according to the type of social actor in question or, conceivably, according to still other variables. If we represent the concepts with the same symbols as before, but with an additional sub-index (between parentheses) to indicate which actor we are talking about, we will have the formula for migratory tension on actor *a* in community *i* induced from *j* (regionally unadjusted):

$$M_{(a)ij} = k_{(a)1} \frac{P^{\alpha}_{(a)j}\, y^{\beta}_{(a)j}}{d_{ij}}$$

A similarly adjusted formula will give the home pull acting on the social actor in the same community.

When concentrating on a given actor, we may drop the corresponding sub-indices. Since, for a given actor, the exponents of *P* and *y* will always be the same, we can also simplify matters by calling the term $P^{\alpha}{}_{j}\, y^{\beta}{}_{j}$ by the same name, which can be *size*, represented by S_j (with the necessary added sub-index if we wish to identify the social actor we are referring to). Size, then, will have the same role as total income (Y_j) had in the previous section. In future discussions we will refer to size with this meaning, and we must keep in mind that in the assumption of $\alpha = \beta = 1$ and of equality of per capita incomes, size is equivalent to population of the actor.

We have, then, for a given actor, in home community *i* (dropping the actor sub-indices):

$$M_{ij} = k_1 \frac{S_j}{d_{ij}} \qquad H_i = k_2 \frac{S_i}{c_i}$$

representing respectively the migratory tension from *j* and the home pull. These values should be regionally adjusted following the general principles previously enunciated.

The method we have just outlined, treating each type of actor separately, may in some cases be unrealistic. It would give odd results if we were to continue subdividing the actors and to insist on applying separate gravitational fields for each new subactor type. The solution is to allow the fusion of actors for gravitational purposes in certain circumstances. For example, it could be maintained that urban executives and government officials pull together. Or, with a greater degree of probability, that urban and rural working classes should be added to each other. This latter procedure could be applied when computing the field for the rural working class but not for the urban working class. Thus, a rural working class in a small community is attracted by the urban working class in the large city, and not only by the rural working class in this community (which may be very small). A working class might even be attracted by a middle class in another city (and by the middle class in its own home town). We do not propose here to consider rules which would need more empirical information before they can be formulated with any likelihood of accuracy. For the moment we can insist on separate gravitational fields, except that a rural working class is attracted (and home pulled) not only by itself but also by the corresponding urban working class; that a similar phenomenon occurs at the middle class level; and that a middle class may add its weight to its corresponding working class under conditions of very high social mobility, which make the middle class look like a natural extension of the working class.

An added complication possibly worth including is the fact that social actors may vary in respect of the distance to be taken into account for the determination of their catchment region because of differences in the amount of resources they command (measured by their per capita income). Upper income actors can move more easily than poorer ones, and therefore their *catchment region* will be larger. The week-end commuting distance will not be directly proportional to income, but may increase with it at a reducing rate. The larger catchment region for upper actors does not have unequivocal results as far as their capacity to resist the attraction of the big city is concerned. Not only their own home catchment region will be increased, but also that of their colleagues in the big city, who will also capitalize the resources in their enlarged regional environment. In general, however, it may be said that the increased regional dimension for upper actors helps them to resist the attraction from the metropolis. But the small proportion of upper actors generally found in small towns makes their situation worde than would appear from the total population figures alone.[5]

In any case, with these methods we shall be able to calculate, for a given social actor in a community, the net migratory tension (NM_{ij}), if any, to which it is subjected from various other centres, outside or within its region. It would be convenient to be able to translate this tension into a flow, taking place in time. The tension is somewhat akin to the gravitational concept of potential and we want an equivalent of intensity of current, giving the number of people (members of the social actor) migrating to the attracting centre per year. The net migratory tension should be divided by a magnitude representing the *resistance* to migration. We must of course apply the gravitational and electrical analogies with care, because in a sense we have already made allowance for the resistance to migration in the form of the home pull, and also the resistance provided by the distance has been in a sense taken care of in the formula giving the gross migratory tension (though the exponent it ought to have is open to discussion). There is no point, on the other hand, in considering now the cost of moving, because this is simply another way of measuring distance. Therefore, we are left with two components of resistance: a cultural component, measuring a non-population or income determined attachment to one's own community, and a loss of relative status element, which depends on the relative status within the community which the migrating individual will have at his new place of residence compared with his status in his home community.

The cultural component of the resistance to move may be considered to have a fixed magnitude for each social actor and type of community. It may change slowly over time as a consequence of attitude changes particularly in matters concerning family structure and the whole mental modernization complex. There will be a certain value below which it cannot fall. The relative social status component may be measured in the following way: let us define the social status of an actor by reference to how many people the average member has below himself. Each actor has an average income: we should range actors according to their average income, making the additional supposition that within an actor the 'average' member has half the number of his colleagues below himself. Then we calculate the percentage of the total population represented by the actors placed below the one we are considering in the hierarchy just constructed. That figure, plus half the percentage formed by our actor, will measure the relative social status of the 'average' member of the actor under consideration in his own home community. All actors, rural or urban, belonging to the community, should be included. If the community is completely urban, the relative status of its working class will be the lowest (though not zero, because the average member of the working class has half that class below himself). If it is a community with a large rural sector, then probably the relative status of its urban working class will be somewhat higher, in some cases even very high. The relative status of the upper actors in a backward community will generally be higher than the one those same actors enjoy in a metropolitan centre, because in the small community the upper actors are likely to form a smaller percentage of the total population than in the larger and more developed city. There might be some important variations in this respect for much depends on the extent of the home community considered, particularly on the size of the rural population contained therein.

The difference in relative status between the social actor in his home community and the one which his peers have in the attracting community will provide a resistance to moving. This is very likely to be the case for most provincial middle and upper actors contemplating migration to the metropolis. It should be noted that our formulation does not use this resistance as a means of counteracting the metropolitan attraction (that role was performed by home pull) but rather for slowing down the rate at which migration will, anyway, take place.

Thus determined the flow (F_{ij}) of members of a given actor who actually migrate to the attracting centre in a given year, we should divide the net migratory tension (NM_{ij}) by the sum of the cultural resistance to move (C_{ij}) and the *loss of relative status* (L_{ij}) component of resistance, and then multiply by the population of the actor under consideration, because the migratory tension was supposed to be applied to each individual in it. We would then have:

$$F_{ij} = k_3 \frac{NM_{ij}}{R_{ij}} P_i = k_3 \frac{NM_{ij}}{C_{ij} + L_{ij}}$$

where the total resistance to migration is $R_{ij} = C_{ij} + L_{ij}$.

The formula for the loss of relative status component of resistance to move will be, if the relative status of an actor in his community is represented by Rel_i:

$$L_{ij} = k_4 (\mathrm{Rel}_i - \mathrm{Rel}_j) \text{ (or zero if this expression is negative).}$$

In both the above formulae, sub-indices should be added to all variables in order to make clear which actor we have in mind.

A further specification might be added, to prevent too quick a depletion of a community in case its resistance is small: the maximum allowable out-migration might be fixed at a given percentage of the existing population of the actor.

To complete the picture, a few added factors should be taken into account. For example, there is the problem of unemploymnet. What happens when there is severe unemployment in a given community? Its attractive or retentive powers are obviously diminished, but by how much? It could be argued that the *average* income of the members of the unemployed social actor will go down, and as such diminish its attractive or retentive powers. But severe unemployment would seem to act in a different way, creating a pool of people whose income will be nearer to zero, making the averaging out operation unrealistic. We shall then consider that when unemployment is above a given percentage of the population of the actor (say 15 or 20 per cent) both attractive and retentive powers will be at zero value. A large city with severe unemployment, then, would not exert any migratory tension on the peripheral small towns. If some of these towns (frontier zones, for example) are passing through a period of prosperity without any unemployment (or only mild unemployment) they will attract the urban poor from a great distance, despite their own scarcity of population, because the large city is unable to retain these by any home pull.

Another refinement in the model would be the inclusion of status incongruence as an expelling factor. For this we would need several measures of status (economic and educational are the two more easily measured). and when the average members of an actor have severe status incongruence the retentive powers of their community will be diminished or even annulled. Thus members of status incongruent groups, lacking the retentive force of a home pull, will have a marked tendency to migrate although their flow will be somewhat moderated if they face a loss of relative status (average status, that is, as more than one measure of it has been taken).On the other hand, they are not unlikely to be the type of people (downwardly mobile aristocracy, for example) with strong emotional attachments to their own communities, having therefore a very high cultural resistance to migration.

Summarizing the development of the model up to this point, we have a method for calculating migratory flows between population groups (social actors) in different communities. If there were no other factors, each time period (year) would result in a given movement of population through migration, to which vegetative growth should be added in each community (the proportions between social actors may be assumed to be constant). In the next period, the calculation might be repeated. Income levels for each actor would be assumed to be fixed, or exogenously determined. This would give us an excessively simplified model lacking the more dynamic sociological and economic factors which are capable of altering the migratory gravitational field. It is to some of these factors that we must now turn. We will start with the process by which new investments take place in a given community.

4. THE ATTRACTION OF INVESTMENTS

It is at this point that the sociological and the economic interpretation of the process of regional development should be combined. A regionally oriented economic theory should be able to predict in what branches of production and in what places new investments are likely to be made in a given time period, using 'purely economic factors' as explanatory variables. The economic factors would include the state of the market and the availability and relative costs of labour, capital, natural resources, management, transportation, and what has been called localization and urbanization economies (or diseconomies), which represent the economic effects of the spatial concentration of industries.[6] Owing to the nature of location economics, in most cases the economist will simply state that a given type of investment is likely to take place somewhere within a given large area: within its borders it is economic but not outside. The area need not be a contiguous one, but a sum of favourable locations. It is at this point that sociological factors should step in. We may consider that the various communities where the investment is likely to take place compete with each other on 'purely sociological grounds' (we have assumed that on economic grounds there is no reason for preferring any of them). The *associationist leaders* are the people most likely to represent the degree of sociological sophistication reached by their community. If what is necessary for getting the investment is a bit of 'pull' and organization, they will provide it (over and above the more economically motivated amount). They will also provide the social atmosphere and civic responsibility which give a good appearance to the community and attract investments when economic factors are not actually against it. Therefore, we may assume that a given amount of investments will be distributed among the several economically possible home communities in proportion to the *size* of their associationist groups. If the investment is not divisible it will go to the community with the strongest leadership, or it may be assigned through an aleatory procedure in which the chances of each community getting it are proportional to the size of their associationist leadership. This formulation illustrates the importance, for a growing community, of having a strong (and well paid) associationist structure, and avoiding the migration of the members of this structure. In a sense, the creation and nursing of a healthy associationist leadership is one of the more strategic components of a development policy. If this is difficult for the smaller communities in a region, then the advantage of creating a powerful regional capital ('polarized' development) becomes manifest. If a community is too poor to maintain an associationist structure of any size, it is always better to have some civic leaders near at hand in a regional growth centre, than to have the whole region depleted of that dynamic social group through a policy of equal spread. The growth centre will be more likely to nurture and maintain an associationist leadership capable of attracting new investments, given adequate economic conditions. It becomes therefore more acceptable for small communities to agree to the creation of a privileged centre, because in that way the total amount of investment resources available for the region will increase. Even if this increase were to benefit the growth centre much more than the other communities, it is always easier to fight for a redistribution within a region than within the nation. Redistribution within the region, should, of course, take place in a second stage, without endangering the consolidation of the growth centre.

This suggests the need of a regional correction to the calculation of the attraction of investments, similar to the one applied in the calculation of the populations. But we should be careful with the type of regionalization we use. The catchment region will not be so meaningful, and it will be better to replace it by the actual sub-national administrative unit (province, department, etc.). This is because the provincial leaders will fight to have an investment located in their province even if it is not going to be made in their own community. If a given investment can equally well, from an economic point of view, be placed either in an area of one province or in one of a different province, then we should first let the two provinces do the sociological pulling against each other. It would be unrealistic to think that all provincial leaders actually pull on behalf of the area of their province which is concerned. We may suppose that only those living in the area, plus a percentage from the provincial capital (proportional to the weight of the area compared with the rest of the province, however measured) take part in the pulling operation. Thus, if a small area of a rich and powerful province is competing against an entire weaker province, the latter has some chance of winning through the exertions of all its available leaders, while the richer province mobilizes only a part of its leadership potential. Once the investment (or part of it) has been obtained for the province, the various communities concerned will fight out the final allocation between themselves.

We may wonder at this stage whether all associationist leaders are equally well suited for attracting investments of any type. Let us compare two cities with the same population, and with equally strong leadership, one of them an industrial centre and the other a university city. Let us assume that economic analysis considers them equally well suited for receiving a new factory. Are we justified in considering that on sociological grounds they still have the same chance of getting it? Experience and common sense would favour the industrial city, unless it were so overcrowded that economic analysis itself would have declared it unsuited. Why is this so? Probably because the leadership of the industrial town is likely to come overwhelmingly from people with business ('executives') connexions, who will be eager to have the new factory in their town while the leaders in the university town will be recruited from dons who might even be opposed to having it in theirs. If we wish to cope with this problem we might take up a suggestion made in a previous section, and subdivide the community leaders into as many sub-groups as there are social actors from which they can be recruited. We would further assume that for given types of prospective investments the various sub-groups of leaders will be of different degrees of usefulness. Thus, if we are analyzing the establishment of a new factory, leaders with urban business, middle class or working class origins will be counted at their full weight, but others will be given a smaller weight. Conversely, if the project under consideration is a new college, the chances are that the university town will get it because of the composition of its associationist leadership.

If we consider actual cases of investment, particularly very big projects (the building of Brasilia, the Aswan dam, or the like) we may be somewhat unhappy about the capacity of our combined economic and sociological model to predict them. Those investments are not the result of a strictly economic calculus, nor are they the consequence of local community leadership. They are part of a *national* political decision. Not that they should be considered as uneconomic. But a purely economic calculus may not be decisive, because of the high risk often involved and the low predictability of results, or because of their very long term maturation. Although these are extreme examples, there are many other instances where decisions are made for non-economic reasons and still do not depend on the local pull of an active associanist leader ship. They are simply the result of a national planning policy which may have as its object the redress of some existing disparity between certain parts of the country. Many welfare (hospitals, low cost housing) and educational (new schools and universities) investments are made for reasons of this kind, and the same can be said for some 'big push' developmental economic projects. They should be considered, therefore, as *exogenous* to an economic or sociological model based on market mechanisms and local social pulls. Nevertheless, we should avoid assigning too quickly an exogenous status to this type of decision. Most welfare, educational and developmental expenditure, though administered from the national capital, is of a rather routine nature, and the pattern into which it has settled might be explained by the economic and sociological model outlined. It is the very special national projects, commanding particular attention from public opinion, that might escape the very strong determination which economic considerations and local social pulls are bound to exert on any society, even a centrally planned one.

Taking into account all the above considerations, we should be able for a given period (a year) to establish a geographical pattern of investment. Part of the available investment would be assigned exogenously, and the rest according to the economic and social forces combined, as described in this section. If we wish to forecast a process covering several time periods, we must now turn to an analysis of the changes produced in the various communities by the investments that have been made during the current period. These changes affect the internal numerical distribution between the social actors, as well as their income levels. It is only after estimating these changes that we will be able to start another cycle, calculating the new migratory gravitational field

5. CHANGES PRODUCED BY INVESTMENT

New investment will require a certain amount of labour and management, depending on the existing level of salaries and the general state of the market. That is, it will give employment to given numbers of the various social actors. Let us assume that full employment obtained in the home community under analysis before the investment was made. To simplify matters, let us think in terms of *net* investment, and consider only one social actor. From where will the new investment get the people it requires? There are two obvious sources: (a) from the vegetative growth of the social actor during the period concerned (this may be assumed to be growing at the same rate as the community as a whole, unless differential fertility rates are available, the basic assumption being that new entrants into the employment market will tend to keep to their father's status); (b) from migrants of the required social actor type who have come into the community during the period concerned. The requirements set by the investments represent the new demand, while the new supply is the sum of vegetative growth and immigration. If total demand is less than total supply (for a given actor) then there will be unemployment, or the corresponding salary rate will go down. If the demand is larger than the supply, a more complex situation arises. Industry cannot get the people it needs by bringing them from outside the community. We assume that there is no compulsory direction of labour, and that migration is governed by the gravitational field already described, which has provided only a certain number of new members of the required social actor. The only way out, then, is to get the necessary people from other social actors in the community. A simple solution, in order to avoid unnecessarily complicated calculations, would be to state that the required people are taken from the actor in the tier immediately below, unless there are unemployed people in another actor at the same tier level. Thus, if what is required are urban executives beyond the numbers provided by vegetative growth and immigration, these will be taken from the urban middle class through a process of social mobility, unless there are unemployed among the rural executives, government officials or cultural specialists. When we reach the lower tier (urban and rural working class) the one with a higher per capita income will draw from the other without any need for unemployment to appear. This means that in most cases the urban working class will draw from the rural one, if it exists in its own home community, which is generally the case. To get a more realistic picture, we may set a maximum percentage of any given actor that can go upwards in any year, and another maximum percentage for movements sideways.[7] As a consequence, if there has been a lot of investment, demand will be greater than supply, at least for some social actors, and wages will go up. Actors' incomes will be affected also by the productivity of the new investments. An economic calculation should provide the resulting figures, including profits, which are part of the income of the executives. The detailed calculations at this stage can be very tedious, and require a lot of economic information not easily available. A radical simplification, useful for running the model for short stretches of time, might assume that the productivity of capital and labour does not change, and the result of new investment is simply to create a given demand for each social actor.[8] If the demand exceeds the supply (after allowing for social mobility) by a certain proportion, the per capita income of that actor is increased in that proportion.

We need, for each type of capital investment (heavy industry, light industry, farm machinery, government offices, schools, hospital, etc) to know the amount of new employment required, from each social actor. This will give a set of coefficients, which might be assumed to be constant for all communities in a given country and at a given historical time. If the supply of a given group is below the demand, it will combine with the other factors of production in a different proportion, leaving an unsatisfied employment demand (under-staffing) which will continue into the next year.

It will be noted that there is no provision for the associationist leaders in the foregoing analysis. This is because of the special nature of this actor. It cannot be said that new investments create a direct demand for them. It is true that new capital has been attracted partly through their exertions, but it does not give employment to any of them. The growth of this actor (apart from migration) should then follow different laws. It was stated earlier that associationist leaders are recruited from the other social actors, and that they tend to remain in the field for a certain time after which they are bound to retire. We may therefore think that in any given year each social actor creates a number of new associationist leaders, via a coefficient of 'propensity to community action' which differs for each actor and which may depend on cultural and historical characteristics. The previously existing group of associationist leaders will suffer a certain loss during the year under consideration. To avoid unnecessary complications of an actuarial order, we should consider this loss simply as a percentage of the total number of the group. Coefficients should be such that in a typical hypothetical community with no vegetative growth and no migration, every year a certain number of community leaders would be created and an equal number would retire. On the other hand, if there is immigration, each new group would make its contribution to the further creation of leaders, depending on its propensity to community action. In the process, the size and the relative importance of the associationist leaders might be increased or reduced. The group is, of course, also subject to migration through the migration field. As for their income, it may be assumed to be the same for each contingent recruited from a different social actor as that actor's, and for the whole group the resulting average.

We have now completed the cycle assumed in our combined socio-economic model. At the end of the period under consideration each actor has a new value for its size and per capita income. The new gravitational field for the attraction of population will be calculated once more with the ensuing migrations starting the whole process again.

The system lends itself to complete mathematical formulation and simulation of time paths. The usefulness of this exercise in model construction is two-fold. On the one hand, by making explicit the process through which social and economic factors interact in regional development, the way is open for further theoretical clarification or empirical testing of some relationships. Admittedly, sociological knowledge is still very scanty and often irrelevant, so the doubt may arise whether this attempt is premature. The answer to this is that the effort is worth while only if it is clearly understood that it claims to be no more than a provisional codification of ideas and hypotheses, so that the sinews of the theory can be more clearly seen and conceptual clarification made easier. It should be regarded as a highly experimental approach in constant interaction with new ideas and empirical data. On the other hand, for those more mathematically inclined, the model might help in the prediction of the results of alternative planning programmes. For this it is necessary to build the complete mathematical formulation, and to estimate the main coefficients. Each planning programme involves making some set of investment decisions or creating some types of inducements in given areas. The investments planned in a chosen course of action should be considered, in the corresponding years, as exogenous decisions (they are exogenous to the model's predictive powers in this particular application). The especially created inducements should be fed in as information for the economic part of the model. Some investments might imply alterations in sociological coefficients, for example, road construction will alter the dimensions of a catchment region. Then the application of the model, using computer facilities, will predict the main results of the policy envisaged.

It would be too cumbersome to give in detail in this paper the complete list of variables, coefficients and formulae involved, all of which anyway have been hinted at in a general and verbal form in the text. We will here simply summarize the steps of the procedure:

i) the whole country is divided up into home communities, centered around urban nuclei and reaching out to the limit of their usually acceptable commuting distance. Purely rural areas are treated in an equivalent way, centered around existing human clusterings;

ii) every home community is subdivided into social actors arranged in three tiers: urban and rural working classes, urban and rural middle classes, urban and rural executives, government officials, cultural specialists, and associationist leaders. Each actor is characterized by its population and income;

iii) every home community has its own catchment region, which includes all other communities within 'week-end commuting" distance. This latter magnitude may vary for each social actor according to its income;

iv) social actors are subjected to a migratory field created by their equivalents in other home communities. This field is proportional to the size of the attracting actor and (inversely) to the distance. The migratory tension thus created is counteracted by a home pull proportional to the size of the home actor and (inversely) to the home commuting distance. Both migratory tension and home pull are corrected to take into account the influence of the catchment regions;

v) the migratory flow between two communities, during one time period (year) is proportional to the regionally adjusted net migratory tension and (inversely) to the resistance to the move. This resistance has a cultural component, which never descends to zero, and a loss of relative status component, which is a function of the loss of status the actor is likely to incur in the process of migration;

vi) during a given time period an economic model should predict the investments which will take place and their likely locations. In most cases there will be several possible locations as a result of the 'purely economic' analysis. The communities concerned will then compete, using their sociological resources, which will be summarized by the size of their associationist leaders actor. The administrative unit (province) where the communities are located helps in the process, by lending the support of some of its associationist leaders in the struggle against other provinces;

vii) allowance should be made for some cases of exogenously determined investments, resulting from political decisions at a national (or sometimes regional) level which cannot be predicted by the combined economic and sociological model;

viii) once the investments have been made, they require a certain amount of each type of labour and managerial inputs, thus creating additional demand for each social actor. The supply will be represented by vegetative demographic growth and by new immigrants. If total demand proves to be smaller than supply, unemployment or reduction of salaries takes place. In the opposite case there will be a tendency to fill the vacant posts with people from other social actors in the same community, via social mobility;

ix) associationist leaders evolve according to a different law. Every other social actor has a certain propensity for community action, which measures the number of new associationist leaders created from that actor every year. On the other hand, associationist leaders tend to retire after some time, and this is calculated as a percentage of the total present, who will disappear every year, apart from those who migrate;

x) as a result of the demand and supply situation described above new salaries or per capita incomes result from the various social actors. Everything is ready for starting a new cycle, which will begin with the calculation of the migratory field.

NOTES

1. Tormod HERMANSEN, *Interregional Allocation of Investments for Social and Economic Development*, Geneva, United Nations Research Institute for Social Development, 1968 (mimeo.). Also in A.R. KUKLINSKI (ed.), *Regional Disaggregation of National Policies and Plans*, The Hague, Mouton (UNRISD Series, Regional Planning, Vol 8), 1972.
2. See Peter HAGGETT, *Locational Analysis in Human Geography*, London, Edward

Arnold Ltd., 1965, and Robert DICKINSON, *City and Region*, London, Routledge and Kegan Paul, 1964, for the problem of delimiting areas of influence.

3. See Walter ISARD, *et al.*, *Methods of Regional Analysis: An Introduction to Regional Science*, Cambridge, Massachussets, The M.I.T. Press, 1960, for a standard treatment of this problem. For locational economics, see his *Location and Space Economy*, New York, John Wiley and Technology Press, 1956, where the historical development of the discipline is traced in full detail.
4. See John FRIEDMANN, *Regional Development Policy: A Case Study of Venezuela*, Cambridge, Massachussets, the M.I.T. Press, 1966, for a forceful case in favour of the policy of 'concentrated decentralization', which coresponds to the one described in our numerical example. See also European Free Trade Association, *Regional Policy in EFTA: An Examination of the Growth Centre Idea*, Geneva, EFTA, 1968, for an over-all view of various approaches to regional development. A study of the European situation can be found in Sergio BARZANTI, *The Underdeveloped Areas within the Common Market*, Princeton, Princeton University Press, 1965.
5. It could be argued that the daily commuting distance also varies according to the income of the actor, and that therefore not only regions but also home communities would vary in size (and number) according to which actor we have in mind. Though this may be true, it would make the model excessively complicated and more difficult to grasp from a common sense point of view. Therefore, it would seem better for the moment to keep the size of a home community constant for all its social actors.
6. Leo H. KLAASSEN describes these effects in his chapter in the present volume. The combination of an economic and a sociological model always raises serious problems, as the models will probably have been developed with different strategies in mind: they may vary in their degree of spatial specificity. In the present volume the 'economic model' is an ideal construction to which various actually developed models, or sets of policy decisions by planners are a first approximation.
7. If education had been taken into account in this model, it could be included here as a variable determining the ease with which members of a given actor can fill positions at a higher level. It should be taken into account, though, that historical experience has often shown that education has not been too relevant as a factor in social advancement.
8. It must be mentioned that in the next cycle of the model, when the 'attraction of investments' has to be calculated again, the new values of the economic variables will have to be taken into acoount. But this may require less detail than is necessary for the exact *endogenous* prediction of income levels with full respect for economic theory. Some standard texts on macro-economics can serve to dissuade the over optimistic sociologist. See for example R.G.D. ALLEN, *Macroeconomic Theory*, London, MacMillan, 1968, or Gardner ACKLEY, *Macroeconomic Theory*, New York, MacMillan, 1961.

SJOERD GROENMAN

3 B

Regionalization as an operational procedure
Some comments on Di Tella's report

I. THE IDLE APPROACH OF HUMAN GEOGRAPHY TO DIVIDE SPACE INTO SPATIAL ENTITIES

Traditionally we are used to the idea that our planet can be divided into regions. Travelling on earth means moving from one region to the other. Geographical maps show by names the different regions: the Ardennes, the Eifel, the Vosges.

It is quite clear that in enumerating those names we are thinking primarily of landscape, of 'natural' circumstances. If there was no human interference with these circumstances the regions would border upon each other and would cover in this way the surface of the earth. Of course the problem of the exact delineation would create difficulties, but these difficulties are well-known in lots of other scientific problems and might be taken for granted. If necessary we are prepared to cut knots. In fact however there are fewer and fewer natural regions, because man is affecting the milieu where he lives. So long as man was a hunter, a fisher, an agriculturist, the natural milieu was playing an important role, i.e. man's life was closely linked to his immediate surroundings. In the network of social relations these surroundings were reflected in several ways. With the coming of industry and transport however and later on the expansion of services the role of the immediate milieu was declining. Industry became not the 'product' *of* the geographical space, but simply found its place *in* space, the words 'of' and 'in' indicating an essential difference in dependence.

Industry, recreation, traffic, services increasingly have no specific relationship with the natural milieu, although they may be pinpointed within space. This holds true also or still more for religion, for family ties, for association with different purposes. All these phenomena represent networks of social relationships, social systems wherein social actors are active. These social systems can be drawn on a geographical map, because the actors are living, are playing their roles, somewhere in space, but the role of space in their interaction is not fundamental. There is no reason to suppose that after plotting the social system in a map we will find entities covering together the surface of a country, of a continent or the earth as a whole. There is in fact a pell-pell of networks, not showing a regular picture of well-defined regions. Only the frontiers of the political entities we call stated are still real lines of delimitation. Geographers will tell us however, that the original regions don't stop at the political frontiers. The country is a political creation of social relationships, more interesting for political scientists, historians, and sociologists than for geographers. The existence of states however does not create a perfect delineation of all sorts of social systems with different reach. The number of bonds crossing their frontiers is so to speak endless.

It is no wonder that the effort of geography to find clear-cut regions covering the earth is idle. *Rochefort* gives a good exposé of the difficulties geographers have met in their efforts to define the concept of region. 'Pendent longtemps, les géographes ont cherché à définir la région par le contenu de l'espace, à l'intérieur de limites déterminées, contenu s'exprimant plus ou moins par une certaine homogénéité du paysage. Cette conception a conduit à un certain nombre d'impasses dans l'effort entrepris pour dégager des unités valables caracterisées par une certaine homogénéité des activités de production qui s'y localisent'.[1] His conclusion however is that the concept of what is a region is still an unsolved problem. And his final remark that 'le géographe s'aperçoit qu'il travaille sur un domaine où interviennent certains facteurs ne relevant pas de sa compétence et impliquant un appèl à d'autres sciences' does not help us to find the solution because in our opinion there is no satisfactory solution now that man's activities have emancipated from his immediate surroundings given by nature.

2. THE DYNAMIC APPROACH: REGIONALIZATION OF HUMAN ACTIVITIES IN THEIR BROADEST SENSE

So long as we consider the region as something *of* space there is no more chance of defining a scientifically satisfactory concept of 'region'. As we will make clear in the following pages the region is something of people, reflecting a network of specific relations, to be plotted *in* space if we whish so, and eventually to be defined precisely *in* space for practical reasons.

More promising than the investigation of geographers about the delimitation of regions is the reflection on the word *regionalization.*

Society is a conglomerate of all sorts of social relationships, differentiated in space. No matter whether we take economic activities, religious life or the realm of education, all these have their deposit somewhere in space, in other words: they are regionalized. By putting it this way we are looking from the social whole to its spatial ramifications. It is quite true that there have been in human history two movements: from the smaller elements in space to the big entities *and* from the big entities down to the out-of-the-way places. States grew up out of smaller political pieces, but later on the increasing state influence crept to its borders and gave shape to the societal life. Economic activities at innumerable places of this earth got interwoven, but as this process went on they were more and more influenced from a number of economic centres. The economic breakdown of one of this centres will have (and had!) disastrous effects all over the world. The integrative powers from top to bottom are every day increasing in comparison with the growing-power from bottom to top, although the latter in history preceded the first.

The efforts of the geographers to find clear-cut, well-defined regions do fit in with the idea that a number of regions are composing together bigger entities.

These efforts had to fail also because a highly dynamic integration process from top to bottom will break up what seemed to be well-defined regions. This integrative process from top to bottom is not only spontaneous. In our age it is promoted purposely for reasons of conscious planning. State and Church, but also big organizations like sport associations and trade-unions are regionalizing their activities. Countries and even continents are divided into districts for very different purposes and there is no reason to suppose why a district for tax-collecting is identical with that of a soccer-league, a churchprovince, a polder, a constituency, a commercial travellers' territory or a military defence area.

Regionalization of economic activities is essential for the modern State. Now that the State has accepted a leading role in the country's economic life it gives intensive thought to economic development and it makes models not only in time but also in space. Economy as a science has introduced at first *time* into its consideration and has given it a place in economic theory. The dynamic vision has succeeded the static one. In the 20th century it is no longer the concept of equilibrium that figures as the key to reasoning, but movement. *Milhaud* states it this way 'On parle aujourd'hui de taux de croissance, de vitesse, de croisière, d'accélération, d'emballement, de ralentissement, de freinage... (...). De même coup, le raisonnement théorique a eu tendence à s'inscrire dans un cadre géographique. Une deuxième coordonnée, l'espace après le temps, s'est introduite dans les schémas abstraits.'[2]

Timing and spacing, temporization and regionalization are coordinates. Planning in time is not linked to definite periods. There are no such things as temporal 'regions' with 'natural' or scientifically defined limits. In the same way the spatial entities have no precise and relatively fixed boundaries. Periods in time and regions in space are chosen on practical grounds. More important than the exact ad hoc decisions about the reach of planning measures in time and space are the *processes of timing and regionalization.*

These processes are changing the temporal and spatial milieux in accordance with models made at the centres from where the economic and social development is controlled or at least carefully watched and corrected. Each of these constellations, or to restrict ourselves, the spatial milieu, is involved in a process of change. We may even say that the spatial milieu is a process itself. It is not a fixed datum. And with 'spatial milieu' we do not mean the surroundings of nature, but the system of relations – of economic relations in economic development, of social relations in social development – wherein the natural elements play an ever decreasing role. By 'region' now we may mean an economic or social system in process we can plot *in* space. The relation with the surroundings of nature is very weak in the case of traffic system. Highways need space, but the traffic system on these roads is superimposed on the surrounding landscape without any important relationship with it in between the centres connected by the roads.

3. THE REGION AS A SOCIOLOGICAL PHENOMENON

In principle it is possible to draw each social system on a geographical map, representing the social relationships by lines. Specifically however it is possible to indicate on a map where people are living together. Living toghether creates a remarkable social configuration. There are certainly all sorts of direct and indirect bonds between the people having their home somewhere in space, but the basis for these bonds is no other than simple proximity. The network of relationships or social systems has no specific goal. The people belonging to the network have different interests (religious, recreational, economic), but none of these interests is fundamental for their coherence, insofar as it is present. The proximity-collectivity or the community *sec* in space is to be called region if we envisage an entity composed at least of several settlements. The sociological region is a collectivity of *people*; it is not the surface where they live. *Ziólkowski* calls it a group of people who live together in a given area under condition of mutual dependence, are subjected to the same influences, and, consequently, develop some similarity of traits and share a sense of common solidarity.[3]

Di Tella makes the distinctions between *home communities* encompassing people who are on daily contact, *and regions* which include several home communities solidary with each other due to several types of interrelatedness.

The fact that the region is called a number of people, living together somewhere, has a couple of implications. Now that the mutual interdependence (Ziólkowski) or the interrelatedness (Di Tella) are underlined, or, in other words, now that we consider the region as a social system, we may say, (with slight variation) in accordance with *Gurvitch* that we are not (only) living in a region but that the region is within us. This means that if all the people belonging to the regional social system migrate together to another place the region itself is moving. The boundaries of the region as a social system are not fixed. They may expand as an effect of a change of scale creating relationships over longer distances in space. The region as a communtiy *sec* in space, composed of people, can be manipulated by measures specifically adapted to societal configurations: by socialization, by information, by imposing laws and norms, by introducing incentives, by persuasion or by coercion, by creating institutional frameworks.

As we pointed out before small social systems to be found somewhere on the surface of the earth grew together to coherent bigger entities. These entities, especially as they were of a political character, increasingly have tried (and with great success) to model the small systems, 'from top to bottom', using the measures just mentioned. The two way integrative process (from bottom to top, from top to bottom) has had the effect of a streamlining of regional social systems-in-process, based on proximity, are nowadays all alike. Regional differences however are on the decline. The downward movement of integration has manifested itself as very effective. This downward movement has got an acceleration in the period of the welfare state, now that differences in prosperity and welfare are considered as phenomena of discrimination.

The integrative power of the welfare state implies regionalization of prosperity and viability. It is not interesting what are the exact boundaries in space of the 'regions'. What matters is the policy of creating primarily a model for the country as a whole to be elaborated in time and in space. In this model the whole has priority before the parts. What will be the proximity-systems, the social systems to be dealt with in space (regions), must be defined within the framework of an overall view of the country. What we reject here is the idea that in social and economic policy the country is an addition sum of regions, and the region is an addition sum of 'home communities'. We must realize that as soon as we have in mind the development of a country or of a number of countries we are dealing with policy. Policy is an activity from centre to periphery. Regionalization is a piece of policy. It deals with the differentiation of political measures in space. The question what will be in *concreto* the regions as foci of political measures is secondary. It is certainly interesting to analyze how a region is built upon home-communities, and how a country is built upon regions. In regionalization however, as a political activity, we follow the inverse way: from top to bottom, from centre to periphery.

There is one more remark to be made on the sociological concept of 'region'. *Ziólkowski* and *Di Tella*, both of them, mention for the social system of proximity the element of solidarity. Now it is clear that as a community increases the sense of solidarity is decreasing. It depends on the size of the 'region' whether a real sense of solidarity is present. The chance it will is greater in Di Tella's 'home communities' than in his 'regions'. The size of the 'home community' by him tentatively is defined or circumscribed by the distance of daily commuting whilst for the regions (at least the 'catchment regions') the distance of week-end commuting has been mentioned.

There is a reason for serious doubt as to the possibility of a sense of solidarity, even in the 'home communities'. There are several cases of commuting over distances of 50 km and more. If we take a distance of 10–15 km it is already doubtful whether the degree of solidarity is intensive. With concern to the week-end community we must state that distances of 100–200 km would mean that practically the whole of Belgium, big parts of the Netherlands and Hungary would be 'catchment regions'. Of course it is quite possible to take areas of this size for development purposes (Slowakia,

Mezzogiorno) but it is not correct to suppose that within such regions there will be a feeling of solidarity, nationalist or ethnic feelings entering the picture of course are spoiling the theoretical model.

I think it is an advantage we can forget about the feeling of solidarity. The absence of these feelings makes that the 'region' is easier to handle with for development purposes. Somewhere within these regions, whatever may be exactly their size, we find of course entities where proximity really leads to group consciousness and where political confirmation created the room for local democracy. The smaller local entities however are *not directly*, but *indirectly*, objects of regionalization.

What Di Tella writes about regional opportunities seems very meaningful. For the economist an area is not a contiguous one, but a sum of favorable locations: labor, capital, distances, transport opportunities, natural resources.

Regionalization is not focussed on local communities or on 'home communities'. Regionalization is a process of drawing main lines; it is an activity linked to key positions (Mannheim). It therefore is not too dirigistic, but in leaving a broad margin of freedom within the region it does not touch, by centralistic measures, the smallest solidary communities.

4. THE REGION AS A PROBLEM BOUND ENTITY

Regionalization means spatial elaboration of national plans, models or measures with no fixed delimitation of the sub-national areas to be chosen as entities for concrete action. Of course this spatial differentiation somewhere meets the social systems of proximity but the meeting-points are flexible. It depends on the character of the action to be taken what will be the sub-national area we may call 'region'. This region is in fact not a part of the surface of the earth but a network of social relations or a complex of social networks, – network not meaning *per se* that a sense of solidarity is present.

The flexibility of 'regions' manifests itself in different ways.

1. Social systems are living phenomena. They grow or decrease, they may deplace, even if they are founded in simple proximity (nomads showing the extreme case of mobility).

2. Systems based on proximity are composed of several social strata. These strata are not living in the same social surroundings, i.e. their ex-

periences, perception and interpretation are not the same. Time and space as social situations differ in their meaning from social layer to social layer. *Di Tella's* circumscription of a region as 'that part of a country within easy reach from a given point so that people living at that point may use its resources and therefore consider them to some extent their own' may be interpreted in this way. Different social strata are considering different resources their own within different 'catchment regions', they live in different regions although their proximity systems are interwoven. It is wellknown that a social role has to be played within a specific social *and spatial* reach. In the sphere of migration, analyzed by *Di Tella* in an interesting way, for the different social strata of the social systems of proximity there are separate gravitation fields.

The change of space, or, to say it simpler, the growing opportunities of communication, have accentuated the coming into existence of different regions for the different social strata. With the increase of prosperity the original day of the lower strata of course is striking.

3. Sofar we were looking from the simplest proximity to wider spatial horizons. Our reasoning had its starting point at the local basis. Regionalization however goes from the top to the basis, from the centre to the periphery, from the national entity downwards to the smaller social systems. For the problem of social and economic development this approach is more relevant. This approach must lead to a highly flexible concept of what is a region. The delimitation of regions depends on decisions at the top, and this delimitation differs in accordance with the specific problem to be solved. The size of the region as a network of social relations, as a social system with social actors, depends on the character of the phenomenon to be regionalized. The region is problem-bound and considerations about how to solve a specific national problem decide how many regions there will be for this purpose and of what size.

Di Tella mentions the provinces as sub-national entities of administration. They are taken sometimes, for opportunistic reasons, as areas for some kind of regionalization. The province has a preference value for administrators and social scientists. It has an apparatus. It is an expression of vested interests. It has the advantage of the coinage of tradition. Historically the provinces may be the brickstones of the national building. They often preceded the nation-state. Now that the nation-state is a reality and its 'downward' influences are ever increasing one may question the meaning of the province. Is it still a realistic mid-way station between the central government and the local communities in the light of the national efforts of regionalization? Within the framework of a problem-oriented policy of regionalization the province is an accidental phenomenon and therefore an obstacle to efficient organization and action. For the flow of regulations from centre to periphery, and for the flow of substantial information about facts and desires the other way around the traditional provinces need to be replaced by flexible and from problem to problem different regions cross-cutting eventually the provincial borders. As the region is now first of all a network of social relations it is even not necessary that these regions can be plotted neatly in geographical maps. They may show on these maps considerable holes. It is the people *in* space that are to be touched, supported, stimulated, organized, not geographical space itself.

The problem-orientation of the 'region' very clearly is demonstrated by the French term 'région-plan'. The policy of economic regionalization has decided upon the areas (= the people and their social systems) to be taken for action.

What holds true for economic policy can be applied to a number of other fields: administration, marketing, church organization, services (postal districts, transport, public utilities as electricity and gas), national defence, police areas.

The main problem of regionalization is how to delimitate specific regions taking into account a number of fixed data like technical possibilities, social structure and culture, *and* geographical circumstances as they appear *in* space, the starting point being the purpose of the action to be taken. The ecology 'at the bottom' is not dominating the considerations. It plays however a correcting role in respect of the problem oriented policy 'at the top'. It is quite clear that in a development policy the regions cannot be read on geographical maps. These maps merely may suggest some solutions, and still more if they have got the character of more abstract cartographic representations (in plural).

5. REGIONALIZATION AND ECONOMIC DEVELOPMENT

Economic development delivers a good illustration of the regionalization of national policy, and therefore of the choice of meeting places of national action and existing social systems of proximity.

There is to begin with a paradox to be overcome. Economic development, if regionalized, is instrumental to the prosperity and welfare of proximity-systems that show economic and social problems. On the other hand the areas to be chosen for regionalized economic action are problem-bound, i.e. the complex of measures to stimulate the development of sub-national entities asks for areas of a certain size, in particular if we believe in the effect of growth poles and in their multiplier function. The choice of 'regions' therefore must reflect the urgent need of proximity-systems for economic stimulation as well as the postulates of efficient regionalized economic action. In fact, if we study the history of the policy of regionalized economic development we encounter two approaches: originally the haphazard measures of the central government to help backward areas, no matter whether these areas were a satisfactory focus of efficient action, later on a more systematic approach, in agreement with economic theory, not directed to small local areas with obvious problems, but envisaging bigger territories, the particularly depressed areas only being parts of them. In the second approach the solution of the economic and social problems not necessarily might be solved exactly where they manifested themselves in space. An efficient, realistic regionalization of economic measures places the solution of local problems within a national framework, corresponding to careful theoretical considerations.

Does this mean that a policy of economic regionalization not necessarily has to take into account the structure, culture and functions of the social systems of proximity? Does economic regionalization reflect only a line of thinking from centre to periphery, and does it create only problem-bound 'regions', defined at 'the top'? For a national policy of economic development the problem is not primarily how to solve the specific local problems of proximity-systems, but how to regionalize systematically the national economic polity. This is true particularly for a policy of the spread of population by means of the spread of resources. But ,is there not the danger of neglecting the specific character of the social systems at 'the bottom'? The best answer to the formulated questions is to say that an effective regionalized economic policy not only is based on pieces of economic theory (in particular on growth poles) but considers the needs of the proximity-systems as important data to be integrated into the theoretical model. In this way the instrumental character of a policy of economic development, being a means for the promotion of prosperity and welfare of proximity systems as well as of the economic strength of the nation as a whole, is underlined. An economic policy is not a goal in itself. Regionalization even less is only a procedure based on theoretical considerations. If regionalization is problem-bound, part of the problem is to meet the needs at the bottom. The delimitation of the regions to be focussed however will not be the same as that of the real backward areas.

If the problems of the backward areas are integrated into a systematic policy of regionalization the sociological study of the proximity-systems remains valuable. This study however must be linked to the chosen regionalization. The starting point to be accepted for this study is the region as it is delineated by considerations from top to bottom and from bottom to top, both of them being part and parcel of a problem-bound policy of regionalization.

NOTES

1. M. ROCHEFORT, 'Les Géographes Fàce à la Notion de Région', *Revue Juridique e Economique du Sud-Ouest*, Bordeaux, 18 (3), 1969, pp. 507–514.
2. Jules MILHAUD, 'Le Rôle de l'Economiste en Matiére de Théorie et de Politique Economique Régionales', *Revue Juridique et Economique du Sud-Ouest*, 18 (3), 1969, pp. 559–574.
3. J. A. ZIÓLKOWSKI, *Methodological Problems in the Sociology of Regional Development*, Geneva, United Nations Research Institute for Social Development, January 1969 (mimeo.). Also in A. R. KUKLINSKI (ed.), *Regional Sociology, Environment and Regional Planning*,The Hague, Mouton (UNRISD Series, Regional Planning, Vol 7), 1972.

ERIC BYLUND

4

Promemoria concerning growth centre problems within the framework of the Swedish policy

From the time after the second world war up till the middle of the 1960's the dominating method of attacking the imbalance between the supply of jobs and the demand of labour within certain regions was migration promoting measures, that is by means of active employment services involving economic support of different kinds to people willing to change their places of work, labour has been relocated from economically contractive areas to expansive ones.

The expanding areas in Sweden are first of all the Stockholm, the Gothenburg, and the Malmö regions. In contrast to these a large continuous territory from the country of Värmland in the south to the county of Norrbotten in the very north is characterized by a high employment in agriculture and forestry and a comparatively low degree of industrialization and urbanization. Due to changes in structure and operation the great decrease of manpower requirements has disengaged labour, which has not been absorbed within the area by a sufficiently expanding economy; unemployment has been the result or a great number of the idle workers has been 'channeled' down to the growing regions, partly due to the attractive power of the regions themselves, partly through a planned migration policy.

The economic fluctuations in the big growth poles in southern and central Sweden are reflected in the out-migration figures from the so called 'forest provinces' in the north. During the boom of the early 1960's the five northermost provinces yearly lost 2% of the population by means of southward migration.

The recession from 1965 to 1968 implied a less attraction on the labour in the north from the southern industrial regions which resulted not only in less out-migration from, but also in net population increases in some provinces. Last year's economic upswing has again caused a strong outflux from the 'forest counties' by the growing demand for labour in southern

Table 1

province	population			pop. change 1961–65			pop. change 1965–68			total
	1961	1965	1968	total	%	total per year	total	%	total per year	pop. change 1961–1968
Gävleborg	293.395	291.875	294.053	− 1.520	− 0.5	− 380	+ 2.178	+ 0.7	+ 545	+ 658
Västernorrland	285.745	277.749	276.474	− 7.996	− 2.8	− 1.999	− 1.275	− 0.5	− 319	− 9.271
Jämtland	139.918	132.461	127.003	− 7.457	− 5.3	− 1.864	− 5.458	− 3.5	− 1.364	− 12.915
Västerbotten	239.704	233.849	234.710	− 5.855	− 2.4	− 1.464	+ 861	+ 0.4	+ 215	− 4.994
Norrbotten	261.958	261.394	259.794	− 564	− 0.2	− 141	− 1.600	− 0.6	− 400	− 2.164
these 5 provinces	1.220.720	1.197.328	1.192.914	− 23.392	− 1.9	− 5.848	− 4.414	− 0.4	− 1.104	− 27.806
total Sweden	7.498.770	7.694.987	7.941.561	+ 196.217	+ 2.6	+ 49.054	+ 246.574	+ 3.2	+ 61.644	+ 442.791

Table 2

	1968
1. The Forest Provinces plus Värmland	1.763.202 inh. = 23% of total Sweden
2. Remaining parts of Sweden	6.003.222 inh. = 77% of total Sweden
3. Total Sweden	7.766.424 inh.
4. Places in Sweden > 30.000 inh.	2.966.047 inh.
5. Places in 'The Forest Provinces' plus Värmland > 30.000 inh.	262.600 inh. = 9% of number 4; 15% of number 1
6. Places in remaining parts of Sweden > 30.000	2.703.447 inh. = 91% of number 4; 45% of number 2

and central Sweden. – These changes can be seen in the population figures in Table 1.

Earlier was pointed out the divergent economic structure, which causes the present regional shift of labour. The result implies a regional concentration and economic growth on one hand and a contraction of population and settlement on the other. Agglomerative effects and external economies accentuate the discrepancy to the advantage of the large concentrations of population. In the 'forest provinces' there is a lack of growth centres, which could counterbalance the development in the expansion poles of Stockholm, Gothenburg, and Malmö. This state of affairs shows itself very clearly in Table 2, which points out that only 9% of the population living in towns bigger than 30,000 inhabitants are to be found in the 'forest provinces', which hold some 23% of the total population of Sweden. Only 15% of the people in north Sweden live in places with more than 30,000 inhabitants, while 45% for the rest of the country. These figures disclose the present regional imbalance and indicate that the regional development problem is to a high degree an issue of establishing growth centres in the north, which by virtue of their own external economies can attract other activities and absorb labour releases from agriculture and forestry.

A new location policy was introduced in 1965 to slow down the migration out of the north which had serious consequences on the age structure and the supply of public and commercial service. This was not a planned growth centre policy. Such a policy does not yet exist in Sweden but is being formed. The location policy of 1965 with its grants and loans for new industries and development of existing enterprises in the 'forest provinces' has admittedly favoured and promoted a commencing economic expansion particularly in the coastal towns and has helped to reduce the out-migration from the northern parts of the country; but a planned concentrated effort has not been made with the explicit view to creating a growth centre and to lifting it up to the same hierarchial level of competition as the towns in southern and central Sweden. The decision for the location of the investments has been based on pure business economies and not on the size and structure of the place. Only exceptionally has there been made an appraisal founded on social economies. The result has become rather an extensive regional propagation of the grants and loans, however, with some concentration to the areas mentioned above. The method used could be characterized as a concentrated propagation of the investments.

The issue of a growth centre policy for the 'forest counties' is, however,

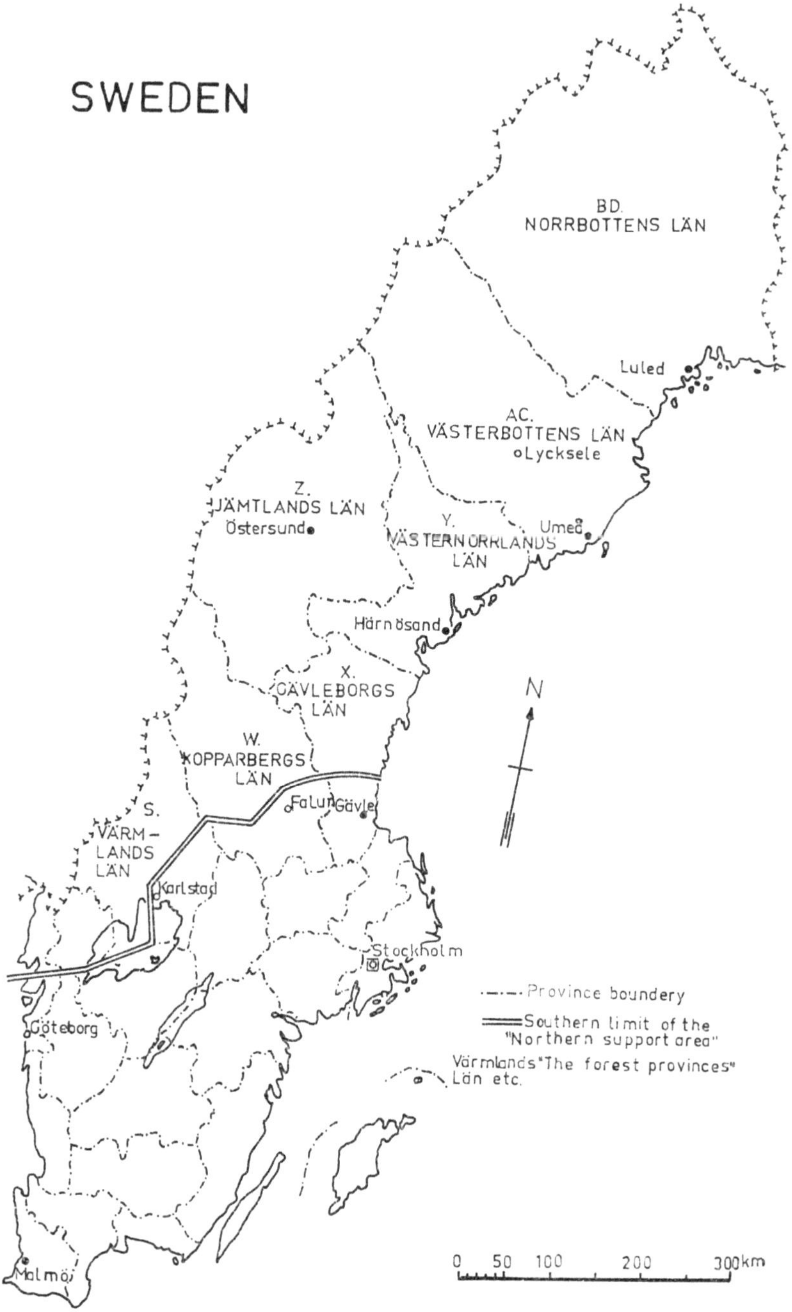
SWEDEN
BD.
NORRBOTTENS LÄN
Luleå
AC.
VÄSTERBOTTENS LÄN
oLycksele
Z.
JÄMTLANDS LÄN
Östersund
Y.
VÄSTERNORRLANDS
LÄN
Umeå
Härnösand
X.
GÄVLEBORGS
LÄN
N
W.
KOPPARBERGS
LÄN
Falun
Gävle
S.
VÄRM-
LANDS
LÄN
Karlstad
Stockholm
Göteborg
Malmö
Province boundery
Southern limit of the "Northern support area"
Värmlands Län etc. "The forest provinces"
0 50 100 200 300km

not limited to only the highest level of the regional hierarchy but also to the lowest possible one. The background to this is the circumstance that the western interior of the 'forest counties' cannot be guaranteed acceptable service facilities only through investments in a small number of large places along the Baltic coast. Such a simple solution is prohibited by the great distances, which do not permit daily commuting to these growth points on the coast for the majority of the population. The basis of existence for the people in the interior and mountain areas is first of all forestry with agriculture of a less remunerative kind, fishing, and some tourism. Due to increased use of machinery in forestry this industry cannot any longer create a sufficiently great basis of consumers for a number of service functions. The need for labour per production unit has been reduced in forestry by 90% during the last 25 years. Figures fall below minimum requirements as a consequence of population decrease and increased costs for the production of service. The result is a drop off of service, in itself an incitement for continued out-migration; and an evil circle has developed.

At Umea university a joint geographical-sociological investigation has been made to try to answer the question: At what lowest hierarchical level does the supply of service satisfy the consumers? Or: What is the smallest size for places where such a service set, accepted by the consumers themselves, is to be found. This also involves the question of the composition of such a service unit. What facilities should the unit hold? A sociological interview survey pointed out some such service facilities, indicating people's basic needs: a grocery shop, a men's and women's shop, a shoe shop, a paint shop, a hardware shop, a garage, an electrical appliance, radio and television shop, a cinema, a doctor, and a dentist, and in addition to these various school forms, which have not been included in this study.

To attain this service unit with 95% probability a place with some 3,000 inhabitants is required, the population in the umland not included – something which appears realistic bearing in mind the rapid depopulation. Today a place with 3,000 inhabitants may be classified as quite acceptable but as early as the middle of the 1970's such a place will find itself in a quandary due to rising costs and effects of rationalizing. In order to offset these trends which act negatively – underminingly – on the service basis such a place must be procured between 30 and 40 new jobs per year or an increase of the total number of consumers of at least 120.

The result of the survey mentions only a very limited number of inland places today acceptable as service centres, as a matter of fact only three in the interior of Västerbotten. If, on the basis of today's communication prerequisites of daily commuting and possibilities for effective service distribution, one would like to create a net of places guaranteeing the majority of the forest workers the standard of services offered at the so called 3,000 places at least 30 such planned places would be needed. The cost of this will again propose the question how much our resources could be distributed regionally without endangering the economy, the optimality of which lies in a concentration of the resources.

It is probable that vigorous efforts will be taken in at least a small number of these inland places on the minimum level of the service hierarchy. However, it is still an open question whether these actions will be characterized by support for long-planned growth – a growth centre policy – or support for adaptation during a reasonable short time. These places should initially be termed 'sustenance places' as distinguished from the above discussed the real growth centres on the highest hierarchical level.

The work with the 1965 location policy has also included calculations of the degree of depopulation which could be tolerated before distruction of capital occurs. It has been estimated that the population decrease should not exceed 2% per year. In order to show the dignity of the problem to master this development it is worth mentioning that the inland region of Västerbotten county with one of the 'sustenance places', the town Lycksele, would need some 3,100 new jobs up till 1980 to counterbalance a net loss of population of at the most 2% a year. Of these 3,100 needed new jobs in the staple industries only 800 might be created by spontaneous expansion of the present activities. This again is certainly rather an optimistic calculation.

MARC PENOUIL

5 A

Growth poles in underdeveloped regions and countries

I. INTRODUCTION

The theory of economic development attributes, in France, a great importance to the phenomena of polarization. Following the works of François Perroux and J. R. Boudeville, the concept of growth poles is at the centre of several analyses.[1] It can also be found behind various political decisions: the organisation of French space around eight equilibrium urban centres, the industrial complexes planning in numerous under-developed countries are illuminating examples.

Although the terms of polarized development and growth poles are frequently used, the ambiguity of this terminology becomes apparent as soon as the authors try to apply the theoretic terms to concrete situations. We have already emphasized the ambiguities and inaccuracies of this analysis, and have often pointed out that, however much of a vogue word the term has become, its real meaning changes profoundly from author to author.[2] It now seems indispensable to define precisely what we mean by growth pole and to separate this concept from all other similar concepts.

The growth pole should be distinguished from growth activity ('activité motrice'). A pole is a whole complex of activities which complement each other in technical interrelationships (upward and downward activities) and economic interrelationships (in connection with the growth of outputs). It is true that the pole is very often created around some growth activity, such as a sector of industry, a harbour, etc.; but such an activity may exist also in the absence of any phenomenon of polarization. It is very often found in under-developed countries, where an intensive exploitation of the natural resources in a given zone may only rarely lead to the creation of a pole. The pole has a sphere of influence only because it is a total of productive activities, collective equipment, and exchange systems which make the diffusion of the growth and structural changes possible.

The size of the pole is an important element of the analysis. Independently from the flow of volume out from the pole or converging towards it (flow of products, labour, capital), the zone of influence of the pole must be taken into account. This has led us to establish a double set of distinctions. The first set refers to the size and to the structure of the propulsive complex. It stresses the complementary technical relationships which are established in a given geographic area. We distinguish therefore:

a) *Points of growth*, when all the leading activities are located within a limited space: complementary relationships are established in this micro-zone, without repercussions on the outside. This concept does not exactly match that of the 'growth centre'. The growth centre is then an agglomeration capable of providing possibilities of varied occupations and collective services such as: health, educational, cultural, commercial or industrial services. These centres are opposed to the poles which are large cities, such as the equilibrium urban centres in France. This idea of growth centre is interesting from the point of view of economic policy, because the presence of such centres is indispensable for the creation of a milieu in which the growth could spread. An isolated pole, without relay growth centres, could not exercise its polarizing effects. When we speak of the growth point, however, we are referring to a different criterium. The growth point does not polarize the growth in a large and homogeneous geographical space, but only in a small zone. This is perhaps because its activity is reduced and purely local (it is then a growth centre), but it can also be because the growth activity has not been able to establish relations except with a quite small number of regional or national activities.

b) *Zones of growth* (or *poles* in a narrow sense) characterized by the existence of complementary relationships in a large geographical zone around one main nucleus.

c) *Axes of growth* created by a series of points or poles of growth between which the complementary relationships multiply owing to the existence of an important transport axis.

Most often, only points of growth exist in an underdeveloped economy, whereas in the developed economies genuine poles or axes of growth have been created: Rhine axis, poles of Northern Italy.

The second set refers to the area of the economic space in which the flows out from the pole and the flows converging into it are found. As a matter of fact, this is the zone of influence of the pole through the monetary flows caused by it. The pole may limit its exchanges to the zone in which it is implanted. It may spread its effects throughout the region or the nation in which it is established. This will be the case when the bulk of its direct and induced exchanges is carried out within that space. But it may also become an international pole, if its supplies and its outlets depend on foreign countries.

geographical space	economic space local	regional or national	external
point	point of local growth	growth point with regional or national effects	growth point with international effects
zone		growth zone with regional or national effects	growth zone with international effects
axis		growth axis with national effects	growth axis with international effects

The formation of a given type of pole depends on many factors, among them particularly:

- the nature of the growth activity (or growth activities)
- the natural resources available
- importance and quality of infrastructures
- structural elements, such as social structures, education, level of education and vocational training of labour
- level of income in the geographic area and its distribution.

On the whole it seems very difficult to define a pole by its structural characteristics. It seems more to the point to focus one's attention on the pole's mechanisms. A growth pole implies the presence of mechanisms governing the growth of income and structural changes. The growth of income results from the double action of two phenomena: multiplication and economies of scale.[3] Multiplication is connected with the flow of investments and with the distribution of income for the integrated activities in the growth centre. The importance of the economies of scale increases in the same measure in which the activities are integrated, thus making possible to minimize numerous costs and hence to maximize the relative advantages of the production units of the zone over those situated in other regions.

This is an important phenomenon because it causes the appearance of relative advantages which, in strong zones, are often decisive, which in turn tends to hamper the growth of other parts of the area and accounts largely for the cumulative character of growth in certain parts of the geographic area. Moreover, these relative advantages show a tendency to enlarge the zone of influence and the attractive force of the pole. The cumulative increase in the productions of the pole, the attraction exercised on the population, the size of the production units, all these are factors which make it possible for the pole to supply larger and larger areas and which force it to get its supplies from more and more distant sources. On the whole, the pole is a spring of growth, which can be located in different points. According to the nature and diversity of its activities, the realized investments influence the distribution of income on the spot or abroad, the local producers being or not being able to cope with the increased demand for consumers' goods created by higher incomes.

On the other hand, the growth pole determines structural changes in the region where it is located. Very often one can see major changes in the demographic situation and in the distribution of the working population: there is a strong tendency to migrate towards the region. Moreover, the share of the various activities in the total product is unevenly balanced in favour of the most productive activities. The development of the infrastructures contributes to creating a milieu conducive to economic and technical progress. Finally, more understanding for innovations may be noticed as educational, vocational and information facilities are created and the efficiency and profitability of progress is demonstrated. The psychological, almost mythical attractivity of strong zones induces labour to flock into the zone and enterprises to establish themselves there on account of advantages which are sometimes real, but sometimes illusory. The attractivity of urban areas in under-developed countries or of the industrial cities in the 19th century are examples for this effect which does not seem to be justified in the face of the misery and the disastrous unemployment resulting from it.

The second group of consequences do not always occur: in this case the pole is a growth pole without being a pole of development. This is a very delicate distinction, in so far as the growth automatically implies structural changes. The difference emerges on the level of activities which are not directly integrated into the pole – geographically as well as technically. If their structure and the behaviour of their productive agents change, one is justified to speak of poles of development. If, on the contrary, the effects on the structures are only local and the behaviour in the relatively independent activities is not directly influenced, the term growth poles should be used.

The analysis made so far is of a general nature and cannot be easily applied to complex and various realities. Polarization seems to play a major part in the process of development, but the extent of the polarization effects and their modalities depend largely on the reactions of the milieu. The rigidity or the adaptibility of the milieu determine the importance of the pole's effects. The milieu, however, is extremely variable.

From the point of view of political economy, it is important to know the relations between the pole and the milieu so that it can be predetermined whether the establishment of new enterprises might be successful. From this point of view, it is natural to ask if the problem is the same in an underdeveloped or depressed area situated within a well developed economy as in an underdeveloped national economy.

The question is important and interesting on the theoretical level, as well as on the level of policies to be applied. Does the development proceed in the same manner, by the same channels, through the same mechanism, regardless of the character of the national economy? Is it therefore possible to apply the same kind of economic policies to all the cases or will it be necessary to stick to the technical adjustments imposed by the given resources? Among the host of economic growth theories, is it possible to find the one which corresponds to the Truth and which, when applied, will ensure success? Is it not only a difference of scale amplified by constitutional particularities which separates a region from a nation?

Various theories have been advanced on this point[4] and this study will be mainly devoted to discussing this problem.

We shall try to show that, even though the two situations have some points in common, major differences may, however, be observed. They will be found on two levels:

- on the level of the nature and peculiarities of the pole
- on the level of the mechanisms of polarization.

2. PECULIARITIES AND NATURE OF GROWTH POLES IN DEVELOPED AND IN UNDER-DEVELOPED ECONOMIES

One of the most intricate problems a development policy has to solve is that of the choice of activities to be implanted, taking into account not only their direct effects on the product growth but also the polarization mechanisms induced by these activities. This problem presents itself in very different terms for the two types of economies under consideration.

Different criteria may be applied in selecting the growth activities: some of them relating to the technical and economic nature of the chosen productions, others referring to the profitability of the productive units, others still to the size of these units. The importance of one or the other criterium, the results of their application vary considerably from economy to economy. But once this choice has been made, another question arises: which will be the form of the created pole as caused by the reactions of the milieu?

2.1 *The choice of growth activities in developed and under-developed economies*

The possibilities for the choice of activities, on which a development pole is based, are certainly very limited and partly imposed by the natural conditions of the economic environment. The choice is essentially limited by the economic milieu which determines the possibilities of investment and the capacity for labour employment, as well as the amount of competition on the market and the importance of the outlets which influence the size of the enterprises.

These elements are variable depending on the level of development already reached. The difficulties in certain backward areas of well developed countries are doubtless very similar to those which may be found in under-developed countries; however, the fact that in the same political territory strong zones exist is often a factor limiting the possibilities of choice, whereas the absence of infrastructures and lack of means is a factor in under-developed countries. It might be worth while to analyse these limitations in detail.

2.1.1 *The influence of the level of development on the nature of the chosen activities*

The backward area in a well developed country is, contrary to appearances, often very handicapped. It suffers from the fact that the enterprises situated in the strong zones occupy the market. Since those enterprises profit from important external economies and since they are on the spot already, it is relatively easy for them to ensure that the entry into the sector is limited. If, on the other hand, one wants to stimulate a zone by new activities, it is important to keep only modern industries, at a high technical level. Only young industries will be able to secure the outlets and stimulate the traditional local structures. But these activities are often to a very high degree capital intensive. Their impact on the local employment may in this case be limited, either because they do not require large labour forces, or because there is a lack of highly qualified labour on the local level. These young industries which have a progressing rate of growth may have important effects on the region. It is necessary, however, to point out that, in general, these are not basic activities but industries appealing to productions of a great number of other, very specialized sectors. This often makes 'decentralization' difficult; the under-developed or depressed region may thus experience great difficulties in obtaining the growth industry or industries liable to stimulate its economy.

In an under-developed country the situation is usually different. The lack of capital, the abundance of labour, the possibility of satisfying national needs by the national production, all lead to a preference for capital saving and labour intensive industries. It is possible, in particular, to retain the 'mature' industries, such as textile or food industries, which will find outlets compensating former imports. It remains but a deeply entrenched myth, which makes of basic industries, such as metallurgy, the starting point for all real development. The difficulties in financing a big size industrial enterprise with the most modern technical equipment, the shortage of outlets with a strong purchasing power, make these choices rather haphazard. Experience shows that, on the contrary, the utilizing of outworn equipment in developed economies, which has been purchased at a very low price, may bring about a major industrial upswing, provided the price of labour stays sufficiently low. The example of Japan in the 19th century is rather significant in this respect.

Difficulties in the choice of growth activities are therefore very often due to the shortage of qualified labour and to the lack of certain local resources. The first obstacle results in a considerable rise of costs, when it becomes necessary to resort to foreign labour; the second may lead to a postponement in the exploitation of certain resources which could have played a great part in the development, e.g. the exploitation of the deposits of Tambai in the Upper Volta is handicapped by the absence of roads and the lack of water.[5] Major works would have to be carried out which would influence the cost of operations and the span of time needed to complete them.

In under-developed economies, agriculture remains the main activity, but one may ask if it could serve as a sufficient source of supplies for the growth industries. The African example of the Ivory Coast[6] is rather interesting in this context. The present and future development of the industrial sector largely depends on a flourishing economy: coffee and cocoa planting and food industries, palm-tree plantations and oil mills, para-rubber plants and tyre factories, cotton and textile industries. To put it the other way round, agricultural development may facilitate the creation of new industries within a very short time: fertilizers, agricultural machinery. Also in accepting the limitations of the environment and making the most of the relative advantage which it possesses with regard to certain manufactures, this country may establish coherent development policies of which the future will decide whether or not they have been efficient in the absence of what is called 'basic' industrialization. On the whole, it seems that the choice of growth activities in an under-developed economy depends on four sets of elements: the natural resources, the possibilities of employing local labour, the availability of capital, possible outlets. If the technical restrictions seem more severe than in a backward area of a developed country, the economic restrictions, without being negligible, are may be less importtant. This becomes quite clear if we take into consideration the requirements of profitability for the chosen activities.

2.1.2 *The influence of the level of development on the profitability and the size of the growth activities*

The profitability of the new activities is an imperative condition for the industries established in under-developed regions. In fact, such activities are subject to a double competition: the competition of the enterprises exercising the same activity in the interior of the country and the competition of foreign enterprises. In a developed economy, these two types of competition are more and more important. The enterprises of the under-developed region are exposed to the pressure of their national rivals to an extent which is the greater, the weaker are the external economies from which they profit. Within a system, in which, for economic or financial reasons concentration is desirable, these regions are very vulnerable and they may watch their old growth industries vanish into thin air and ruin their chances of starting the mechanisms of polarized growth.

On the other hand, the institutional evolution leads to a reinforcement of foreign competition, either on the level of regional rearrangements such as the European Economic Community, or on a global level: the agreements of the Kennedy Round. These agreements lead, by enlarging potential markets, to a rationalization of the production which entails the elimination of marginal activities, the concentration of financial means, but often also a certain preference for geographic zones of a strong industrial concentration.

There are plenty of examples for such an evolution. We should like to cite two. Firstly, the example of the Liège region, analysed by L. E. Davin.[7] In this case it becomes apparent how the relatively stronger growth of other regions, the increased foreign competition lead to a serious set-back, to the discarding of former activities which polarized the growth. The coal mining crisis becomes here a general economic crisis which eliminates the classic phenomena of development and leads, on the contrary, to a cumulative evolution of demographic, psychological and institutional structures making development more and more haphazard. The case of the Bordeaux region is, although different, no less significant.[8] The crisis of the region, the difficulties in establishing new activities are expressed by a stagnation of harbour activities which, in our modern world is a sure sign of decline. This situation grafted on the evolution of techniques (transports, ship building etc.) and on some natural handicaps, explains the decline of other industries (of which shipbuilding is the best example). The port which was the most important mechanism of polarized growth in the region is no longer competitive and can no longer play its part in stimulating the economy.

The situation is very different in under-developed economies. In most cases, there are no competitive enterprises in the country or at least the local market may be shared. The only genuine competition comes from abroad, but contrary to conditions prevailing in a region, it is possible here to establish a protective tariff system. The regional agreements resulting in a customs union generally result in larger markets rather than in greater competition.[9] The criterium of the profitability of growth activities seems here to be secondary. It must not, however, be underestimated. Even if the tariff protection permits the establishing of any industry, it must not be overlooked that the existence of industries producing at a price which is higher than world market prices has its repercussions on the production costs of other activities and on the purchasing power of various incomes. The profitability of other sectors may thus find itself affected and the national exports deprived of outlets.[10]

On the other hand, one should not forget the cumulative character of development. Even without it being so, it is important to make the activities yield a financing capacity which will be reinvested into the national economy. If an inflow of foreign capital is counted upon at the start, the prospects of profit must be considered to attract it, taking into account economic and political risks. The fact that the production costs are far higher than world prices makes the profits of the enterprise dependent on the protective legislation which might always be repealed and whose value is therefore dubious. Also, the tariff protection is often very imperfect owing to checking difficulties in countries where border lines are not always as real as we have them in Europe. Custom frauds may therefore become rather serious. The problem has been brought up by Senegal recently in connection with the border traffic to Gambia concerned with textiles and various other goods, such as wireless sets. Guinea has also emphasized the problem of frauds on its various borders. In general, it may be said that if the criterium of profitability in under-developed economies is not of the same importance as in an under-developed region, this does not mean that it is negligible.

The size of enterprises is, by the way, often connected with profitability. In an under-developed region, the established units have to employ a number of labour and control a large portion of the market to enable them to exercise an influence on regional economy. Also, as we shall see, their effects are not automatic. In an under-developed economy, a medium size enterprise may even play, in a given geographic zone, an important part in breaking through the old structural equilibrium. The juxtaposition of medium size units is here even more efficient than the creation of one big size unit only, because of the shortage of markets and because of the danger incurred that one large unit, isolated in the national economy, will not be integrated.

We find therefore that the growth activities as the basis of the polarization phenomena have quite different characteristics in developed economies from those in under-developed economies, which in turn result in remarkable differences in the nature of the polarization phenomena.

2.2 *The nature of polarization phenomena in a developed economy and in an under-developed economy*

At the beginning of this study we have distinguished three large groups of polarization phenomena: the points, the zones or poles, the axes. These three forms are found in the two types of economies that we shall examine but it seems to us possible to demonstrate that the dominating forms are not the same. In developed economies the axes are predominant; in under-developed ones, the points are most frequent. As for the 'poles' in the narrow meaning of the word, they have a different character in both cases.

2.2.1 *The predominance of axes of growth in developed economies*

The opposition between developed and under-developed regions in Europe shows very well the difference between those regions which are organized around axes of growth and those which are deprived of them. The importance of the Ruhr and Rhine axis, the upswing in the Seine valley between Paris and Le Havre, the economic development along the axis of the Rhone-Rhine rivers are some good examples. It seems that development of a region in a modern economy cannot any longer turn around only one more or less isolated centre, but that it implies the establishment of interdependence relationships and complementary relationships between the nuclei of development, which are united by efficient and easy operate means of transport. The other way round, nuclei of development may exist also in under-developed regions, but their isolation prevents them from outgrowing a certain stage. In these regions, the cities are doubtless industrial and commercial centres, they exercise an attractive effect on the surrounding countryside, but their dynamic qualities are insufficient to be able to entail changes in the whole of the region and, often even not sufficient enough to ensure a rapid adjustment of their own economic and social structures. It is one of the main causes for failures of regional development policies to believe that it is enough to establish a plant in order to bring about a phenomenon of polarization. Even if this new and dynamic activity manages to be integrated in the local milieu, which often is not the case, it risks not being able to give the economy the incentive which it might have doubtless given in another region. This may happen because the nucleus of polarized growth which has been created cannot be easily linked to other nuclei of the same type.

Strictly speaking, in under-developed regions only points of growth of a national effect are found. The created activities bring about genuine changes only in limited geographic areas, most effects of the polarization mechanisms being felt on the outside (see chap. 3.). We have had occasion to demonstrate that this is what, in our opinion, happened in the Aquitaine in the case of the exploitation of gas in Lacq.[11] There certainly are, also in these under-developed regions, polarization phenomena resulting from the presence of urban centres. Cities always exercise a certain attractivity on numerous activities and the growing part of the tertiary sector only augments their importance: their administrative and recreational facilities make every city a centre of polarized growth. However, this attractive effect has its limitations which first of all depend on the importance of the urban network in a developed economy. The law of Reilly will work and the commercial attraction of a centre is limited by the presence of other centres surrounding it.[12] Moreover, very often in these regions, the population and the equipment of medium size cities grow more rapidly than large centres, which in the long run may reduce the action of polarization of these centres.

It seems therefore that in developed countries the action of polarization depends particularly on the nature of established activities and on the interindustrial and interurban relations that may develop. The urban milieu is doubtless a privileged centre of polarization, but by itself, it does not imply the existence of a new structure which is more favourable to development. The growth of the production has in the urban milieu a tendency to be polarized but this does not imply structural changes inherent in the development. The polarized development depends here on the growth activites and on the economic and social milieu. The situation is very different in an under-developed economy where the city is already a new structure as such.

2.2.2 *The predominance of points of development in under-developed economies*

In under-developed economies as in under-developed regions the establishing of mechanisms for the diffusion of growth and of development is difficult. The reason may be found at the same time in the milieu in which the activities have been set and in the mistakes made in the development policy. The milieu, we will return to this later, is generally a powerful brake in the development, not only because of the social structures which stand in the way of innovations, but also because of a production structure which is not enough diversified and does not permit the establishment of complementary relationships. The implanted growth activity cannot but turn outside and thus it permits the creation of a point which contributes little to the desirable structural changes. The dominating role of the production of these growth units in relation to local needs is perfectly justified with regard to the criteria of productivity, profitability, gains, interior and exterior revenues; but selling to the exterior of almost the whole production is the reverse side of the medal. The orientation towards the exterior, for the supplies as well as for the outlets, has been often criticised. It implies important gaps in the growth mechanisms, but it constitutes also a short term incentive to growth. We think therefore that in some countries at least, the development – with the changes and global flows of investments it implies – will not be brought about until a certain increase in the production will be achieved, even at the cost of a certain loss of energy caused by the outflow of revenue to the exterior. In certain under-developed parts of the world – it is Africa we have particularly in mind – it may be wise to accept the temporary existence of growth points of a limited effect which permit the concentration of financial, cultural and technical conditions of a later development. In reality, the establishing of axes of growth is almost impossible because the network of communications is insufficient and the productive activities are not diversified. The problems of developed economies are in sharp contrast to this situation. Does this mean that instituting poles of growth is almost impossible, at least in the first stages?

In reality, in under-developed economies, the growth poles generally are urban centres, nuclei of secondary and tertiary activity.[13] The city as such is a centre of structural changes of great importance. It makes possible the blending of populations coming from different regions or even nations who, so far, have had rather few and often hostile relationships. Settling in an urban milieu does not certainly mean abandoning all past habits and mores; the African city often recognizes in its districts the diversity of the ethnic origins of its inhabitants; relations marked by xenophobia are frequent and of a serious nature but the fact of daily cohabitation alone is significant. On the other hand, the city weakens traditional structures: the family falls apart, the authority of the village chief is replaced by composite influences: party, church, boss. Social relations on a new level are established in which the occupation plays a decisive role. In the field of economy, the city is the monetary exchange zone, in contrast to rural environment in which self-sufficiency is predominant. The attraction of the city on the surrounding populations, the prestige of the city dweller and the amenities of the city, the myth of success and riches penetrate to rural environments inducing their slow transformation. The major city of an under-developed country is by nature a growth pole, but more so by its psychosocial influence than by virtue of the growth industries which it harbours.

This urban milieu has, however, its weaknesses. First of all it is not sure that the city actually acts on growth. Very often, it is deprived of important activities. To make it act on growth, it is necessary to establish in it numerous complementary activities which may here profit from considerable relative advantages. This will be the case particularly in harbour cities which constitute points of contact between the national economy and the exterior.

Often the attraction of surrounding populations is more rapid than establishing new activities. The city becomes then a centre of unemployment, of misery, of social disturbances which are here more serious than in rural conditions. In underpopulated countries this may deprive the soil of labour it greatly needs. The city is also the privileged domain of speculation, particularly of real estate speculation. The resulting great waste does not contribute to a smooth growth of the national product but orients this growth towards activities which are more profitable than beneficial to growth. The ultimate danger is a hypertrophy of this urban pole, growing isolated in the whole of the nation. The great city, in fact, is not affectedin its commercial, administrative and psychologic attraction by the presence of competitive urban centres. The Reilly law does not apply where the great centres are at a distance of thousands of kilometres and where the intermediate cities are very often deprived of all that which constitutes the attraction of the metropolis. The gigantic size of such a metropolis may under the circumstances upset the national economy by emptying the country of its human resources and by 'concentrating all the industries'.

This quick analysis shows that, although the polarization phenomena seem to exist in any developing economy, the modalities vary with the milieu on which they act. Behind identical terms frequently used very different realities exist which to neglect would be dangerous indeed and might mean the failure of the most wisely contrived policies. Although it has been proved that growth industries have an inducing effect, the criteria required to ensure an optimum efficiency of these industries vary from one type of economy to the other. But once these activities are established, the mechanisms of their influence on the economy also show peculiarities according to the level of development.

3. THE MECHANISMS OF POLARIZATION IN DEVELOPED AND UNDER-DEVELOPED ECONOMIES

It is essential to know according to which mechanism the development gets under way. Only after having studied this problem will it become easier to understand why the efforts of an industrial location policy or measures of economic policies strongly vary according to the level of development of the economy. These mechanisms act in two different directions: through the flow of income and the intersectorial relations on one hand, and through structural changes resulting from a modification of the initial equilibrium, on the other.

3.1 *The mechanisms of growth in the flow of income and in intersectorial relations*

The two actions are close together although their point of impact is different. The first implies some repercussions of the pole on the consumption industries through the distributed income, the second implies a more direct repercussion on the activities providing the goods and services necessary for the production of the pole or on the activities utilizing the products supplied by the pole. However, the purchases made by the pole amount in fact to payments of income made to economic agents in the upward stages of the production. They have moreover an influence on the investments made by these upward industries. As for the downward industries supplied by the pole, their growth results mainly from external economies which are made possible by the pole. One may therefore safely set an action through the flow of the expenses resulting from the poles' existence and the effects resulting from external economies created by the pole.

3.1.1 *The effects of the flow of expenses resulting of the presence of the pole*

Let us remember that these are the expenses incurred for consumption goods and resulting from income distributed by the pole or from the distribution of income by the industries from which it has purchased goods. Included are the expenses made by the pole for production goods.

The first great comparison between developed and underdeveloped countries is in favour of the latter because of the existence of important losses. The incomes distributed among the workers and capitalists are partly repatriated or are spent on purchase of goods in developed countries. In the same way the investments made correspond on the whole to the purchase of production goods abroad. The effects of these outflows to exterior are visible in the balance of payment: although foreign aid consists of very large sums, the monetary flow in the direction of developed countries generally takes it away. The result is that the growth achieved by the multiplied effect of additional expenses is produced in the developed economy and not in the economy in which the pole is located. Public foreign aid and private foreign investments have a direct effect on the economy of a country to the extent in which they permit to accrue the capacity of production and to provide for infrastructures. On the other hand, the induced effects resulting from the circulation of the flows of income derived from the expenses of the pole are only produced in a limited way depending on how fast these flows are directed towards the exterior.

In developed economies, these losses may also exist but they are of less importance. The under-developed regions may doubtless lose part of the advantages of the induced effects resulting from investments made in this region, but in general other regions benefit from them. In under-developed regions, the diversity of economic activities ensures a certain growth of the entire regional production under the effect of the pole's spending. Although the consequences of the phenomenon are comparable, the extent of it is very different. The question even arises whether the nature of the phenomenon and its causes are identical: in fact, in an underdeveloped economy, the main obstacle to a mechanism of diffusion of the growth effects through induced consumption expenses consists in the structure given and particularly, in the existence of a vast non-monetary economic sector which is largely self-sufficient. If we take the example of the Ivory Coast, one of the most advanced African states, we find that the number of salaried employees does not exceed 10% of the active population,[14] the salaried industrial employees being mainly concentrated in the capital. The rural world representing sometimes 70 to 90% of the population is little affected by the growth of the pole. The dualism of the economy is the primary cause for the non-diffusion of the growth effects. In addition, there is too little diversity in the industrial production which reduces the possibility of having supplies on the spot. But these new activities have very little chance to emerge rapidly, if their potential market remains small as long as the non-monetary sector of the economy areas will not be raised.

In developed economies, there are still other causes involved. Especially the fact that activities already created in other regions have a capacity of production sufficient to ensure the satisfaction of new consumption needs. The impediment lies not so much in the dualism of the regional structure as in the control exercised on the market by the strong zones. The development of inducive effects is, on the other hand, in developed economies, handicapped by the possibility to employ greater numbers of labour. The rising qualification requirements imply a continuous rise in average salaries. Full employment achieved in prosperous regions implies the application of more capitalistic methods; in depressed areas the main difficulty is often the poverty of qualified labour. However, those sub-qualifications have nothing in common with the problem of under-developed economies where the total absence of qualified labour is an absolute stumbling block. Illiteracy, the existence of a cultural milieu alien to all spirit of rational organization of the production and to scientific and objective measures, are obstacles which are very difficult to overcome.[15]

In view of this new blocking structural factor the number of qualified employees can be raised only very slowly. The total result remains the same. The impact of polarization phenomena is in general national in developed economies, and international in underdeveloped economies. Such a situation cannot be simply explained by the organization of the markets but also by the structure of the productive apparatus.

3.1.2 *The effects resulting from external economies created by the pole*

The pole often ensures the establishing of an important infrastructure from which all the activities of the region benefit. The flow of its purchases may permit to modify the production conditions of other sectors and reduce their production costs. Also, the production of the pole makes it possible for these industries to get their supplies cheaper. In addition, there are the advantages of the transport and banking network, etc. In a general way, the services created by the pole's functioning give also benefits to other activities. There are remarkable differences according to the types of economies.

In developed economies, the external economies are mainly of the first type. They have repercussions on the costs of purchases and sales of the growth activity. These effects are the more important, the closer are the complementary relations between the production of the pole and the pro--duction of other industries. In fact, only massive purchases can affect production techniques or ensure a noticeable reduction of average costs by distributing fixed costs on a greater number of products. In a similar way will the sales of the pole affect the costs only, when they relate to products amounting to an important part of the production costs of the users. To put it the other way round, the existence of these potential external economies may favour bringing to the region of complementary activities. The process of polarization develops by the creation of new sectors of activities which complement the main activity. In this case, the presence of the pole may foster the regions less developed so far, to the extent in which these external economies sharing the advantages that may be provided by public works, will cause a new redistribution of the production in the area.

But sometimes the existence of the pole produces also 'external diseconomies'. The establishment of infrastructures is certainly sometimes necessary but very often these infrastructures have already existed and are only more or less improved, when owing to the pole's presence the utilization becomes more intensive. This will be the case with the network of roads, the telecommunications, often also with general administrative services. This may result in inconvenience for the other users. Other repercussions are predictable: increased difficulty in finding labour, increase in the real estate prices, repercussions on the salaries, shortage of water for industrial users, etc... These various elements may raise the costs of the enterprises considerably which would like to settle in the region or develop their production. Economic difficulties for other sectors might also arise: for agriculture suffering from an exodus of the population, for certain enterprises which are now faced by more powerful and better organized competitors, for certain micro-regions which are emptied of their population. On the whole, the economic and social equilibrium is at stake. A visible improvement of the situation should result, but this evolution is not automatic and does not affect identically all the parties involved.

In under-developed economies, such situations are not so frequent. If the reduction of costs actually takes place, it is not always sufficient to justify the creation of new industries. Again the limited market is an obstacle which the pole by itself is not in a position to enlarge to the required proportions.

Especially the preponderance of the agricultural sector, which ensures the creation of a great part of the income and employs the major part of the active population, is a rather unfavourable element, because it establishes only few relations with the polarized activities. The attraction of foreign economies is usually strong and the financial circles which have created the pole do not always disfavour closer connection with the centres of foreign production.

The principal action that may be expected from the pole is the improvement of infrastructures. There are many examples for road, railway and harbour construction carried out to make possible the transport of products from an important centre. The case of Mauritania, the Gabon, and less so of Guinea, are significant.[16] In the case of the Tombao project, on the Upper Volta, the extension of the Abidjan-Niver railway and the hydraulic projects will not fail to have their effects on the entire economic activity. This is the more important, as also the rural areas are profiting from the infrastructures which help in distributing their products and ensure a certain transfer of progress. When these reorganizations include the construction or improvement of a harbour they may even contribute to the creation of a new pole or point of growth.[17] Unfortunately, apart from these cases, the effects on industrialization are often reduced by the all-determining obstacle of the market. The milieu acts here as a brake, it hampers a genuine diffusion of progress, which is very slow, and which could be achieved by raising the general standard of living of the entire population through numerous but coherent measures. The problem of structural changes is in this connection of utmost importance.

3.2 *The mechanisms of growth and structural changes*

The problem which remains to be studied is the resistance of the structures to the stimulating effect of the pole. From this point of view again the two types of analysed economies are profoundly different. On the surface there exist points of comparison, in both cases an inertia of the structures, a maladaptation of the milieu may be observed. These vague terms, however, cover different realities emerging in the context of the pole and the conditions of structural changes as well as with regard to the diffusion of innovations.

3.2.1 *The pole's action on the structures*

The presence of the pole puts in crisis numerous structures as we had occasion to point out examining the urban phenomenon in under-developed economies. But it is necessary to find out in how far an important growth may be achieved by non-economic structural changes. Does the pole facilitate structural changes? Are these changes conducive to growth? These are the two questions which we will have to answer.

The presence of the pole facilitates structural changes in a very different way in under-developed and in developed economies. This is given to the fact that the structural resistance of these two types of economy is not the same. In developed economies the structures are, in our modern world, a direct result of the demands of technology, but they have less mobility than the rapidly progressing technology. The legal structures of the production units, the political and administrative structures, the structures of social strata are all largely dependent on the form in which the production is organized: the joint stock corporation is an answer to the need for accumulation of capital, the parliamentary system has ensured a certain representation of economic interests, and its difficulties and adjustments may be – at least partly – explained by the diffusion of the mass media; the predominance of the middle classes caused a certain form of enterprises and a level of technology which tolerated private enterprises, the coming to power of the 'technocrats' is a sign for the transition to a more concentrated form of economic organization. Thus, the structures of the 'Western world' may be described as a product of a general evolution of productive techniques.

These structures may certainly be petrified or have become too rigid; private enterprise may be a brake to the concentration made necessary by technological progress. The normal functioning of the administration may degenerate into bureaucracy. Some members of the leading classes may be more concerned with preserving their privileges than with ensuring expansion. The workers may refuse being transferred from one sector to another or from one region to another. We are thus faced with a variety of elements which all may prevent the establishing of complementary phenomena by providing obstacles to the new activities or by making their profitability questionable. Nevertheless, the presence of the pole may modify the situation to a great extent. The old social structures may be affected and a new governing body may direct the economy. However, such efforts cannot be automatic and mechanized. In under-developed regions of developed countries such impediments are very frequent and the growth industries cannot achieve more than a very reduced polarization effect.

In under-developed economies the problem is different in the sense that the existing structures are not structures of technical societies. They are societies in which an objective analysis of facts and an orientation towards ever intensified technical research are entirely absent. The pole with its technical implications depends on a very different form of society. Here the problem is not to adjust the structures, to correct them, but to replace one form of society by another. It is quite clear that such results cannot be obtained rapidly, starting from the pole, in large areas. The pole is, from this point of view, still a creator of dual economies, because in the rural milieu its influence soon becomes too weak to bring about rapid changes in the field of occult and magic practices and to change the prevailing customs so that they may be adapted to the requirements of modern life.[18] In a microzone, the type of new society necessary to economic progress may be created, not without difficulties for men, but this geographically limited effect does not correspond to a wholesale action on the economic environment. At the distance of a few kilometres from the town, the tradition again comes into its own.

The effects of the urban pole can be rather found on the level of the mechanisms of traditional economy. It is not by rational impulses, that the economy of the polarized zone acts on the environment, but through the 'demonstration effect', by the detour of conspicuous consumption. Life which is organized around the pole creates new needs, needs not based on the objective utility of the goods, but on the social prestige they confer. The attraction of the city and of the goods which may be bought there, is a factor in making the economy a monetary one and it is also a factor of migration. It favours the setting up of dual economies much more than it generally transforms the structures and the question arises if the results are all desirable.

In developed economies the effects of structural adaptations are an essential element of the action in favour of the growth. The obstacles are removed and the new structure is more favourable to growth than the old one. In under-developed economies, these favourable consequences are less evident. The urban pole is more a centre of imbalance than a centre of growth. The unemployment shows that migration does not always increase the productive capacity of national labour. To the hidden unemployment on the sector of agriculture, the complete unemployment of the urban workers is added. The individual income of the family members of the employee remains very low. The under-equipment in the administration is more obvious, although the urban centre absorbs all the forces of the country. In the rural milieu, the effects on the growth are weak and often independent from the action of polarized industries. More than elsewhere the problem of the pole's influence seems to be an essential element, but the slender means restrict this influence, except where certain polarized industries use raw materials which come from the rural areas. The results may appear discouraging. But the effects on the diffusion of innovations must not be neglected.

3.2.2 *The effects on the diffusion of innovations*

The possibility of transferring new inventions to the domain of industrial application, the measures calculated to place the enterprise in a new commercial position, in a word, the innovations made by the enterprises are a source of progress and growth. The problem is to study to which extent the growth activity promotes inventions and consequently their diffusion.

The growth enterprise in a developed economy is often creating inventions. Every big size corporation in a new and dynamic sector has its own facilities for study and research. It is obliged incessantly to launch new products, to invent new marketing techniques, and new publicity slogans. Innovation is in a way linked to the very nature of growth activity.

The situation is very different in under-developed economies where the enterprises try above all to exploit the resources of the soil or mining deposits in utilizing modern but rarely entirely new techniques. In comparison with the traditional manufacturing methods of the country, they may be called technical innovations but there is no question here of real inventions nor even of special processes adapted locally. The technological progress is imported without establishing research facilities on the spot which, of course, have dynamic effects. There are numerous cases where this simple transfer of western techniques has dubious if not disastrous effects. Many objections might be raised here to the transfer of agricultural and even industrial techniques. The lack of adjustment of certain local productions to local needs may seem paradoxical in economies deprived of the bare essentials, but may be explained by the fact that one tried optimistically to adapt production which satisfied western consumers to local needs. Apart from the field of production, we have seen that a simple copy of western educational systems or European fiscal systems cannot replace a real concern for genuine innovations. A bare copy which wants only to change the old systems is no equivalent to the creation by local technicians of methods adapted to national needs. The obstacles to the creation of innovations are therefore strong and of a different nature than those which are met in developed economies. In the latter countries, these limits are financial and involve the profitability of former investments which may make it necessary to shelve temporarily certain new inventions. But usually these obstacles are quickly overcome by the forces of progress. In under-developed economies, however, it is the absence of suitable means and facilities which presents an impediment to innovations.

The pole tends to favour by its only presence the diffusion of new production forms on all levels of economic development. First of all, it provides the proof of the efficiency of new and progressive techniques. Then by the new publicizing techniques which it introduces it awakes public opinion to an appreciation of new types of goods and the efficiency of new techniques. By creating needs and ensuring the diffusion of its products, the pole may also, even in under-developed economies, introduce some evidence of the usefulness of transformation. In putting the new goods within the reach of everybody, it gradually induces numerous traditional manufacturers to abandon their old habits and introduce, on their level, some innovations. All this is certainly very insignificant as far as the results are concerned, but may be an inducement to an important structural evolution. It seems, however, that these results can only be achieved if sufficient means may be utilized and where the milieu is not very hostile to all things foreign, which is generally the case.

This action of the pole on innovation – may we stress that in an under-developed economy this is totally different from the invention and even from the adaptation – is doubtless one of the best ways to spread progress in the whole of the economy. It implies, however, as the other effects of the pole, a minimum of commercial and monetary relations with the other national economic activities.

4. CONCLUSION

At the end of this study, we may conclude that the forms of development vary according to the characteristics of the natural and human milieu. It is true that we meet everywhere elementary mechanisms which cannot be subject to comparisons... if a great effort of abstraction is acceptable: development and growth are everywhere the result of the mechanisms of multiplication, of complementary relationships, of structural changes which we have mentioned so often. Also in all places the resistance and the impediments are caused by the inertia of existing structures. The forces of progress can triumph only where activities are powerful enough to create the mechanisms of growth and to overcome, with the help of external aid, the influence of the blocking factors. The success in such a fight depends on the kind of stimulation activities and on the particularities of the milieu.

But behind this pattern, common to all the problems of development, arise many different situations. The reasons are evident. In developed and under-developed economies, the socio-economic milieu is very different. There is only a difference in degree between the obstacles raised by the behaviour of a given social group in Europe and those resulting from magic beliefs in some regions of Africa. The growth activity may, by its sheer power, influence the behaviour of hostile groups in developed economies; it has no chance to impose itself and create a pole of growth, in an underdeveloped economy, if the major obstacles created by the existing structures have not been removed from the very beginning. Otherwise, a dual economy emerges and the pole projects its effects towards the exterior. The economic mechanisms linked to the presence of a growth activity would exist, but their point of impact will not be the same and their results will be fundamentally different. This does not mean that in a developed economy, the absorption of the pole in a given region is not an essential element of a development policy; the nature of the problems to be solved and the means to be used must be carefully distinguished.

It is after all political economy with which this analysis is concerned. There are no ready made formulas that can be applied to all problems of development. The theoretical conflicts appear often to be academic. Balanced growth or unbalanced growth, concentration of action or 'sprinkling', the theoreticians and practicians may argue about them; the objective observation of facts leads to shades of meanings and to caution. A simple multiplication of limited actions would not be able to ensure a genuine development, because even if the economic milieu would improve, the social milieu would be little affected and the incentive forces would be insufficient. Or, in other words, a simple implantation of great industries, without any action on the milieu, will not resolve any of the real problems of development, for this would be insufficient for transforming the milieu. The development policy based on the creation of a pole is a total action, which must be carried out in two series of interventions, some of them trying to attract growth activities and complementary activities, others envisaging to adapt the milieu. Because it is a total action the development policy cannot be of the same kind in societies which are different in every point. The abstract theoretical analysis may only provide the frame of reference for a better integration of the concrete problems which must be solved in each particular case.

NOTES

1. F. Perroux, *L'économie du XXe siècle*, PUF, 1961, pp. 123–245; J.R. Boudeville *L'espace et les pôles de croissance*, PUF, 1968.
2. M. Penouil, 'Politique régionale et pôle de croissance', in R. Petrella (ed.), *Le développement régional en Europe*, La Haye–Paris, Mouton, 1971.

3. *Cf.* H. Bourguinat, 'Economies et déséconomies externes', *Revue Economique*, (4), 1964.
4. The thesis of the unity of the phenomena of regional and national developments has been particularly supported by J. Lajugie, 'Les conditions d'une politique de développement régional pour les pays du Marché Commun', *Revue d'Economie Politique*, 1959, (3), pp. 263–334.
5. Reference to this problem will be found in the *Bulletin d'Afrique Noire*, No. 480 and 489, 1967.
6. This case may be studied from the *Perspectives décennales* issued by the Ministry of Planning of the Ivory Coast. An interesting critical study was written by S. Amin, *Le développement du capitalisme en Côte d'Ivoire*, Ed. de Minuit, Paris 1967.
7. L.E. Davin, 'The structural crisis of a regional economy: the case of Walloon', in E.A.G. Robinson (ed.), *Backward Areas in Advanced Countries*, London MacMillan, 1969, pp. 113–143.
8. M. Penouil, 'Dix années d'évolution des structures économiques: l'Aquitaine reste une région en retard', *Revue Juridique et Economique du Sud-Ouest*, (Bordeaux), 1968, (4).
9. H. Bourguinat, *Les marchés communs des pays en voie de développement*, Geneva, Droz, 1968.
10. P.T. Bauer, *Economic Analysis and Policy in Under-Developed Countries*, London, Commonwealth Studies Centre.
11. M. Penouil, 'An appraisal of regional development policy in the aquitaine region', in *Backward Areas in Advanced Countries*, pp. 62–112.
12. M. Robine, *Note sur l'estimation statistique des paramètres de la loi de Reilly*, Institut d'Administration des Entreprises, Bordeaux, 1965 (Coll. 'Travaux et documents').
13. F. Perroux, 'Note sur la ville considérée comme pôle de développement et comme foyer de progrès', *Tiers Monde*, 8(32), 1967, pp. 1147–1156. See also SEMA, *Etude socio-économique sur la ville d'Abidjan*, Paris, SEMA, 1964.
14. According to *Perspectives décennales* there were, in 1965, 216,926 salaried employees in an active population of ca. 2 millions. Of these, 98,328 worked in agriculture and 33,000 in public servies.
15. W.A. Lewis, *La théorie de la croissance économique*, Paris, Payot, 1967.
16. On Guinea, see the interesting study of poles by Fria de G. Bell in *Cahiers de l'Institut de Science Economique Appliquée*, 141, September, 1963. It must be pointed out, however, that in this case – as in many others – the actual effects have only poorly corresponded to the expectations.
17. A good example of such a policy may be found in the construction of the port of San Pedro, in the south-east of the Ivory Coast, with the view to enhancing this part of the country. See *Bulletin d'Afrique Noire*, No. 447, 490 and 498, 1967.
18. Examples for these political and sociological stumbling blocks may be found in the reports of D.G. Lavroff, A. Mabileau and C. Nicolas in *L'Afrique noire contemporaine*, Paris, Colin, 1968 (Coll. 'U').

PAVEL TURČAN 5B

Remarks on Penouil's report and on polarized growth in a socialist economy

I. INTRODUCTION

In his report M. Penouil exposes in a very stimulating way the problem of common features and specific differences of polarized growth in industrialized and developing countries. He approaches the problem along two main lines, i.e. the character and nature of the pole, on the one hand, and the mechanisms of polarization, on the other. The report focusses the present state of knowledge on polarized growth, its systematization and its enrichment in different directions.

I should like to enlarge the optic of the studied problems by adding the case of problems resulting from the introduction of polarized growth within a socialist economy. Although the undermentioned remarks are based on experiences made in socialist countries of Europe, they do not directly reflect the practice of one determined country but attempt to trace some fundamental features of the problem.

The regional economists (or, better, spatial economists) try to make more operational the theory of polarized growth which was originally conceived as a theory expressing, *ex post*, the tendencies dominating the spatial organization of the national economy. Their attempt is to obtain a tool of the voluntary control, *ex ante*, of the geographical distribution of the economic and social activities within a nation.

Spatial economists of socialist countries feel very clearly this necessity because the problems connected with the direct management of the national economy as well as the need of a social approach to the efficiency of the utilized means oblige them to establish a policy of polarized growth as a tool of territorial organization of the whole national economy. This is not any more just a question of critical zones or backward areas but rather of a system of growth poles and axes which concern the whole country. For this task one has to tackle completely new and specific problems of operational type.

I intend to examine briefly three problems which seem to me characteristic for the question:

a) the role of the market in polarized growth, in general,
b) criteria for the territorial organization of the economic activities in a socialist economy,
c) models of functioning of a socialist economy and the introduction of a polarized growth.

2. THE ROLE OF THE MARKET IN POLARIZED GROWTH IN GENERAL

François Perroux originally conceived the theory of polarized growth as a theoretical expression of the long term tendencies prevailing in the spontaneous process determining the technical relations between the economic agents at the spatial level within a *developed market economy.*

He started from the analysis of a *developed economy* with a high degree of labour division, a strong specialization and cooperation (sub-contractors, etc.) and a large scale production. This analysis implies the existence of a chain reaction launched by the action of innovators, the imitation effect in the domain of the production, the influence exerted by growth enterprises on an environment able to intercept these impulses. It ascribes an important role to the modern infrastructure, to service industries and research activities.

Perroux' theory is based on the functioning of a *market economy.* The mechanisms of polarized growth depend on the market forces and categories on the quest for the biggest advantages undertaken by the autonomous economic subjects.

When analyzing the economic essence of the polarization effects and the channels through which the impulses coming from the growth enterprises and regions are diffused, we are inclined to impute these impulses to the occurrence of a supplementary *demand* and its orientation in the space, and to profit of it in order to initiate the growth and to start the multiplying and accelerating mechanism without neglecting its spatial destination.

This decisive role of the supplementary demand may be recognized by analysing subsequently all different types of polarization: the technical, psychological, geographical polarization or the polarization by incomes.

From the economic point of view, even the problem of the psychological and socio-economical capacity of a region to intercept and use the impulses coming from growth enterprises is expressed by the capacity of the region to satisfy the appearing demand. A potential pole introduces economic growth in a region in so far as this region is able to satisfy the new demand of qualified labourers, production means, raw materials, consumption goods as well as productive and personal services.

3. CRITERIA FOR THE TERRITORIAL ORGANIZATION OF THE ECONOMIC ACTIVITY WITHIN A SOCIALIST ECONOMY

For the elaboration of a long term economic plan one takes, in general, as an essential criterion, the annual average rate of growth of the national income. Among others, the following factors are determining this rate: the admissible part of investments within the national income, the offer of manpower and the export-trade balance. The central planning organization strives for reducing the influence of these factors by utilizing them in a more intensive way. It tries to increase the national income by rising the efficiency of the investments, by a more intensive utilization of the quantitative and qualitative resources of manpower, by improving the exports' and imports' values ratio.

It is obvious that the optimalization of the territorial structure of the economic activity, based on a system of poles and axes of growth, may contribute decisively to accomplish each of these tasks. The efficiency of the investments for an enterprise, a region or even the national economy depends strongly on the location, the degree at which are introduced and utilized the internal economies deriving mainly from the production scale, as well as on the external economies deriving from the utilization in common of the infrastructure, on the productive services and also on a rational cooperation in the production and consumption spheres. The increase of the final production which is imputable to a unit of social investments is inversely proportional to the growth of transport and social costs as well as to productive services, whereas it is directly proportional to the growth of the industrial complex' scale up to the optimum level, from the technical and economic point of view. The creation of a stratified industry within a system of poles and axes of growth, complementary to the exploitation of the material advantages in a given zone as well as to the activation of the local resources of manpower, can become essential for the growth of the social productivity of work.

The degree of efficiency of the used factors of production depends on the structure of the complex in which they are functioning and on the level of technical progress which facilitates the functional integration of the economic activities within the poles.

Therefore, the perspective plan of a socialist country which takes into account particularly the extra-economical aspects of social and political requirements, should estimate the economic effect of the location of investments on the global aspect of the national economy and on long term growth. In this context one has to apply the concept of polarized growth at the macro-economical level and to create consciously a geographical structure of the national economy which would ensure a minimalization of the costs of investment, production, transport and distribution which are imputable to a growth unit of the national income.

In order to utilize efficiently the resources of a country on the basis of polarized growth, it is necessary to activate their effects and to channel them into different regions of the national territory, taking into account the constraints which are represented, on the one hand, by the limitation of the global funds for investments and the other available production factors and, on the other hand, by the effects resulting from investments made in the particular regions in a given period as well as in the future. The effort to increase in the perspective plan the growth rate of the national income excludes a complete and simultaneous utilization of the resources from each region of the country, since such a procedure would imply an excessive territorial dispersion of the existing means. This effort, on the contrary, presumes that the big investment projects are concentrated on the complex growth of the regions chosen according to the marginal efficiency of the investments on the level of the national economy.

Here one can, of course, only talk about the chief projects. Their part of the totality of the investments and their connection with investments realized in other regions are determined by multilateral considerations of social, political and economic nature. Generally speaking, these considerations have to comply with the aim of restraining an aggravation of the interregional differences or even of narrowing the gap between the different levels of the regions. In any case, it is difficult to ignore the point that the principle of a polarized growth implies a consciously unbalanced growth of the economic activity in the space.

4. MODELS OF FUNCTIONING OF A SOCIALIST ECONOMY AND THE INTRODUCTION OF A POLARIZED GROWTH

Up to now, one can distinguish, on the basis of the recent experience in socialist countries, two fundamental models for the functioning of the socialist economy: the centralized and the decentralized model or, in other words, the administrative and directive model and the model which applies the market mechanisms. Both are based on the common property of the production means (although there are important differences in the various countries) as well as on one plan of economic growth (again, with differences in its character and structure according to the different countries).

The fundamental differences between these two models lie in spheres which are particularly important for the polarized growth, namely in the role of the market and the market categories in general, as well as in the position of the enterprise (the degree of its autonomy being of special interest).

The *centralized model* is, first of all, marked by a centralized management and rigid planning of the national economy; by the passive role of the market and the absence of a real autonomy of the enterprises; by the dominating role played by vertical and sectorial relations between the different links of the economic organism.

The *centre* decides on the total volume of the investments, on their sectorial granting and territorial location and even grants all the financial means of the State's budget without obliging the enterprises to refund these sums. It decides on the current production, its assortment, the production factors to be used, the resources of the productive supplying and the destination of the products including the purchase- and the selling-price. The passive role which plays money normally within the production consists in being an instrument for controling the costs of the reproduction process.

In such a situation the preliminary economic conditions are missing, which are necessary for a spontaneous polarized growth to be based on the autonomous decisions taken by economic subjects acting according to the maximization of the expected advantages. The *centre* tries to take over the function of the market and decides directly on the construction of industrial complexes in view of initiating and utilizing internal and external economies.

Under these conditions, it is most important to find out whether the controling decisions of the *centre* can fully take the place of the market mechanisms. This question is, however, only a partial aspect of a more general problem which is essential for the centralized model. It is shown that the *centre* can rationally decide the location of a limited number of big investments whereas it is difficult for it to compensate the fact that the enterprises are not able to react in an autonomous and vivacious way to the impulses given by the market which makes rather hard a real physical and regional planning.

The enterprises are not competent to react autonomously to the additional demand which follows up the creation of an important enterprise, to the impulses caused in ascending and descending line, to the increasing purchase power of the new employees in the area. They cannot take the initiative toward the exploration of advantages resulting from the creation of a modern infrastructure, toward the interception of innovating impulses resulting from the example given by modern factories and the scientific and technical knowledge applied in the new firms. On the one hand, this passive role of the enterprises is due to the fact that they have only to execute decisions taken by the *centre* which are prescribed in the plan and on the other hand, to the fact that the enterprises unilaterally try to achieve their aims foreseen in the plan and not to increase their profitableness.

This explains the enterprises' lack of elasticity in view of adjusting the spatial structure of the economic action which is accompanied by a desequilibrium between the development of the infrastructure and the productive investments, as well as the excessive role of new investments in the increase of the production, the existing system of production not being fully exploited.

The lack of a correct structure of prices, particularly of prices for the means of investment, and more generally speaking, the passive role of the money bring about an insufficient rationality of the decisions taken by the *centre* concerning the location of additional lateral and derived investments. These investments, being of lower importance if considered individually, may, as a whole, contribute substantially to the formation of the geography of the national economy.

The sectorial principle which dominates the model pursues unilaterally the optic of a sectorial rationality and does not create the conditions necessary for studying and utilizing the advantages which are formed at the horizontal level by the points of contact between the enterprises, the branches and sectors.

Under these circumstances, the national economy does not fully profit in the sphere of its spatial structuralization of the potential advantages which offers an overall plan with a central distribution of the investment funds.

The problems are completely different if a *decentralized model* is functioning in the socialist economy. This model which has mainly been developed as a theoretical one and whose practical experiences are very limited up to now, presumes an active role of the market and the market-categories. It revives the autonomy of the enterprises whose decisions are now determined by the maximation of their profitability. The *centre* only intervenes in the sphere of decisions taken at the macro-economic level, in the determination of general conditions for the functioning of the market and the decision-making of the enterprises. The *centre* does not use any more, as an instrument of its economic policy, the injunctions of the plan as well as the administrative orders, but rather a flexible plan, a fiscal and financial policy, a policy of prices, of external economic relations etc... The enterprises make the investments on the basis of their own means and of credits which are, as a rule, refundable.

The conception of a decentralized model implies conditions under which a polarized growth might be based on a combination of decisions taken by the centre and the autonomous activity of the enterprises. The enterprises would react autonomously to the impulses coming from the market and would try to find out and to use the advantages deriving from the purchasing and selling relations as well as from the cooperation between the links of the economic organism in general. The active role of the market, the creation of a rational system of prices, of equal and more objective conditions for the functioning of the enterprises, would create conditions which are more favourable to an efficient regional economic policy.

On the other hand, a decentralized model would present new problems for a polarized growth.

First of all, we have to face the problem of the subjects realizing the investments and the problem of dividing competence and means of investments between the organs of the State and the enterprises. The existing enterprises would make investments in view of renewing modernizing and extending their equipments. Their role in the creation of new firms has still to be cleared and determined. It is quite likely that the trusts and other organisms uniting different enterprises on a voluntary basis play an important role in this field.

The State would invest in the infrastructure and decide and finance the very costly creation of key-enterprises. Besides this direct action, the State would also influence decisively by means of its financial policy the sectorial and even territorial distribution of the means of investment applied by the enterprises.

If the decisions on productive investments are mainly taken by the existing enterprises, the tendency might become obvious toward a reproduction of the given territorial structure of the productive system and its dispersion (a tendency which is emphasized by the importance of the workers' organs assuming the self-management within the enterprises).

The *centre* would keep its essential role of influencing directly or indirectly the consolidation of the integration of the activities as well as on the increasing efficiency of the territorial structure in the national economy.

A combination of the active role of the market with an autonomous position of the enterprises on the one hand, with an intervention of the central organs of the State acting on the basis of a long term plan, might supply, in a socialist economy, important elements for the efficient organization of the economic activity in the space – an activity which is also based on a system of growth poles and axes. A detailed formulation of the role of the enterprises and the State, as well as of the conception of a collaboration between them, constitutes a scientific and political task which has to be accomplished in the future.

ZYGMUNT PIORO

5c

Comments on Turčan's remarks

M. Turčan's presentation of the mechanism of the process of polarized growth does not correspond with reality seen by an unbiased eye.

In the first place, M. Turčan imputes that Perroux based his theory of polarised growth solely on the functioning of the market economy. It can hardly be assumed that Perroux, who formulated this theory in the period of advanced economic planning in France, failed to perceive the intervening role of the state, which, through the medium of indicative plan, had a whole range of measures to reward industries conforming to the plan – such as access to credit, tax concessions etc. Active elements of the French plan come out especially in the context of regional development policies. Based on the Perroux theory, they express not only the market economy, but also a tendency to enlarge the imperative part of the plan at the cost of the indicative part. The so-called 'contrats de programme' can be considered as a sophisticated form of production, investment and price control.

M. Turčan's presentation of the two models of socialist economy, centralized and decentralized, without their historical context, is misleading. The audience may be under an impression that planning in socialist countries does not develop, that the model of administrative planning is still paramount, that the mechanism of polarized growth has not been applied in industrial location policies of the socialist countries. On the example of the development of planning in Poland, I am going to show, in its historical aspect the process of decentralization of planning and economic management, and the role therein of the process of polarized growth.

The policy of accelerated industrialisation adopted by socialist countries required an introduction of a new dynamic structure of economy and a maximum utilisation of economic resources. The formation of this new economic structure took place in conflict with traditional market tendencies, through abandoning the policy of rentability of individual enterprises.

As the reconstruction of the country devastated by war was the first priority, consumption has been purposely limited to the bare necessities. This brought about the growth of accumulation of the gross national product, which has been used mainly for producing the means of production.

Such control of production was only possible in result of the central planning, with a strict discipline maintained in the implementation of the plan. At the same time, it was paramount to the minimalisation of the market influence.

At that stage of economic development, central planning went hand in hand with central management. Such strategy safeguarded the acceleration of industrialisation, brought about a speedy development of production and the intended transformation of the socioeconomic structure.

In a few years the rapid industrial growth created new circumstances. The methods of centralised planning became unadequate to developed industry, with growing complexity of links between numerous enterprises, between industry and its customers, and also with ever growing importance of international links. It proved more advantageous to resign from the strictly centralised system of planning and to replace it with one that would join the central power with a serious growth of autonomy of industrial enterprises, which had to adapt themselves to the demands of their customers by making use of the mechanism of the market. Thus in the process of forming a socialist economic system the consumers' market has been accepted as a basic mechanism of discovering the people's needs, and a social mechanism of acceptance and of the usefulness of production.

At the present stage of the socialist economy, taking advantage of the market mechanism is a consequence of the rise in living standards, of a stronger orientation of the economic policy towards the rise of consumption, and of the growing role of intensive factors of development, namely of peoples' initiative and activity in the process of production. Which does not mean that the progress of socialism depends on replacing the centralised planning by the mechanism of the market, or on taking over by the market of an active role in the socioeconomic development, as suggested by Mr. Turčan. The market cannot, in any degree whatsoever, take place of the social development planning.

J. Pajestka, a theoretician of economic planning in a socialist order, says that the socialist economic system has to consider two basic mechanisms of self-regulation: the reckoning of gains and losses and the mechanism of the market. For that purpose it is necessary:

a) to coordinate the activities of different economic units, and
b) to see to the current allocation of the means of production by (among other factors) a locational policy.

The mechanism of the market must be organised and regulated for the maximum satisfaction of social needs, for keeping social costs at the minimum, and also to counter balance its own undesirable influence.

An important element in the organisation of the market mechanism is the forming of horizontal economic links, on which is based a system called 'horizontal planning'. It is a system of spatial coordination of various economic institutions, which utilises the conditions of the market.

The acceptance of the market mechanism by the socialist economy does not exclude the use of other criteria in the planning of consumption in socialist countries, such as:

a) a criterion of maximum social value (granted economic resources and other limitations);
b) socio-cultural criteria not based on the market mechanism, specific socialist order.

Mr. Turčan rightly says that admitting the market mechanism to directive planning will allow a better and more efficient organisation of economic space along the lines of the theory of polarized growth. Here horizontal planning is an efficient instrument. But there are many instances when, in the period of centralised planning in Poland, the theory of polarization on various levels, where economic criteria were accompanied by social ones, has been used in industrial location policies. New industrial centres were created and many existing ones developed where the mechanisms of economies of scale, external economies, complementary etc. were active. In cases of excessive agglomerations, when social costs rose out of proportion to economic effects, the policy of active and passive deglomeration has been applied with fairly good results.

Lastly, the social criteria were instrumental in the effort to re-activate small towns through the location of industry, which may be considered as a polarized growth of a small region, bringing in effect a sustained socio-economic growth capable of accelerating the development processes not only of the towns, but also of the countryside.

So in the socialist economy the way to a more efficient spatial organisation of the economic system leads not through the absolute role of the market mechanism, but through the perfectioning of the planning system.

To the excellent report of M. Penouil I should like to add the following remarks:

a) It is very important to notice that even the under-developed regions in developed countries differ widely from the developing countries, both in the techno-economic aspect and in the socio-economic structure. Hence the impossibility of applying the same strategies and mechanisms of development.

b) What M. Penouil calls 'milieu economique' has its continuation in sociological structures, named by J. Ziółkowski the 'psychosocial infrastructure', which exerts a very strong influence over economic development. The only trouble is how to introduce these factors into the input-output tables, as their nature resists quantification.

c) M. Penouil's views in the matter of the axes of development do not find confirmations in my observations of the spatial structure of economy in Tanzania. There, railways and roads connecting plantations or mining districts with ports brought about the concentration of the population along the routes, and the economic stimulation of neighbouring areas. Thoses are not 'axes of development' of the scale that appear in developed countries. But, toutes proportions gardées, along the axes of technical infrastructure (provided that favourable conditions of climate, soil and water are present) better effects are achieved with lower costs. The axes of development are a reality in Tanzania and they become an effective strategy of selective development.

TORMOD HERMANSEN

6A

Summary record of discussions

1. ORGANIZATION, PARTICIPATION AND METHOD OF WORK

1.1 The meeting of the Expert Group was sponsored and organized jointly by the United Nations Research Institute for Social Development and the European Coordination Centre for Research and Documentation in Social Sciences.

1.2 *Participation* in the Expert Group was confined to noted and established authorities in the field. The experts met in their own individual capacity, rather than being representatives from their institutions or countries. However, in the selection of participants, attention was paid to the desirability of: a) keeping the Group within the limit of about 25 experts, b) having experiences, views and approaches represented from countries of different size, with different economic and social systems, from different parts of the world, and at different stages of development, c) having a multidisciplinary composition of the Group with all the major fields involved represented such as economics, geography, sociology, etc. Although the majority of the participants came from the industrialized European countries, it can be said that the Expert Group as a whole represented a balanced diversity of views, approaches and experiences, a fact which contributed considerably to the successful accomplishment of the meeting. A complete list of participants is given in the Annex to this report. It should be mentioned that even if no expert from African countries participated, one of the European participants, Dr. Z. Pioro, conveyed factual information as well as particular African problems and approaches to the meeting on the basis of several years of experience in regional development planning in Tanzania.

1.3 The *proceedings* of the meeting were established and directed by a steering committee consisting of A.R. Kuklinski and R. Petrella, representing each of the two organizers. For each topic to be discussed, a basic paper and a commentary paper prepared by two participants were circulated to the participants beforehand. The authors of the commentary paper were furthermore asked to act as special rapporteurs of the discussion on their respective topics. For each meeting a chairman was oppointed. Because of the language composition of the Expert Group, it was decided that it might divide itself into one English-speaking and one French-speaking group for the discussion of more general topics. L. H. Klaassen and J. R. Boudeville were appointed chairmen of these two groups respectively.

2. PURPOSE, TERMS OF REFERENCE AND PAPERS

2.1 The *purpose* of the meeting was to assess and evaluate the respective roles of growth poles, growth centres and service centres in regional development and planning. The Expert Group was furthermore asked to give particular attention to the feasibility of transfer of theories and concepts developed and experiences gained in practical planning in industrialized countries to the developing countries. Finally, the meeting should discuss and, if possible, suggest priorities for research in this field with a particular view to prevailing problems and conditions in developing countries.

2.2 The Expert Group was invited to consider the concepts of growth poles and growth centres within the context of the theory of polarized development as applied to sectoral as well as spatial patterns of development. Although no formal terms of reference had been established, six main subjects for discussion were delimited:

a) The concept of polarized development in regional planning – an *economic* interpretation (external economies, economies of scale, regional thresholds, leading industries, multiplier effects, inter-industrial technical interdependencies, the mechanism of growth transmission from the pole or centre to the surrounding region).

b) The concept of polarized development in regional planning – a *sociological* interpretation (social advantages of scale and interaction, social multiplier effects, the redistribution of population, the generative and parasitic cities, the role of growth poles and growth centres in the modernization of a given society).

c) The concept of polarized growth in regional planning – a *geographical* and urban interpretation (the central place theory and its application to regional planning, the role of the city in the region, rural and urban relations and modifications).

d) The *institutional framework* – factors and mechanism in the formulation and implementation of growth poles and growth centres.

e) The theory of socio-economic region and its application.

f) Growth poles and growth centres in regional policies and planning in developed and developing countries (a comparative assessment and evaluation).

2.3 A set of *papers* was commissioned in accordance with the above lists of topics. The list of authors, papers and rapporteurs was as follows:

1. L.H. Klaassen, *Growth poles in economic theory and policy*. Rapporteur: M. Datta-Chaudhuri.
2. T.S. Di Tella, *The concept of polarized development in regional planning – a sociological interpretation*. Rapporteur: S. Groenman.
3. P. Vellas, *Institutional aspects of development poles and growth centres*. Rapporteurs: A.R. Kuklinski and J.G.M. Hilhorst.
4. T. Hermansen, *Growth poles and service centres in regional planning – some geographical aspects*. Rapporteurs: O. Erson and G. Weissglas.
5. L. Frey, *Aspects of the theory of socio-economic regions and its application*. Rapporteur: P.R. Odell.
6. M. Penouil, *Growth poles in underdeveloped regions and countries*. Rapporteur: P. Turčan.

2.4 The *agenda* of the meeting was established on the basis of the list of papers, so that the first three days were devoted to the topical papers, and the two remaining days to a more general discussion and to a discussion of research priorities respectively. The chairmen of the English- and French-speaking groups were asked to prepare written summary statements of the discussion in their respective groups. These statements are included in Section B and C of this chapter.

3. SUMMARIES OF PAPERS, COMMENTS AND DISCUSSIONS

A. Meeting No. 1, 19 May (morning)
Chairman: R. Petrella
Topic: *The concept of polarized development in regional planning – an economic interpretation*

Paper: L.H. Klaassen, 'Growth poles in economic theory and policy'
Discussant: M. Datta-Chaudhuri

A.a) Klaassen's paper falls into two parts. In the first, which deals with the underlying theoretical issues explaining the tendencies towards spatial concentration inherent in the process of economic growth, a unified econometric model is outlined. In the second part, this model is applied as a tool for analysing the feasibility and promises of a growth pole policy within the context of a general policy for national economic growth. The econometric model outlined incorporates final demand with adistinction between goods of different spatial range; multiplier and input-output relations; supply of production factors; the concept of interrelated industries (bundles of industries) and social activities, and the role of such bundles and of amenities in attracting capital, entrepreneurs and skilled labour. Conceptually this model can be viewed as an attempt to dynamize and build the spatial elements into the input-output model in a proper way. In the discussion of growth pole policy, particular attention is given to the integration of such a policy in a more comprehensive regional policy aiming at national growth, the costs and revenues of cities, the minimum size of cities which could be expected to serve as growth poles, and the social costs of large cities. The difficulties involved in obtaining adequate and reliable estimates of levels of living and of social costs, average as well as marginal, were considered as one of the most important obstacles to overcome before the model framework suggested could be practically applied.

A.b) In his commentary paper Datta-Chaudhuri concentrated upon two basic issues which, in his opinion, were not clarified in Klaassen's paper. First, that the growth pole theory essentially is a theory of the dynamics of development involving innovations and structural change in the economic as well as in the social systems, rather than a theory of economic growth. Secondly, that the theory applies mainly to structural change in the spatial organization at large, i.e., to the interregional aspects, rather than to individual regions considered in isolation. Datta-Chaudhuri pointed out also that from the point of view of planning it might be unnecessary to work with econometric models of the type suggested by Klaassen, in which the coefficients had to be estimated on the basis of past situations which were to be deliberately changed through active planning.

A.c) The discussion following Klaassen's paper and Datta-Chaudhuri's comments dealt particularly with the interregional versus the intraregional approach, the distinction between growth poles and growth centres, the notion of optimum size of cities, the validity of concepts like development potential and development worthiness, the applicability of the growth pole theory to less developed countries, and the use of quantitative models in formulating growth pole policies. There was a broad consensus of opinion that although the theory of growth poles lent itself most easily to interregional application, it should not be overlooked that it also offered a planning tool for regional authorities aiming at developing their respective regions, and since regional development planning could never be pursued entirely from above, the application to the regional level could well be the more important. It was furthermore suggested that the eventual conflicts between the inter- and the intraregional approach could be resolved partly by recognizing the validity of the concept of bundles of industries for explaining processes of regional industrialization, and partly by accepting the distinction and the differences in scale and scope of growth poles set in the field of interregional forces, and growth centres set in the field of intraregional forces. The discussion of the notion of optimum size of cities showed that this notion is a very vague one, and there was little consensus of opinion about its usefulness for practical purposes, at least at the present stage of development of urbanization theories and techniques of measurement. There was common agreement, on the other hand, that it would be more fruitful to pursue the problems of minimum sizes and maximum sizes defined in relation to vehicle effects and social costs respectively. During the discussion of the concepts of development worthiness and development potentials, it came out that the former, even if it might be a relevant one for developed countries, was of much less value to developing countries than the more promising concept of development potentials which could be an important tool for guiding location decisions. There was broad agreement among the experts that the theory of growth poles, if properly modified to take into account prevailing natural-geographical conditions and the specific types of national development problems, could be a very useful planning tool for developing countries. However, since the problems of spatial development are of a qualitative as much as of a quantitative nature in such countries the application of quantitative models would have to be limited, at least in the initial stages.

B. Meeting No. 2, 19 May (afternoon)
Chairman: L. Wingo
Topic: *The concept of polarized development in regional planning – a sociological interpretation*
Paper: T.S. Di Tella, 'The concept of polarized development in regional planning – a sociological interpretation'
Discussant: S. Groenman

B.a) Di Tella's paper aims at drawing relevant sociological theories on social stratification and social mobility, the formation and roles of organizational and community leaders, together with socio-ecological theories of spatial communities; with relevant geographical theories of spatial interrelationships and migration and with economic theories of allocation of investments and income formation, so as to provide a framework for studying the mutual interdependence and interplay between sociological, ecological, geographic and economic factors in spatial development. Particular attention is given to the role of organizational and community leaders in the determination of patterns of geographical allocation of investments, and to the interplay between external and internal (to the home community) pull and push factors of socio-economic nature which determine the patterns of migration. The framework elaborated above is formulated in a way which lends itself to being utilized for simulating the process of formation of growth poles and growth centres as an integral part of the complex socio-economic and spatial development by means of an electronic computer.

B.b) In his commentary paper, 'Regionalization as an operational procedure', S. Groenman concentrated upon the problem of how to define suitable regions. Two fundamental approaches to this problem were recognized and analysed, viz. the definition of regions from the bottom to the top, i.e., the identification of socio-economic systems of proximity, and the delineation of regions from the top to the bottom, i.e., the regionalization of social and economic policy. Although he accepted Di Tella's concept of home community as a relevant social system of proximity with real existence, Groenman seriously questioned the attempts of defining regions as collections of home communities if the aim was to obtain a conceptualization suitable for analysis of the spatial dimension of national development policy. For this purpose the regionalization approach in which regions were conceived and delineated as problem-bound entities appeared much more promising. However, it was stressed that the method of regionalization does accept and recognize the existence of social systems of proximity, even if the social ecology at the bottom is only one of the relevant considerations. For certain types of regionalization, for example in connection with growth pole policy, the reconciliation of the problems and potentialities of socio-economic systems of proximity with the overall national development goals, was to be seen as an issue of utmost importance.

B.c) In the discussion most speakers dealt with the problem of social systems of proximity regions versus regionalization of national policies and planning. There was a broad consensus of opinion in the usefulness of the concept of home community as outlined in Di Tella's paper, while both the relevance and the practical usefulness of the concept of catchment regions were questioned. It was made clear that both the factual conditions and the problems of planning would differ considerably between industrialized and developing countries, the latter often being faced with problems of tribal regions commanding solidarity which might constitute centripetal forces threatening national unity. It was furthermore emphasized that although ecologically based social systems of proximity were of diminishing importance in industrialized countries, this was not the case for a large number of developing countries, where agricultural improvements and natural resource exploitation would have to serve as main vehicles for national growth. The discussion indicated that the discipline of sociology as of now had only a modest contribution to offer to the development of growth pole theory and policies. It was suggested, however, that sociologists might have an important role to play in the evaluative stage of growth policies, appraising effects and shortcomings and thereby filling a gap in the continuous control cycle.

C. Meeting No. 3, 20 May (morning)
Chairman: G. Gaudard
Topic: *The institutional framework – factors and mechanisms in the formulation and implementation of growth poles and growth centre policies*
Paper: P. Vellas, 'Institutional aspects of development poles and growth centres'*
Discussants: A.R. Kuklinski and J.G.M. Hilhorst

C.a) P. Vella's paper takes a broad view of all institutional factors involved

* This paper was sponsored by the Public Administration Division, United Nations, New York.

in the formulation and implementation of growth pole policies. It surveys a number of institutional approaches found in different countries and it provides a typology of relevant institutions. Particular attention is drawn to the need for coordination, vertically as well as horizontally, within the public administration at large, between the public administration, the public sector and the private sector, and within the private sector in order to promote lasting growth and exploitation of the multiplier potentials of growth poles. To this end it is suggested that a large-scale coordination committee be established in which all interested groups and key decision-makers within both the private and the public sector are represented.

C.b) In his commentary paper A. R. Kuklinski suggested another, more demand-oriented approach to the study of the institutional dimension of growth pole policies, taking as a point of departure the need for efficient planning, and posing the question: if a decision to design and implement a growth pole policy is taken in a certain country, what feasible institutional opportunities exist and which are the best ones? Recognizing the differences in scale and scope between growth poles and growth centres, Kuklinski suggested that growth pole policy can be implemented through either: a) existing regional government and planning institutions, b) the creation of new tailor-made agencies, or c) the adaptation of the general administrative division and system already existing to the new tasks.

C.c) In J.G.M. Hilhorst's commentary paper, attention was focussed on the problem of vertical coordination and the possibility of achieving this by means of the establishment of a hierarchical pattern of the decision processes relevant to the implementation of growth pole policies. The hierarchy should be based on the spatial scope of the decisions so that decisions of wide spatial scope, i.e., with nation-wide implications, are coordinated at the central level, setting the stage for coordination of decisions with more limited scope at the regional and at the local level respectively. In this framework the distinction between growth poles and growth centres would be explicitly recognized, the growth pole policy being a task for the central government and planning agencies, while the planning and implementation of growth centres could be left to regional authorities within the limits set by the national growth pole policy.

C.d) All participants in the discussion agreed that an efficient administrative set-up was a most important precondition for successful promotion of growth pole and growth centre policies. However, there appeared to be considerable disagreement among the experts when it came to defining criteria for efficient administration, and to outlining suitable administrative structures. The discussion ended, therefore, with a recommendation that more research resources should be devoted to the study of the specific institutional requirements of growth pole policies and the various feasible ways of meeting these requirements either through adaptation of older institutions, regional governments and planning procedures, or through the establishment of new ones.

D. Meeting No. 4, 20 May (afternoon)
Chairman: E. Bylund
Topic: *The concept of polarized growth in regional planning – a geographical interpretation*
Paper: T. Hermansen, 'Growth poles and service centres in regional planning – some geographical aspects'
Discussants: O. Erson and G. Weissglas

D.a) The point of departure taken in Hermansen's paper is that the creation of growth centres requires a deliberate adjustment of the settlement structure within the regions concerned. Such a policy is closely linked to the location of service trades. The settlement pattern and the location of the service centres are tied together in a complex system of mutal and reciprocal interrelationships forming a hierarchical structure. This hierarchical structure is partially explained by the so-called central place theory. Adjustment of the pattern of settlements therefore means manipulating a system of interrelated centres, where what happens in one centre depends on what happens in, and has repercussions in other centres. The interrelations between the settlement pattern and the system of service centres appear to provide a useful point of departure for analysing how growth centre policies can be implemented. The paper clarifies and describes the interrelations between the settlement pattern and system of service centres, and analyses how changes in the system are generated and how these can be controlled and steered as a means of creating growth centres. In the last part of the paper, problems of service supply and resource allocation in sparsely populated regions are discussed with a view to assessing under what conditions and how a growth centre policy may be an appropriate solution, and under what conditions the problems have to be resolved by other means.

D.b) In his commentary paper O. Erson pursued further some of the reasoning in the Hermansen paper to see what the implications would be for a fully developed service society. In this connection he questioned the proposition made by Hermansen that the development towards a more widely spaced system based on larger centres with the smaller ones gradually disappearing would be a relatively slow process. On the contrary, the process of spatial 'rationalization' could easily be quite rapid, and even so rapid that serious problems of service supply and of maintaining acceptable social and cultural standards in sparsely populated areas could arise. In order to slow down the eventually too rapid destruction of the smaller central places serving rural and natural resource-bound population, one would probably need to establish a strategy of maintaining and promoting growth in some service centres.

D.c) G. Weissglas, in his commentary paper, developed the thinking on the consequences of a too rapid concentration in another direction, making the point that if one accepted the concentration as both necessary and desirable from the point of view of long-term social and economic development of the level of living of the people rather than specific areas, it would seem necessary to plan deliberately, not only for growth in selected growth centres and growth points, but also for the resolution of problems resulting from stagnation and depopulation in those areas which hold no promises for future growth. This means that a growth centre policy should be integrated in a more comprehensive system of spatial planning, aiming at maintaining balance in the process of spatial change.

D.d) The general discussion focussed upon four main subjects: the relation between the central place theory and the growth pole theory, the validity and usefulness of the centre-system model as a tool for spatial planning, the distinction between spontaneous and planned growth centre formation, and the feasibility of applying the type of models discussed in developing countries. With respect to the first point, there was broad agreement that although the central place and growth pole theories at the present stage of development may be both conceptually and substantially inconsistent, the first being essentially a static micro-theory with some aggregative qualities, and the other a dynamic macro-theory, they might be viewed as complementary for practical planning purposes aiming at directing the development of the spatial system by means of inducing growth in selected points and centres. There was also a relatively broad consensus of opinion about the conditions which had to be fulfilled if the model suggested should be useful for planning purposes, namely that the structural inter-centre relations were of a relatively stable nature. An apparent contradiction was pointed out here between the stability that seemed to exist in the real world and the potential instability arrived at in theoretical models. The desirability of keeping a distinction between spontaneous and deliberately planned formation of growth poles was supported by most speakers, while it was contended that if the model framework should be applicable to planning in developing countries, it would have to be adapted so as to integrate the particular structural feature of primacy of the urban system found in most of these, and the many ecological connections that prevail particularly in the agricultural sector.

E. Meeting No. 5, 21 May (morning)
Chairman: J.R. Lasuén
Topic: *The theory of socio-economic regions*
Paper: L. Frey, 'Aspects of the theory of socio-economic regions and its application'
Discussant: P. Odell

E.a) The leading theme in Frey's paper is that when one wants to use regional development policies to reach fundamental welfare aims, such as levelling out differences among regions in income and access to social and cultural services as an inherent part of economic growth policies, the role played by technical progress and innovations would have to be given attention. This would lead to the abandonment of models focussing upon the take-off of individual dominant units of production or of industrial complexes, to the identification of larger planning regions and to search for guidelines for regional policies derived from the adoption of aims and criteria of socio-economic homogeneity. This should not be seen as a rejection of the potentiality of the growth pole idea based on the recognition of the advantages of spatial concentration of interlinked units as such, but to the extension of this theoretical framework to include the socio-economic environment of the space in which the growth pole is located. Particular attention is given to the transformation of the labour force during the process of development and the changes in supply and demand conditions for labour of various skills in various types of regions. On the basis of the demand and supply of labour, a set of homogeneity criteria are suggested. In the last part of the paper the regional development policies in general and the attempts of growth pole policy, particularly in Italy, are examined. It is concluded that these policies could have been more successful if they had been integrated in global development plans.

E.b) In his commentary paper P. Odell took a point of departure in the possibility and the danger that regional development policies would aim at developing in areas other than those whose development would give the highest contribution to national growth. He then raised the question whether the model presented in Frey's paper was sufficiently well structured to take into account the existence of different types of problem areas. In his opinion the active labour market policy advocated by Frey would have to be constituted in radically different ways depending on the type of problem area the policy is directed towards. Odell also expressed some misgivings with respect to the applicability of Frey's analysis to developing countries suffering not only from the lack of well articulated urban hierarchy, which had been a basic precondition for selecting growth points in southern Italy, but also from a severe lack of planning resources necessary to work out and control the implementation of the kind of global development plans suggested by Frey.

E.c) In the general discussion it became clear that the somewhat depressing conclusions about the feasibility and potentiality of growth pole policies in southern Italy, which arose out of Frey's paper, were not at all clear-cut as there was a difference of opinion as to how far and for how long it could be said that the growth pole policy had been pursued in Italy. It was furthermore suggested that the Italian experiences indicated a misapplication of the concept of growth poles, giving all too much emphasis on the establishment of a single or a group of industries in single places with too little regard for the growth centres positions in the urban hierarchy and the possibility for exploiting inter-urban linkages arising out of forward and backward inter-industry linkages. There was some disagreement among the experts about the length of the period which must pass before reliable evaluations could be made, since it was more the long-term trends than the short-term gains which were of greatest interest. However, the considerable amount of investments needed to induce radical new trends seemed to indicate the necessity for a continuous dynamic control strategy by which policies could be adjusted to new and prospective events.

F. Meeting No. 6, 22 May (morning)
Chairman: S. Lefebvre
Topic: *Growth poles and growth centres in regional policies and planning in developed and developing countries*

Paper: M. Penouil, 'Growth poles in underdeveloped regions and countries'
Discussant: P. Turčan

F.a) Penouil's paper starts with a clarification of the terms and concepts used in an often too ambiguous way in the general discussion, and proceeds to a discussion of the main differences between the roles of growth poles in backward regions within industrialized countries and growth poles established for the purpose of inducing economic development in the developing countries. Penouil distinguishes first between a growth pole and the industrial complex which usually is its growth generating core. A growth pole may be characterized with reference to two fundamental characteristics, viz. the scale and its sphere of influence in economic space. Accordingly one can distinguish between growth points, zones and axes depending on the scale, and between poles of local, regional, national and even international scope depending upon characteristic differences in spheres of influence. Penouil concludes, however, that it is difficult to define a pole by its structural characteristics only. Therefore it is also necessary to take into account the particular properties of poles with respect to growth generating mechanisms, i.e., multiplication, attractivity and economies of scale, which together with the structural characteristics, create a milieu conducive to economic and technical progress and social change. Comparing growth poles in developed and developing countries, Penouil arrives at the conclusion that in developing countries mostly growth points and very few zones or axes of growth can be found, while the opposite is true for developed countries. Discussing the choice of motrice core activities in backward regions and in developing countries, the conclusion appears to be that the choice-options are often very restricted in backward regions due to the fact that new activities in such regions are exposed to very hard competition from firms located in advanced regions. Such restrictions are of less importance in developing countries. For the developing countries it is possible, therefore, to outline schemes of industrialization based on motrice activities whose implementation may be ensured by proper national development policies.

F.b) In his supplementary intervention, P. Turčan confined himself to a comparative appraisal of the feasibility and efficiency of growth pole policies in centrally planned and market economy countries.

F.c) The general discussion following Penouil's paper and Turčan's comments was very vivid. There was broad agreement that, taking into account the modifications suggested by Penouil and others, the growth pole theory appeared to offer good promises as a tool for national as well as for regional development planning in developing countries. There was less agreement, however, about the specific methods to apply in order to transform the general theoretical propositions into specific planning frameworks. Some of the speakers suggested that further research should be done on the formulation of the theory in mathematical terms, while others argued against stressing the dynamic and developmental character of the growth theory and the fact that it contains many elements that can be quantified only partly or not at all. The discussion of the relative strength of the growth pole theory in centrally planned and market economy countries did not produce any conclusions.

G. Meeting No. 7, 22 May (afternoon)
Chairmen: J. R. Boudeville (French-speaking group) and L. H. Klaassen (English-speaking group)
Topic: *General discussion*

Summaries of the discussions in this meeting made by the two chairmen are included in Section B and C of this chapter.

H. Meeting No. 8, 23 May (morning)
Chairman: A. R. Kuklinski
Topic: *Priorities for research*

H.a) There was general agreement among the participants that, among the different fields of study pertaining to regional development, research on growth poles should be given high priority. It was emphasized that the idea of growth poles had gained considerable popularity both in mixed economy and planned economy countries, industrialized as well as developing, but without any corresponding theoretical and methodological foundation being laid. There was also a broad consensus of opinion that the research efforts, in order to derive the highest return for the benefit of rapid regional and national development, should be coordinated within a framework of large-scale international programmes of theoretical and empirical investigations. Finally, the need for giving particular emphasis to the problems of transfer of concepts, theories and experiences from industrialized countries, where the growth pole idea was originally conceived, to the developing countries was underlined. Therefore one should aim at comparative studies of experiences in countries of different size, at different levels of development and with different economic and social systems which could be coordinated within the framework of a multi-national coordinated project.

H.b) As far as more specific research topics were concerned, there was general agreement that it was useful to distinguish between topics related to the structure and development of individual poles and topics related to systems of poles. A third group of research topics, concerned with methodological questions, could also be distinguished. In the following, a list of topics suggested during the discussion is put together. It should be stressed, however, that this list does not reflect any consideration of priorities; it is merely an inventory of important projects that should be taken up. It is nevertheless thought useful to include this list in the report as a starting point for further discussion.

H.c) With respect to *individual poles*, the following topics were suggested:

a) structural comparisons between poles of different size and locational position, and of the role of infrastructural investments for growth;

b) the occurrence and sequences in the emergence of new activities and the ways and means to induce them;

c) dynamic interdependencies between demographic, economic and social factors in the growth of poles;

d) role of administrative structures in promoting and directing the development of growth poles;

e) social costs and social revenues of comparable centres of different size;

f) the type of centres where innovations, new techniques and new forms of organizations emerge, and how they are transmitted throughout the system of centres and rural settlements;

g) why functional poles of growth emerge in some places and not in others;

h) the means necessary to create poles and make them work successfully;

i) the decision-processes involved in the setting up and implementing of growth poles, with particular emphasis on the identification of key-decisions and key decision-makers;

j) a cross-sectional study on individual growth poles established in different countries aiming at extracting information about their relative location, industrial composition, the sequential development of new activities and the problems encountered in their extablishment;

k) the multiplier effects generated by growth centres and growth poles in different spatial positions and developmental contexts.

H.d) With respect to *systems of poles*, the following topics for research were suggested:

a) the role of communication and transportation infrastructure between centres;

b) the role of administrative structures and in particular the tax system for the allocation of resources among centres;

c) how systems of poles are constituted by functional inter-centre linkages, and how these linkages change during time and generate change in the whole system;

d) the degrees of freedom for interventions in the process of locational change, and the opportunities through planning to generate particular patterns considered to be conducive to rapid development;

e) how the development of system of poles can be steered towards more rational systems according to prevailing trends in technology and preferences;

f) the mutual relations between system of centre within a nation (or an area) and the development of this nation (or area);

g) the role of comparative and absolute advantages in some poles over others in the system, arising out of external economies and economies of scale in the provision of infrastructure;

h) the efficiency of a) social investment expenditure, b) aids to industry, c) training of manpower, on the growth of the added volume of employment and of social (welfare) and stability in poles with given (and varying) structures (models for both developed and developing countries);

i) a comparative study of the spatial filtering down process of innovation through a system of poles in different cultural developmental and institutional contexts.

H.e) From the point of view of *developing countries*, the following topics were of particular importance:

a) the implications for economic growth and evolution of the system of geographical poles of the rapid improvements in agricultural techniques now under way in most developing countries. Particular attention should be given to:

1. the spatial diffusion of new agricultural techniques and the problem of deliberate speeding up of the diffusion process;

2. the consequences for release of labour and the destination of migrants

from agriculture, i.e., continued growth of the existing metropolitan areas vs. formation of new towns;

3. the change in optimal scale of farms, the implications for the land tenure system and the role of land reforms;

4. the formation of new systems of distribution of agricultural products and the implications for change in the system of centres and communications;

5. the spread of the development impulses arising out of the agricultural revolution into other sectors.

b) the process of industrialization and the role of import substitution. Particular attention should be given to the dynamic sequences of industrialization and the consequences of different sequences for patterns of industrial location, e.g., starting as in the case of Japan with final products based on imported technology and moving towards backward linkage industries, or the opposite way starting with the so-called basic heavy industries;

c) the impact upon spatial evolution of emerging factors like new technology, declining significance of sources of raw materials and energy as factors of industrial location, declining importance of local sources of finance for local investments, increasing complexity of economic organizations, greater involvement of government in decision-making, increasing complexity of economic organizations, increasing governmental concern for declining regions, importance of import substitution as a motive force for growth of agglomeration;

d) the structure and functioning of the national system of centres in countries of incipient industrialization, and the impact of the unbalanced structure of the system upon national and interregional socio-economic development;

e) the formation of new centres at the intermediary level to function as counteracting poles to primate capital cities, and at the lower level to function as service centres for agricultural areas and as relaying centres for modernization and development impulses;

f) the spatial integration of the national economy and the role of the formation of development belts and axes in achieving such integration;

g) the impact on the spatial structure of the colonial economy based on raw material export, and the problems encountered in readjusting the spatial structure to the needs of a more diversified pattern of development;

h) the problems of regional differentiation in agriculture and its impact on the system of centres;

i) the problems of interdisciplinary comprehensive planning with a particular view to the role and integration of physical planning on the one side and socio-economic planning on the other;

j) the integration of growth pole and growth centre policies with national and regional plans and policies for social and economic development.

H.f) Finally, with respect to more *general methodological topics*, the following were suggested:

a) the integration of economic and sociological models oriented towards planning;

b) the development of models and statistical methods for inter-city comparison;

c) development of dynamic models of inter-city relations during economic growth starting with the simplest case of two cities forming the nucleus of a development axis and introducing the complexities gradually;

d) development of models of administrative systems and their impact upon regional and local economic growth.

ANNEX – LIST OF PARTICIPANTS

Expert group on growth poles and growth centres

J. R. Boudeville – France
E. Bylund – Sweden
M. Datta-Chaudhuri – India
O. Erson – Sweden
L. Frey – Italy
G. Gaudard – Switzerland
S. Groenman – Netherlands
M. Halouzka – Czechoslovakia
N. M. Hansen – U.S.A.
T. Hermansen – UNRISD
J. Hilhorst – Netherlands
L. H. Klaassen – Netherlands
A. R. Kuklinski – UNRISD
A. Kuprianov – UNIDO
G. Lambert-Lamond – UNRISD
J. R. Lasuén – Spain
S. Lefebvre – France
P. Odell – United Kingdom
M. Penouil – France
R. Petrella – CEUCORS
Z. Pioro – Poland
V. Ram – UNESOB
T. Di Tella – Argentina
P. Turčan – Canada
P. Vellas – France
G. Weissglas – Sweden
L. Wingo – U.S.A.

JACQUES R. BOUDEVILLE

6B

Concluding statements
Research plan for an analysis of polarization

In Europe, as in the United States, the popularity of the growth-pole concept has made it current coin. The result is a state of confusion, which experts at round-table conferences seek to dispel from the standpoint of theory and from that of economic policy.

In southern Italy, Ireland, Canada, Holland, Spain and Colombia, – in every country, this idea of French origin is adapted and applied in a different way. Indeed, the analysis of polarization is intended to be of practical value. The aim is to provide guidance for statesmen. The development policy advocated is both technical and geographical. The results therefore call for checking, refining and theoretical advance. If this work were done more thoroughly and more frequently, the models inspired by its dynamic of information and inequality would save us certain humanly speaking fruitless experiments or disastrous inaction.

Although our knowledge of technical and geographical poles, of their hierarchy or impact and of development sequences is still far from complete, we can already discern some basic points which indicate the direction that should be taken by future research and policy.

I. THE ELEMENTS OF AN ANALYSIS OF POLARIZATION

The purpose of the following reflections is not to submit any final or formal theory of polarization, but to summarize briefly points on which general agreement has been reached regarding this type of analysis.[1] These can be grouped under four main heads.

1.1 *Polarization is a dynamic process of structural evolution*

The structures in question are not only economic, but also sociological and institutional.

Howbeit, the notion of process is of sociological origin. It is defined as a sequence of interactions produced as an outcome of empirical research. It is thus a dynamic notion going beyond that of stable-structures growth to become part of the development of social techniques and behaviour. Hence the privileged role of the urban environment.

From a *technical* point of view, polarization is a process whereby activities are industrialized or diversified starting from a single industry or a complex of propulsive industries. It has essential foundation: the incentive to invest resulting from the double interplay of inter-industrial pull and push. The downstream and lateral effects, described by François Perroux in connexion with the propulsive industry, can be recognized here. In the medium term (five years) and the long term (fifteen years), which are the analytical periods for polarization, a basic role is played by investment. Polarization can thus be analytically broken down into three parts: the multiplication effect (Leontief), the acceleration effect (Aftalion), the effect of downstream and lateral push (Perroux-Klaassen). To be operationally applicable, every analysis of polarization must be dynamic and include investment among its internal elements.

Polarization is thus a process conducive to the completion of three types of distinct inter-industrial matrices: the current input and output matrix A, the capital matrix B and the infrastructure matrix C. No study can be exhaustive or even really significant in the absence of knowledge of these three essential features and their different phasing in time.

In other words, polarization can be observed on three distinct levels, but it can be explained only by their interdependence.

Diagram

1st level. Current working
Input and output
matrix

Matrix completed
by polarization

2nd level. Sectorial development
Matrix for initial
productive investments

Technical capital
matrix completed
by polarization

3rd level. Collective development
Initial social
investments matrix

Social capital
vector completed

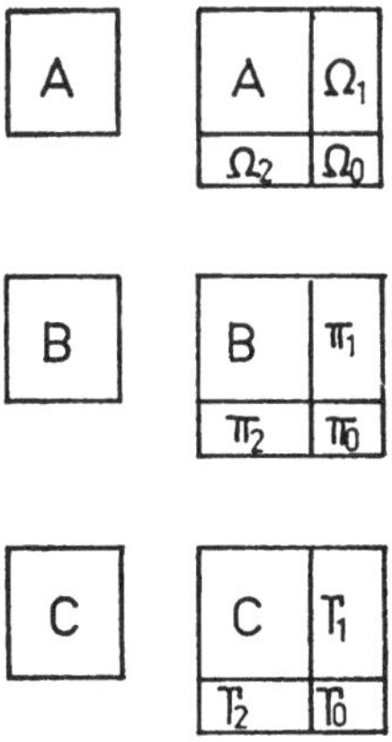

It is therefore not enough to complete Klaassen's multiplier(1) by Leontief's acceleration effects(2)*

$$X = (\hat{\lambda} A + L) X + \hat{\lambda} Y \quad (1)$$

$$X_t = (\hat{\lambda} A_t + L_t) X_t + [\hat{\lambda} B_{t+1} + M_{t+1}] (X_{t+1} - X_t) + \hat{\lambda} Y \quad (2)$$

for this would be to overlook, first, the fact that L varies between the period t and the period $t + 1$, since these are pluri-annual; secondly, that collective or social infrastructure investments play a prominent part in polarization and thirdly, that the influence of demographic migration is no less important.

The polarization process is not confined to a study of production mechanisms; it is also based on the structural evolution of house old demand linked with urbanization, industrialization and increasing incomes. These features will be dealt with in detail under 1.4.

It should be noted that the mere static comparison of structures existing at several distinct moments, and more particularly of social- and productive-capital structures, can only be supplemented by the study and choice of the investment sequences. In this respect, it would seem that the use of dynamic programming combined, stage by stage, with the search for periodical optima under constraint ought to be a privileged instrument of study.

As Klaassen has shown, but even more fully, the temporal analysis of the polarization process needs to be completed by a new dimension: the geographical dimension. This is a localized phenomenon.

1.2 *Polarization is defined as the development of a geographically agglomerated economic and social complex*

The external economies typical of polarization are essentially based on the effects of communication, using the term in the broadest sense irrespective of whether it is goods, services or informations that are exchanged. Communication is, however, hampered by distance, not only geographical but also technical and psychological; this can be statistically determined and usually has an impact reaching higher than the second power.

*: X = the output vector, Y = the terminal-demand vector, A = the technical-coefficients matrix, B = the capital coefficients matrix, $\hat{\lambda}$ = the diagonal matrix of attraction coefficients by demand, L = the current attraction matrix by supply, M = the matrix of the attraction of investments by supply.

The phenomenon, first identified by Reilly, then generalized, explains geographical agglomeration. Other sources of localized external economies also exist, such as the indivisibility of certain infrastructures and their use in common through grouped activities. With the addition to these of threshold phenomena, which for any given technique accompany the emergence of certain quaternary activities (credit, insurance, higher education), the full range of current motives for polarized economic development is covered.

This purely qualitative description deserves to be quantified and as far as possible measured.

A whole set of external economies makes its appearance as the transposed effect of the interdependence of economic sectors, so that in the case of these economies measurement is simple.

In dealing with the complementary nature of infrastructures calculation by the method of direct and indirect economic gains and costs should be contemplated. Quantification then becomes possible.

With regard to hindrances to communication, research by Leo Klaassen has shown that these are measurable in respect of current transactions. Their consequences in the field of technical progress and innovation have yet to be more closely studied.

In a recent economic model concerning the polarized development of the Paris area *(Bassin Parisien)*, the attempt was made by the author to note the components of industrial pull in urban agglomerations of over then thousand inhabitants, distinguishing the effects of multiplication, of demographic acceleration and of polarization due to growth imbalances.

Among the exogenous variables, this model includes the importance of infrastructures and the existence of the high tertiary activities.

All polarization studies show that polarization, far from being automatic, depends on the interplay of exogenous political variables, whose efficacy needs to be gauged and among which a choice should be made.

1.3 *Polarization processes and policies differ with the economic system in which they appear*

The economic and social structure is formed by the complete set of stable technical or behavioural relations observable during the annual period. This structure can as a rule be formalized in a model containing relations identifiable by observation and having evaluable parameters. These structures are of different types. The parameters of the relations comprising them, their number and form, vary in space and time. Hence, there are two necessary types of study: a static comparative study at different given periodes, and a dynamic evolutionary study. The second is the analysis properly speaking of polarization.

At any given moment, polarization is conditioned differently by three main categories of economic structures:

i) Industrialized market economies which pertain to the study of geographical agglomerations of industrial complexes round a propulsive industry on account of the external eocnomies and social costs providing the incentives for this interdependent urbanized complex;

ii) dualistic semi-market economies with price deformities whether with regard to labour, capital or foreign currency, which impede or distort polarization phenomena. The absence of a communication infrastructure creates problems with a damaging impact;[3]

iii) planned economies, without markets and with controlled prices, which eliminates real spontaneity from polarization phenomena and hampers attraction phenomena through communications (transport, information, innovation), which are a typical feature of the modern world.[4]

As time passes, the polarization process develops differently in these three types of economy, which proceed from different models and policies. But whatever the structure of the economy, development cannot be determined by mere analysis and comparison of the profitability of isolated projects. The interdependence of projects *inter se* and with the rest of the economy cannot be reduced to a study of economic gains and costs. Accurate results can only be obtained from programme analysis when this at the same time takes all possible alternatives into account. The analysis of polarization should not therefore be carried out pole by pole, that is to say, for each complex agglomerated and localized in a partial disequilibrium, but rather by making due allowance for the interdependence between poles.

1.4 *Hierarchically diversified and demographically larger poles have, owing to their flexibility and impact, a development process distinct from those of simple and satellite rural centres*

The hierarchy of poles is different from that of the administrative hierarchy, being an economic hierarchy often distinct from the latter (Washington, Brasilia, Ankara, Canberra). It is measured by the intensity of the transactions of the pole, the connection of satellite poles in accordance with the law of polarized development and is warranted by the diversification of its activities and the presence of higher ranking economic functions (quaternary).

The significance and role of tertiary activities differ, moreover, with the type of agglomeration. In order to judge the impact of any new activity it is necessary, in any case, to reset the various types of town within the polarized system to which they belong. A study of the national and structural urban network is thus a prerequisite to every analysis of polarization.

The administrative structure should be stressed on this account and the report by Pierre Vellas shows that its efficacy entails the adaptation of development poles to the modern as opposed to the more tratitional functions of growth centres.

2 THE ITINERARY OF RESEARCH

Four principles have been set:

1. polarization is a dynamic process of structural evolution;
2. it is based on a geographically agglomerated economic and social complex;
3. it varies with the type of national economic structure;
4. it varies with the hierarchic position of the agglomerations in the national system.

These four general themes often raise problems that are still far from having been solved. We propose to examine them further by research regarding them as comprising two groups:

- an *initial complex* related to the *isolated* pole conceived as an investment with an estimated economic and social yield;
- *another complex* related to an integrated system of poles, devised no longer as an isolated project but as a programming of interdependent projects.

We therefore propose the following themes for research, set out in order of increasing difficulty rather than of immediate urgency:

1. The comparative study of social gains and costs in towns with a structure of activities similar enough to reveal the part played by economic and social infrastructures, and the significance of quaternary activities;

2. The study of the sequences of the emergence of new and substitution activities in groups of cities of comparable structure, such as:
Lyon – Turin – Frankfort
Belo Horizonte – Córdoba – Cauca
Bahía Blanca – Pôrto Alegre – Recife

3. The dynamic and serial study of demographic and economic factors (multiplication, acceleration and polarization) in urban development. Distinct models will have to be made for the developed and underdeveloped countries according to the size of their national market.

We are thus led to undertake research in urban interdependence:

4. The study of the linked development of two polarized systems:

a) the role of communication infrastructures in areas dependent on two linked poles.
This case is particularly frequent in developing countries, for example:
Pôrto Alegre – Pelotas
Belo Horizonte – Governador Valadares
Bahía Blanca – Neuquén
It is found, to a lesser extent, in developed countries, for example:
Dijon – Lyon

b) the study of the development of the bi-poles, for example:
Lyon – St. Etienne
Metz – Nancy – Thionville

5. Assessing the efficacy of expenditures in
i) infrastructure;
ii) aid to industry;
iii) the efficacy of expenditures in manpower training on the increase of value added, on employment and social stability of the observed poles in an interdependent system (polarized region);

6. Analysis of the efficacy of the administration in studying, co-ordinating and promoting of polarized development. Examples, planning of the *Bassin Parisien*, the Keban project, the Indus project (Tarbela).

It will be seen that these researches all tend towards the setting up of a system of operational models integrating the economic, administrative and sociological data. It is assuredly towards this type of decision model making political choices possible that all efforts should be directed. To this end, models should be made to vary corresponding to groups of countries of distinct structure. The basic task would consist in coordinating the endeavours of nations belonging to the same economic type along easily comparable roads of development.

NOTES

1. The comments that follow were drafted at the end of a round-table conference held in Geneva on 22 May 1969 by a group of French-speaking economists composed of Messrs. Boudeville, Gaudard, Lambert-Lamond, Lefebvre, Penouil, Petrella, Turčan and Vellas. The author, who was privileged to chair the meeting, is alone responsible for any errors that may be found in the summary of the discussion.
2. The brilliant report by Marc Penouil is very clear on this point.
3. The very firm statements by Pavel TURČAN, 'Le developpement d'une région en retard: la Slovaquie', *Cahier de l'ISEA*, Economies et Sociétés, 'Economie Régionale et Pays Socialistes', Janvier 1969, 3 (1), pp. 57–82, are most enlightening in this respect.

LEO H. KLAASSEN

6c

Concluding statements
Some reflections on growth pole policy

1. In order to pursue successfully a growth pole policy it seems indispensable to increase our knowledge about the problem of how settlements function and grow. Studies to be made in this field should concentrate on the question of how new activities in settlements emerge from the existing structure and determine the new structure. A profound understanding of this basically dynamic process is fundamental for our ability to judge the possibilities of setting such a process in motion in the places where this seems desirable.

In addition to these studies, which basically concentrate on the relations between human activities, economic as well as social, the relationships between cities and regions should be studied. This sort of knowledge seems particularly important for the studies of systems of cities and the characteristics of those systems as a function of their spatial structure.

2. The discussions of our conference focussed upon the question of how the spatial structure of our societies can be induced to move from the present one to one which is more preferable from the economic, social, as well as organizational point of view.

There seems to be a general agreement that such a change should take place by means of creating new, larger centres in places where these centres contribute both to national economic growth and to a more balanced spatial distribution of income. This means that the development potential of different regions as well as the mobility of labour should be taken into account. In smaller countries with a high mobility of labour the development potential can be the only criterion for selection; in larger countries with low mobility of labour the national growth criterion should be considered secondary as compared to the criterion of a more equal spatial distribution of income.

3. There seemed to be a rather general agreement on the severe lack of

sociological knowledge in this field. This lack is twofold. *First,* basic criteria are lacking about what is to be understood by a favourable or an unfavourable social structure, which social structures are stable and which not, and what is to be understood by social progress or growth. *Secondly,* hardly any systematic studies have been made about changes in social structures accompanying economic growth in urban areas nor of the possibilities of influencing these changes. Contrary to economics, sociology in the urban field does seem to have defined neither target variables nor instruments that could be used to attain these eventual targets.

4. These basic deficiencies of sociology in this field are a major obstacle in the integration of economics and sociology in the study of the growth of systems of settlements. The cooperation in the practical fields, however, could be promoted considerably more than has been the case so far. Particularly in the fields of mobility studies (commuting and migration), consumer behaviour, locational preferences and the perception of space, a more intimate cooperation between economists, sociologists and geographers seems fruitful. This is also the case for studies relating to the actual changes in the structure of demand for and supply of labour accompanying urban growth in particular and urbanization in general. The influences of technical progress on this process should clearly play an important role in such studies. The same holds for autonomous changes in the educational structure.

5. There seemed to be less agreement on the organizational structure to be preferred in the urban growth centres, although it was generally felt that the quality of the human factor involved was of considerably greater importance than the organizational structure *per se.* This holds even more since generally the quality of local authorities and employees is determined by the size of the city as well as its income level while growth poles require people of a higher level than the ones belonging to the present city size. For this reason higher salaries were suggested for key employees to be attracted to the city.

6. The need for more research in optimum institutional framework was urged. Furthermore it seems important to indicate that each growth pole should make a development plan in which its targets for the future are fit, investment needs are estimated and the financial consequences of the anticipated development are fixed. For this crucial work usually no proper institutions are present in cities and in many cases no competent people are available to do this job: nor usually is the local government adequately

equipped for the implementation of such a plan. It is clear that at least in this respect the organizational structures will have to be adjusted.

Finally it was agreed than an extremely important research issue would be the integration of local, regional and national plans. In such an integrated planning the local initiative should be built in as an extremely important element.

7. The discussions on systems of cities focussed among others on the possible contradictions between growth pole policy and central place theory. Results of studies presented at the meeting indicated that there seems to be a tendency towards greater rigidity in the ranking of centres within national boundaries and consequently less room for a growth pole policy aiming at changing the shape of the size distribution. It seems that these studies should be promoted further and focussed particularly on the comparison of countries and periods with and without a deliberate active growth pole policy. Since we are moving from societies in which things just happened to societies that are deliberately planned, or at least steered, the contradiction between growth pole theory and central place theory, the latter being not really much more than a statistical regularity, might seem quite irrelevant after all.

8. There seemed to be some confusion about the part in growth pole policy to be played by the local authorities and the central government. Although it was recognized that local governments in decentralized governmental systems can have great power, it seemed that as a general point of departure only the growth pole policy pursued by the central government was considered. Since the balance of power between local governments and the central government is a function of the size of the country, the political system as well as historical and geographical conditions, and since, on the other hand, it can hardly be denied that the efficiency of a growth pole policy is dependent upon this balance, studies in this field seem to be of great importance. These studies could focus more specifically on the question of how the efficiency of a growth pole policy is influenced by the structure of prevailing taxation systems. In such an international comparison countries like France and Spain could be compared with Germany, the USA and Finland.

RICCARDO PETRELLA 7 A

Some notes on growth poles

I. PRELIMINARY REMARKS

The idea of growth poles has met with considerable succes in recent years. There are many examples of cases when this idea has influenced the economic policy.

To limit ourselves to Europe: already in 1957 the strategy of development by growth poles characterised, in Italy, the new trend of the 'second phase' of national policy in favour of the Mezzogiorno. More distinctly, in 1965 the declared aim was to make the coordination of State initiatives in the Mezzogiorno more effective by the progressive concentration of aid and investments in nuclei or areas of industrialisation where a certain rhythm of economic development already existed. It was in this sense that the decision to construct the Bari-Taranto-Brindisi pole was taken, thus giving the idea a quite official character. Similarly in the Federal Republic of Germany, where in 1963 the Federal Government presented a 'programme of federal growth poles' involving a total of 48 small and middle-sized towns. This programme provided for the granting of financial aid and incentives to towns presenting a series of favourable conditions.

In England too, important reports on regional development have been published since 1963 introducing the concept of 'growth area' in regions where it was considered valid: for example: 'The North-East: a Programme for Development and Growth', (HMSO doc. 2206), 'The South-East Study' (HMSO doc. 1964), 'Scotland – a Programme for Development and Growth' (HMSO doc. 2188). In the Netherlands in 1958 a policy of 'regional concentration' in medium-sized agglomerations characterised the 'second phase' of the regional policy of the government by determining eight 'development zones' outside Randstadt Holland, the most industrialised region of the country and several 'development nuclei' inside these zones. In Czechoslovakia we find implementation of the theory of poles in the policy pursued since the 1960ies in the province of Eastern Slovakia by the construction of a large siderurgical combine of European importance with the aim of transforming this department from an agricultural region to an industrial agglomeration of national importance.

It should also be recalled that the Norwegian Government has designated – in an experimental capacity – a growth centre in each of the 15 provinces situated outside the zone of Oslo; the Swedish Government has designated 20 localities with more than 30, 000 inhabitants situated in the northern part of the country as growth centres, and in 1965 the Irish Government published a declaration on development centres and industrial zones. And finally it is not necessary to recall the experiences of the policy pursued in Poland for the development of the central western and eastern regions, nor the considerable achievements made in the Soviet Union with regard to the vast desert areas and federated republics in the eastern and southern part of the country, nor the policy of the eight 'metropoles d'equilibre' formulated and in the course of implementation for several years in France, a policy which extends, on the scale of national territory, the theory of polarised development within the framework of a global conception of territorial planning in France.

So it can be seen that the idea has been a success which merits our full attention, all the more so because the idea of growth poles has developed apparently without difficulty in different economic and political systems and in countries with an unequal level of development.

A perusal of the contributions contained in this book gives rise to a first statement of facts: despite its popularity, the outlines of the idea remain uncertain, even confused. The rapidity with which the idea has been universally received and then adapted *sic et simpliciter* to different situations, has without doubt acted in such a way that, while this idea has gained *in extenso* it has lost in precision. But other more serious reasons are perhaps the roots of such confusion. This is what we are trying to show in this paper, responsibility for the ideas put forward is that of course of the author alone.

We shall proceed in the following manner:

1) On the basis of analyses and discussions of reports presented at the conference of experts, we shall try to explain the popularity of the idea of growth poles. This will lead us to present a brief survey of the definitions and contents which have gradually come to constitute the theory as a whole

as we know it today, as well as of practical contexts in the framework of which the idea has been developed and applied.

2) Then we shall strive to verify whether a basic principle exists to which the theory and practice of growth poles can be ascribed. We shall, in particular, see: a) how such a principle can take account of the fact that the idea of growth poles has been applied in a contradictory manner within the framework of regional development policies, some viewing it as a means of eliminating regional disequilibria within the country, others as a means of increasing the rate of national development and, in the long term, the well-being of all inhabitants of the country; b) how this same principle has justified the application of the idea of growth poles in the developing countries and can justify it in the future.

3) Finally, offering a method of intervention in the production processes with the aim of making a global change of the preexisting structures, of the purely economic domain where it had been originally formulated, the idea of growth poles has gained the attention of other social disciplines. Thus, today stress is rightly given to the multidisciplinary aspect of an approach aimed at gaining an extensive and global understanding of the policy relating to it. We shall therefore try, in the final paragraph, briefly to indicate some lines of research so that the policy of growth poles can meet the needs of our contemporary societies as a whole and the historical contexts in which this policy lies and operates.

This contribution, of course, will cover only some aspects of the relationship between growth poles and regional policy. For a more extensive analysis of such aspects, we refer the reader to the paper by A. Kuklinski on macro-regional planning at the end of the book.

2. REASONS OF POPULARITY

The basic idea of the theory of growth poles is quite simple: 'Growth does not appear everywhere and all at once; it appears in points or growth poles with variable intensity, it spreads along various channels and has varying terminal effects for the whole of the economy'.[1] It is, in effect, an empirical establishment of fact relating to the inequality of economic development in its spatial dimension. Development is essentially polarised in the sense that forces inherent in the development process work towards the clustering of economic activities. The mechanism explaining a polarised growth seems also simple. At a certain moment, for reasons that may be either accidental or explicable, the advent of an economic activity in a given locality gives rise to a process of cumulative development by the expedient of phenomena of a direct character (demand effect, supply effect) and other indirect phenomena which have their origin in local income created by the direct effects, part of which income will be spent locally. As a consequence of the need for communication (including transportation) and the fact that the communication costs increase rapidly with distance, a tendency to concentration of economic and human activities which are technically linked with each other takes place in the given locality .Thus a bundle of economic, industrial and tertiary activities is formed, giving birth to a growth pole. This, in reality, becomes identified with an urban agglomeration, most often the regional capital. As Leo Klaassen shows in his report, the phenomena of economic growth by growth pole are closely linked with the phenomena of urbanisation. 'The existence and growth of large cities has become one of the most common phenomena in our industrialised world. Urbanisation and industrialisation are so closely linked with each other that it is hardly impossible to think of the one without implicitly thinking of the other. Recent shifts in employment from manufacturing to services have still further accelerated the process of urbanisation. Large cities become still larger, and even for the largest in the world there seems to be no limit to their further growth. Each growth seems to produce new stimuli for fresh growth in new expanding sectors'.[2] Of course, factors of a political and administrative character also have an important effect on the development caused by economic progress, the technological change and demographical evolution (rural exodus to urban centres, growth of population).

It cannot be denied that the simplicity of these ideas and their apparent connection with facts described, hence their capacity of interpreting the growth phenomena, should have guaranteed their immediate acceptance and dissemination in the scientific community and among policy making circles. However their success is explained by other reasons which relate not only to the strictly descriptive but also to the normative level.

The theory of growth poles, placing the accent in the first place on a conception of growth in terms of disequilibria, breaks with the neoclassical tradition of economic equilibria from a double point of view: on the one hand it opposes liberal conceptions of balanced growth which concentrate on the conditions of expansion solely of the global production and total revenue; on the contrary, it presents itself essentially as a theory of development which makes it possible to explain the whole process of structural changes, both in the economic as well as in the social and institutional systems. On the other hand it enriches the up to now abstract and punctiform economic analysis by introducing the variable of space, neglected even in the theory of monopolistic competition which reduces space to an element of the category of causes of differentiation of the product. Originally, according to Perroux, for instance, this variable was still conceived at an abstract level of geographical space. It is only gradually, through the contribution of other authors and by the usage which, in practice, had been made of this theory, that it has also been applied to the spatial aspects of growth in its specifically geographical sense.

Thanks to the theory of growth poles and of polarised economic development, a more realistic explanation is obtained of the processes, and an economic policy better corresponding to existing mechanisms becomes possible. This has not failed to have an influence on the various public planning bodies at the national, subnational (regional and local) and international level, who have seen in this theory an operational implement for the formulation and carrying out of their development plans. We touch here a group of reasons which result from the requirements of development policies after the second world war in the ex-colonised countries and in backward regions within industrialised economies. Arising at the same time as the theory of big push, although it quickly differentiated itself from it, the policy of growth poles partly entails themes and contents dear to this theory, the essential of which is, in a few words, the idea that a minimum level of resources exists which should be transmitted to the development programmes, if these are to have any chance whatsoever of success. Successive investments will not accumulate their effects to the total of the effects of each of them. A minimum amount of investments is necessary, although not enoug to ensure success. Based on the phenomenon of external economies, the theory of big push involves the creation of a large number of interdependent projects in a simultaneous manner. This method has been largely applied in the 1950ies in several underdeveloped countries and even in backward regions of developed countries, such as in the case of the Mezzogiorno in Italy. Its application has not always been fortunate in the ex-colonised countries because the resources necessary to promote their growth by a big push turned out to be so great that the countries were not able to obtain them themselves and the aid of rich countries was not of such a scale as to compensate for the deficiencies of the ex-colonised countries. Furthermore such an aid had not been conceived in a way to permit these countries to use it in view of their interests and their need for national development.[3] The same applied to the backward regions of industrialised countries where the institutional structures, fundamentally of a liberal-capitalist character, did not enable the state to influence private investments with the desired aim. On the other hand, public investments were so dispersed from the territorial point of view (we are talking, let us recall, of the 1950ies when we witnessed almost everywhere in Europe a policy of industrial powdering and of large investments in the infrastructure) that their impact on the traditional structures of an agricultural and pre-industrial society had not been sufficient.

Presenting itself as an alternative policy to that of big push, the theory of growth poles has advocated the need to concentrate investments in a small number of sectors, the key sectors, that should be determined by the size of upstream and downstream relationships, in function of the maximum inputs and outputs, using, to this end, the input-output tables on which, in the meantime, other authors such as Leontieff and Isard have done original and very fruitful work. Thus, in the underdeveloped countries the phase of a selected development in a limited number of sectors replaced the phase of generalised development; in the countries of Eastern Europe planning authorities moved from a policy of generalised industrialisation in the whole territory and based on heavy industry to a policy of intensive industrialisation in zones and sectors that could ensure a more rapid rate of development of the national economy; in the backward regions a policy of concentration of public aid investments in the zones or areas of development has been implemented.

Three kinds of factors have more particularly favoured the policy of territorial concentration: a) the development of the technical and economic conditions of the industrial location; b) a change in the needs of the population; c) the responsibilities of the public authorities.

The natural traditional restraints to the location, such as the nature and contour of the soil, climate, water, availability of sources of energy, raw materials, which in the past shaped the economic and human geography of our societies, have gradually lost their determining influence. A growing of productive activities breaks away from the restraints of the physical geography and even the traditional activities, thanks to the development of transport and the very great mobility of the productive factors, can be more freely localised than they had been in the past. New conditions arise, general relating to the economic efficiency, such as the importance and nature of the infrastructures, the importance and nature of collective services, the existence of a minimum of surrounding economic milieu which assures external economies, the occurrence of which is often determinant in the present location processes. The result of this is that it has become possible to pursue a policy of largely voluntary location, concentrating in a given area a diversified number of activities, a concentration which, in its turn, is required and called for by the requirements of modern technology and economic efficiency.

The second factor is explained by the fact that a large and qualified population with a great capacity of production and adaptation to the most advanced techniques becomes a primary element in the process and strategy of development. Consequently, if the aim is to develop an underdeveloped zone or region, the best method would be to create a massive active qualified population making possible the establishment of sufficient and very varied economic activities in a growth pole.

The third factor is related to the fact that the functions and the economic and social initiatives of the public authorities become a determining condition here and obligatory elsewhere for the development of the contemporary societies; in the more industrialised countries because the structural mutations of the liberal industrial economic system cause the sectorial and territorial disequilibria that we know; in the ex-colonised countries because no other possibility exists than the direct taking over by the public authorities of the economic destinies of the country; in the countries with a socialist system because the common ownership of the productive factors implies the collective administration of the economic and productive processes. Now the available resources being limited, the problem of their optimal utilisation has made their rationalisation indispensible by the expedient of the hierarchy of objectives and plans of development of the various sectors and regions. The method of growth poles, supporting the need for the concentration of investments in certain well selected places and in complexes of optimal size and structures, has arisen as one of the most effective responses, offering a scientific and operational basis to the policy of regional development and the planning of national territory.

Finally, as one becomes aware of the close links existing between the economic development and urban structures, and has noted that the unlimited and anarchistic growth of big cities is a considerable cost for the whole community, the theory of growth poles, in its implications concerning the urban polarisation and the hierarchic structures of cities* seems to offer concrete methods of initiatives to carry into effect not only a global policy of growth in regions that are poor from the industrial point of view and lacking from the point of view of urban structure, but also in order to pursue, as in the case of France and the Federal Republic of Germany, a policy of modernisation and reconstruction of the present structure of urban and rural agglomerations.

This brief survey – however insufficient – maybe enables us to draw the following considerations:

a) the theory of growth poles has been worked out on the basis of experience and problems in industrialised economies. Explaining *à posteriori* the mechanisms of the development of modern industrial societies, it has been conceived to respond to the problems posed both from the point of view of territorial development as well as from the sectorial point of view,

b) formulated originally as a theory of development through space and firstly applied to the problem of regional development, it has now become a global theory of social development (opposed to the more limited concept of economic growth) on a sectorial, spatial and temporal basis,

c) the first concrete applications to the problems of regional development, openly claiming kinship with this theory, have been carried out within the framework of systems of liberal capitalist economy, such as the countries of Western Europe.

3. THE BASIC PRINCIPLE

In view of the three preceding remarks and on the basis of the concluding statements by Jacques R. Boudeville[4] which, in a very clear and balanced way, sum up the main 'theses' of the theory of polarisation, it is now possible to affirm that there is a basic principle which actuates the whole theoretical and operational construction of the theory of polarisation, that is to say, industrialisation as aim and essential dynamic factor of the development of the structures. Following Boudeville's formulation: 1) Polarisation, from a *technical* point of view, is a process of industrialisation and diversification of activities starting from an industry or complex of

* Benefiting above all here from theoretical contributions of another school of thinking – that of the Zentrale Orte or Central Places – developed in Germany and the United States.

motive industries. It is based on an essentially economic foundation: the incentive to invest resulting from the double effect of interindustrial mechanisms of impulsion and acceleration. (...). 2) Polarisation is defined as the development of a geographically agglomerated economic and social complex. The external economies that characterise the polarisation are, in effect, essentially centred on the fact of communication in the broad sense, whether it is a matter of exchanges of goods, services or information (...) 3) The process and policies of polarisation differ according to the types of structures of the economy in which they operate.'

We find the principle of industrialisation in the specific applications we have indicated earlier, such as the Bari-Taranto-Brindisi growth pole, that of Kosiče in Eastern Slovakia, the 48 German cities, the French 'metropoles d'equilibre', the eight Netherlands development zones, the English growth areas, and so on. Industrialisation is, in effect, the main declared objective in the national plans of many European countries. Although the industrialisation may be presented as an aspect of the process of modernisation, it is no less normally the fundamental aspect. We therefore know of the problems which, under the dictates of industrialisation, the regional economic policy and, in this context, the policy of development poles have posed in recent years, giving rise to great theoretical and political disputes that are still unsolved: does the granting of state subsidies to enterprises in certain parts of the country threaten to prevent the competition from playing its normal role and to reduce the general level of productivity? What proportion of the country's resources can be allocated to the selected regions without prejudicing other regions? Is it desirable to encourage emigration of the population of an unfavoured region or to try, and at what price, to modify the structure of this region?

These questions, indiscriminately, invoke a single one: to what degree can the aim of the industrialisation of the country, often determined by a given rate of growth of the GNP per inhabitant, be reduced, or diminished, by the fact that part of the national resources are destined to less developed regions? Of course this question implies the validity of the thesis according to which the use of national resources in the less developed regions constitutes a relative loss for the whole of the economy of the country, which is questionable both for the medium and the long term.

Whatever may be, the existence of this principle makes it possible to apprehend another basic reason explaining the popularity of the theory of growth poles, which thus supplements those indicated in the preceding paragraph: the aims pursued or permitted by this theory adapt themselves to the major aim of the economic policy of our modern societies and integrate themselves fully into it. While calling to question the modalities of the economic 'administration' of the past, this theory offers a set of ideas and concepts and postulates a series of concrete measures which in no way contrast with the existing productive mechanisms nor with the commonly accepted principles. This applies apparently both for the developed and underdeveloped countries, for the capitalist as well as the socialist countries.

But the existence of this principle also makes it possible to understand one of the main reasons for the uncertainty and confusion surrounding the contents and specifications of this theory. Although industrialisation has its own logic, which arises in any society using new techniques, the roads taken or still followed in the different societies to arrive at industrialisation are often distinct, because of the diversity of political systems and historical factors. Thus, apart from uniform elements, industrialisation takes on specific aspects in each country, even in the different regions within a country. Or, under the imperative impetus of industrialisation at all territorial levels, one has been led to consider every phenomenon of change as a process of polarisation, therefore necessitating a policy of development poles: here, to develop a small town with 5000 inhabitants was to begin to establish a pole; there, to set up a siderurgical industrial complex was to create a development pole; in another country the construction of a hydro-electrical station with power production, processing industries and agricultural use of water was conceived as the basis for the development of a new pole; elsewhere the pole ought to arise as a result of very important port or river infrastructures. Thus, from country to country and from one experience to the other, a series of types of poles, axes, zones, areas, nuclei, points, centres, mixed, complex, isolated, interdependent, principal, subsidiary poles were established, which, involving theoretically delimitable ideas, in reality covered extremely diversified and incomparable situations.

The particular situations of every country are certainly such that one could not claim to give the same definition in Bulgaria to what was defined as a growth centre in France, nor could the urban agglomeration of minimum size necessary in Sweden to be selected as a pole or development nucleus be the same in Italy, when the density of the population is completely different in the two countries. We note, however, that different definitions do not conceal only different uses of a same conception but also dissimilar conceptions, while responding to objectives that can be considered analogous. In other words, behind the common denominator of industrialisation, opposed policies have been and are being practiced, so that their alleged links to the common theory are finally questionable.

Difficulties also arise with regard to the understanding of the effects and mechanisms of polarisation. As we have said, these mechanisms are in theory apparently simple and understandable. In practice, the effects of polarisation are considered sometimes on the scale of a microzone of several thousand inhabitants. Sometimes only the effects on growth and income are considered, sometimes all the effects on the various structures. Sometimes the accent is put on the role of a motive activity, sometimes on the links existing between this industry and the urban environment. Even the criterion of motive industry, which represents the basic element for all polarisation, is not exempt from ambiguities and confusions for, in effect, if a dynamic and innovating economic activity can play a driving role in one place and thus originate the growth of the location zone, it is possible that it does not produce the same results elsewhere. In his report, Marc Penouil has made a good attempt at clearing up some of these problems by classifying the motive industries according to their local, regional, national or international effects and then suggesting respectively the definition of points, poles and axes of growth. Clarification has also been obtained from the distinction between 'growth poles' and 'development poles': where growth is generally defined as an increase in the size of various economic variables such as the population, the production or the revenue. Of course, growth implies certain changes in the economic structures. For example growth of the population implies a change in the age structure, growth of an industrial activity implies modifications in the distribution of the active population. But in the case of growth, these structural changes essentially affect the magnitudes in growth and do not imply a modification of economic relations. If appreciable modifications take place in economic relations, then one refers to the idea of development understood as the changes made not only on the expanding variables but also on the productive sectors, the attitudes of economic agents, the nature of institutions, etc.

Despite these clarifications and definitions, an understanding of the mechanisms of polarisation, in particular the *a priori* determination of conditions making the advent of a polarised development possible and, more precisely, the determination of activities that can play the role of growth poles in a given region, remains difficult to obtain. We know today that the accent is above all placed on the influence the motive activity can have on the environment and, on the other hand, as Luigi Frey indicates, on the role of the 'milieu vivant' as indispensible precondition for the polarised development to occur and for the motive activities to exercise their polarising effects. It becomes ever clearer that it is not enough to locate a considerable number of dynamic activities or a big industrial combine, nor to ensure the transport, communication and other 'tertiary' infrastructures, or let the external economies play their role, so that the polarised development is guaranteed in a given region. Transformation of the milieu, the urban structures, the attitudes of economic agents, the 'human' environment, the administrative institutions and mechanisms, also becomes indispensible.

But in doing so should we not put stress on a new or at least more global dimension within the framework of the industrialisation policy which has up to now influenced the formulation and the practice of growth poles policies in the various countries? Does this not signify that in carrying out a policy of polarisation one should examine the sociopolitical context and the necessary modifications to be made to the dominant production mechanisms and institutional structures, as well as to take into account the level of development of every country and the mechanisms which determine in the present world the productive forces and power structures among social classes and countries. In the case of the policy in favour of less developed regions, the strategy of growth poles has paid little attention to the specific conditions of the milieu and to the transformation of general conditions of the development mechanisms within the country and, in the case of the ex-colonised countries, to the peculiar requirements to be met for their development and to the limitations existing from the neo-colonial situation. Since the development of modern industrial societies was characterised by a polarised growth, it was considered that a policy of voluntary industrialisation aimed at reproduction of mechanisms that had shaped the present societies would have made it possible to extend the industrialisation to zones and countries that had remained outside this process up to now. This postulate, being apparently valid for the more developed countries and zones, proved to be erroneous when the policy of growth poles did not take into account changes of dimension postulated by the development of backward regions and countries.

This leads us to examine, in the next paragraph, two basic problems: a) the deadlock which the application of the theory of growth poles to the problem of the development of backward regions has characterised in certain cases; b) the conditions of the application of this theory in the underdeveloped countries of the Third World.

4. THE LIMITS OF SPONTANEOUS APPLICATION OF THE POLARISATION POLICY

A. In order to tackle the problem of the deadlocks that have characterised application of the theory of growth poles to the development policy of backward regions, may we be permited to examine one of the most significant examples, that is the policy of areas and nuclei of development in the Mezzogiorno.

The strategy of polarised development applied in the Mezzogiorno dates from 1957, when the Cassa per il Mezzogiorno was charged with the establishment of 'consortii' in the various parts of the south, aimed at promoting the location of industrial activities in a given area through the creation, development and administration of infrastructures such as road and railway connections, installations for water and energy supply, etc. This strategy was based on two fundamental arguments of the industrial location theory and of the spontaneous polarised growth: the pre-existence of attractive factors for the location of industrial activities and the wish to obtain external economies so that the pre-existant location factors can have the highest degree of influence.

In order to be recognised as an 'industrial development area', apart from the existence of new industrial initiatives, an area might ensure the following conditions:

a) a favourable geographical predisposition,

b) the existence of raw materials or good opportunities for their supply from not very long distances,

c) the availability of basic and civil infrastructures or the possibility of their expansion by not too expensive nor long term investments,

d) adequate availability and territorial concentration of manpower,

e) the possibility of obtaining additional manpower from neighbouring agricultural areas,

f) the pre-existence of an economic structure capable of enabling the devotion of part of the increase of income to the consumption of industrial products.

According to the legislative, the establishment of areas and nuclei of industrialisation should consequently be aimed at the intensification and amelioration of the infrastructures system of zones already possessing an agglomerative force, with the aim of also drawing in industrial activities not linked to factors of geographical location or to the availability of raw materials, manpower, etc.

At the end of 1969, 12 areas and 34 nuclei of industrialisation had been designated and established.

One of the results of the policy of concentration during the period of 1957–69 had been to increase existing negative tendencies: the abandonment of ever greater territories in the inland parts of the south and concentration of the population in urban areas in which a productive structure capable of absorbing the manpower leaving agriculture existed – or one hoped would arise. So a strong increase of migratory movements took place from poor zones in the inland Mezzogiorno towards the chief provincial towns and the coastal areas and, outside Mezzogiorno, towards the regions of the north. According to recent data[5] the zones of the Mezzogiorno in which a more intense process of growth has occurred – and thus of industrial concentration – covers in total an area corresponding to 20.7% of the territory of the Mezzogiorno. In addition, only 14.1% of the area within the perimeters of the 'consortii' of industrial areas and nuclei of industrialisation is localised in the inland parts of the Mezzogiorno, while the remaining 85.9% covers the industrial areas (45.6%) and nuclei of industrialisation (36.6%) situated along the cramped coastal areas of the continental and insular parts of the Mezzogiorno. During the period of 1952–66 the 12 areas of industrialisation (9% of the area of the Mezzogiorno) concentrated 86.6% of the absolute growth of the population of the Mezzogiorno and the near-totality (95.5%) of the natural growth. Opposed, of course, the demographic development of the external zones to the industrial zones and nuclei of industrialisation which have undergone a very clear demographical deterioration. In other terms, the policy of polarised development applied in the Mezzogiorno has incontestibly increased the disequilibria already existing between the coastal zones and inland Mezzogiorno. If one adds that such a policy has also not made it possible to diminish the disequilibrium between the regions of the north and the Mezzogiorno, the total picture is not encouraging.

It has been argued that the policy of poles of development in the Mezzogiorno has been brought to a crisis by the multiplication of areas and nuclei and, thus, by the impossibility of pursuing an effective concentration of initiatives by the public authorities. This is without doubt right, but that is not the problem. In effect, admitting that if a more restricted number of areas of industrial development had been designated, we would have probably witnessed a more massive concentration of infrastructures, industrial locations and, certainly, of the population, with the sole result of speeding up the abandonment of all remaining territory of the Mezzogiorno.

The failure of the policy of development poles in the Mezzogiorno is also not due to an original deficiency in the underlying theory. It is completely due to the present mechanisms of Italian development. Its failure was due to the fact that it had been applied following the logic of unplanned spontaneous industrial location while it was a question of a planned and voluntary policy by the public authorities. In addition it had been applied without the development processes of the national economy, held back everywhere by the requirements and 'laws' of the growth of the most industrialised regions of Northern Italy, having been deflected or at least controlled. Or, as is the case also in France, Great Britain or Sweden, the concentration of the most dynamic and modern activities in the most developed regions of the country implies and requires a progressively growing infrastructure and thus a process of increasing the incentive force of the zones of urban and industrial concentration where the effectiveness and rentability of new locations are much greater.

But it is not enough to restrict oneself to a critical analysis of the public initiatives. Another reason for the failure, or the partial results, obtained by the policy in favour of the Mezzogiorno based on polarised development lies with the political and social forces who have been making uncertain and weakening the development policy in the Mezzogiorno. Apart from the Maffi groups of Sicily and Calabria who, by their actions and presence, void any possibility of reform and have largely profited from the advantages linked with the creation of the 'consortii', the political and social forces dominant in the Mezzogiorno (conservative or left) often acted in the past as conservative elements, increasingly preoccupying themselves with ordinary administrative activities and the obscure interests of local and electoral intrigues. This has also been supplemented by the contradictions and uncertainties of governmental groups and the action of economic and social groups in the industrial north who have relentlessly opposed, up till recently, any real policy of transformation and reform of the productive mechanisms, a real policy of economic planning throughout the national territory, and any institutional reform of the State apparatus.

Consequently, the problem of Mezzogiorno, although it had been recognised by all sides as representing a national problem, has perforce been a problem of extraordinary state initiatives with the risks, the difficulties, the lack of coordination, the wastages that an action of such a scale, basically of a non-programmed type, implied.

In order that the situation could be different two other elements were missing: on the one hand, the existence of a contractual force of agricultural 'braccianti'* and a determining presence of labour unions and, on the other, the existence of regional powers which should have enabled the population of the Mezzogiorno to take direct responsibility, within the framework of a global strategy for the whole of the country, for the problems of development.

During the past 15 years, more than one and a half million people have left the countryside of the south. This enormous exodus has caused great changes in the antiquated relations of production in agriculture. The labour union force of the 'braccianti', still numerous in the south, was therefore strengthened but up to a few years ago they were but miserable individuals without organisation and unitary action. Dispersed in small factories of an artisinal type, the workers, on the other hand, have not had an effective trade union or political influence. Still now their condition is very precarious: out of 2 million industrial workers, only 200–300.000 work in large or medium sized industrial enterprises. The remainder live from day to day, or at best from week to week, and represent the great part of the urban subproletariat. They lack a real class consciousness and their solidarity is only shown in isolated cases, often by explosions of anger such as the recent events in Calabria, Battapaglia or Apulia.

With regard to decentralisation of the public powers and planning responsibilities, it was only in 1970 that regional executive legislative powers were established throughout the national territory in conformity with Section VI of the Italian Constitution.

Up to 1970 the regional programme committees only played an indirect consultative role without any democratic representativity. Many of them, above all in the Mezzogiorno, were not even able to carry out their principal task (preparation of the plan of regional development to be submitted to the central bodies), because of the lack of financial means and of technical and qualified personnel. So all decisions were taken by the central ministeries and

* Unskilled day labourers.

by the Committee of Ministers for the Mezzogiorno. No determining structural modification had been made to the traditional procedures of the central administration. Even the creation of the Cassa per il Mezzogiorno has not presented the occasion for a real innovation in the practices of bureaucratic centralism. To give an example, the procedure for the constitution of 'consortii' which, as we have said, was the basis of the creation of areas and nuclei of industrialisation, has not escaped the slowness and bureaucratisation of the centralised administration: in order for it to become operative, the regulating plan of the area or nucleus of industrialisation, which represents the main task of the 'consortium', had to be presented to the Committee of Ministers for the Mezzogiorno, submitted for examination by an Interministerial Committee and for discussion by the Council of Ministers, and was then subject to a decree by the President of the Council. The time from the adoption of the statute regulating the internal structure of the consortium to the final endorsement of the regulatory plan was 5 years for the area of Taranto, 7 years for the area of Brindisi and 10 years for the area of Bari. This is another aspect of the failure of the policy of growth poles which could have been eliminated if the southern regions and population had had autonomy in initiatives concerning their economic destiny.

At the conclusion of these remarks it is also interesting to throw further light on a last but no less important factor, among the conditions missing in the application of the polarised development policy in the Mezzogiorno. This is the European dimension of the strategy of industrial location. In the degree to which Italy, integrated in the Common Market, has not raised the problem of a strategy of territorial development on the European community level, it has had to submit to the restraints caused by the 'laws' of European economic development of a neo-liberal capitalist type where the mechanisms of territorial concentration and the imperative requirements of economic effectiveness and intracommunity competitiveness have greatly acted to the disadvantage of the peripherial and underdeveloped regions of the Community. The aim of the national policy being industrialisation, it had been particularly difficult, within the framework of a growth poles policy in the Mezzogiorno, to face up to the needs of the strong regions of the country who, when a choice of location and/or use of national resources was posed, put forward the argument of the need to allocate investments in the most dynamic activities in a priority manner to the northern regions and the need to satisfy their demand and need for collective infrastructures in order not to weaken the international competitivity of the Italian economy.

And even the legislative law compelling state enterprises, or enterprises under state control, to localise at least 40% of the new investments in the southern regions, which was one of the conditions to promote the creation of poles there, has not always been respected.

This description of the Mezzogiorno shows that the elements on which action should be taken in the application of a growth poles policy are extremely varied and complex ones and that such a policy implies a widespread coordinated action aimed at transforming the existing conditions of not only the economic but also the political, social, institutional 'milieu', not only at the local or regional level of areas directly concerned by the poles but also, at the national level and, in the case of Italy, at the European Community level.

B. The case of the policy of growth poles in the underdeveloped countries deserves a qualitatively different description although some remarks made above can be extended to these countries.[6]

The process of industrialisation of these countries up to now has been particularly difficult and full of obstacles of an internal and external nature. The aim of this paper is not to examine the structural and economic restraints or the conflicts between cultural traditions and racial groups which have hindered the progress towards industrialisation. It is not necessary either to recall the impediments and difficulties posed by the colonial heritage and by the imperialist and neocolonialist policy of the large and medium world powers. The fact is that, while industrialisation had brought many advantages to the societies of the Third World and while these had overcome big obstacles in several cases due to the courageous policy of new leading groups, serious difficulties inherent to industrialisation threaten the future of the ex-colonised countries. Among the most disquietening are:
1) the rural stagnation;
2) the proliferation of the urban sub-proletariat;
3) the lack of basic education, of training of experts and of mass education;
4) the excessive rate of growth of the population and manpower;
5) deterioration of the terms of exchange of their products on the world market, even when these countries have succeeded in increasing the quantity and raising the labour output, with the result that the domination of the industrial powers continues to threaten the developing countries;

6) the direct domination and control of many resources and local productive activities by companies of the industrial powers.

In this context the idea of growth poles has been exported into the developing countries, following, almost to the letter, models formulated in the industrialised countries. Obliged, of course, as all contemporary society, to pass from the traditional to the modern mode of existence and from the latter to a mode that could be termed ultramodern, and also having to pass through these two stages very rapidly in order to catch up the accumulated gap, the developing countries have been led to try out a territorially and sectorially concentrated growth.

The result has been, on the one hand, the creation of small islands of industrialisation (the so-called cathedrals in the desert) with no relation and no osmosis with the environment and, on the other hand, the spectacular distension of huge urban agglomerations characterised by generalised unemployment and underemployment, often the capital of the country, while the rest of the country remains in backwardness and the most total poverty.

In these urban agglomerations, besides a growing number of qualified people whose professional expectations are out of proportion to the real possibilities of obtaining work, there is an ever growing mass of itinerant merchants, shoe-shine and newspaper boys, beggars, occasional workers and pickpockets who form a miserable, unstable and disappointed urban sub-proletariat.

Among the other causes of this urban grouping and excessive sub-proletariat are the urban salaries, which are clearly higher than the wages of the rural workers and attract to the cities a large number of people seeking work, the galloping demographical growth, in the majority of these countries more than 2.5% per year, and finally, the use by the modern enterprises of techniques that make it possible to economise in manpower. Due to the financial support of the world industrial powers, the industrialisation concentrated on capital and the modern sectors of technology has therefore given rise to the production of goods and services destined for the great part for a minority of inhabitants who have the chance of drawing their revenues from these enclaves of the modern sector. The result of this is often the juxtaposition of two economies and the widening of the gap between the rich and the poor. The thesis by which the growth of modern enclaves will be sufficient to bring about the transformation of a whole traditional society is henceforth questioned. It would, however, be a serious error to affirm that a policy of industrialisation should consequently be preceded by the increase of revenues of the rural masses and thus to maintain that the growth and above all improvement of agricultural production and stock breeding constitutes the keystone of all transformation of the country and the indispensible condition for the pursuit of industrial development.

The economies of the ex-colonised countries – it is obvious – have been integrated into the world economic system. More exactly, the production and exchanges of the ex-colonised countries are completely subjugated to the functioning of the big industrial powers. The progress that can be achieved or has been achieved in an economy thus subordinated to foreign powers will not be able to destroy – on the contrary – mechanisms that generate the subjugation and increase of the relative underdevelopment. The major problem for the countries subject to the situation of neocolonialism is, therefore, we believe, to free themselves from the 'peripherial'economic condition in view of their real development and harmonious integration into a new world community. Within this framework, the reconversion of their economy should certainly begin with agriculture. But because the active population of the ex-colonised countries remains, for the great majority, rural, one too often infers that these countries have a sort of agricultural vocation. In effect, the alleged distinction between countries of industrial vocation and countries of agricultural vocation arises from a colonial conception of international relations. The present gradual development in the world obliges all countries to assume – in good or bad faith – an industrial vocation. The real importance of agriculture in the ex-colonised countries does not therefore lie in the fulfilment of a specific mission. It lies in the need to feed populations that are still prey to underdevelopment. The pitfall for the developing countries would be to industrialise their agriculture with priority in such a way that they would continue to remain suppliers par excellence of agricultural commodities and continue to undergo deterioration of the terms of exchange. On the basis of these facts one would not renounce the modernisation of agriculture but the priority concern should be the effort of modernisation in other sectors, under the circumstances, industrial ones. Here we return to the problem of the use of the growth poles policy in the ex-colonised countries. Once again this cannot be correctly envisaged without taking account of the fact that the development of these countries at the present time lies in the context of the world forces and of development characterised by the extraordinary upsurge of new productive forces and the deepening of the gap that separates the developed from the underdeveloped countries.

It is on the basis of the opposition between the tendency of ultramodern techniques to become worldwide and the tendency of these same techniques to spread at increasingly unequal speeds in the various parts of the world, that the questions of development, and thus of the growth poles policy, should be posed.

Apart from the conditions which determine the greatest speed of development in the privileged countries, the fact is that the considerable inequalities between the speeds of development go hand in hand with a concentration of qualified experts and the organisational power in several privileged regions. Hence the concentration of centres of initiative of world importance limited to the territory of the big very advanced powers and hence the growing awareness in the ex-colonised countries that political independence is illusory or fallacious if it is not accompanied by economic independence. But, in a world in which all technical and economic forces are in a state of interdependence and interaction, economic independence only belongs to countries which have centres of initiative of world importance. And inside each country, as is the case of the European countries, only the regions possessing such centres hold real chances of participating in modern society. Therefore a first constatation becomes necessary for a correct policy of polarised development in the developing countries. With the aim of achieving a real economic independence and thus preventing a future world domination of neo-colonial imperialism, the ex-colonised countries must conceive a policy of industrialisation at the level of big continental or sub-continental groupings. The national schemes for catching up with the advanced countries by the backward ones are completely belied by the growing techno-economic gaps between the various parts of the world. Only a joint and common plan of the various groups of countries of the Third World and a pooling of available resources could, in addition, enable the poor masses in the ex-colonised countries to overcome the obsession of development and distress linked with the manner in which they live. In concrete terms it would be a question for the ex-colonised countries to fulfil the following objectives as soon as possible:

a) the creation of big political-institutional groupings by an advanced economic integration and the working out of a plan for the development of all integrated space in terms of the common needs and diversity of the member-countries. To do this the ex-colonised should not repeat the experience of West European countries based on a commercial and free-exchangist conception of integration but should aim at reaching the stages of their integration on the basis of their complementarity and the need for a common strategy;

b) the transformation of their relations of production and their economic structures through a new division of labour inside the subcontinental groupings. Here too they should not repeat the experiences of the construction of an isolated heavy industry met with in the countries of Eastern Europe during the 1950ies. Such a project would have quite a different consistency and economic-political significance on the scale of a big subcontinental grouping. On such a scale it would also have the possibility of laying the foundations for several ultramodern centres of initiative and of technological initiatives with worldwide effects that would enable the ex-colonised countries slowly to free themselves from the dependence on the big powers and to establish new relations of exchange and cooperation with them;

c) a radical transformation of the educational system (still taken from western and colonial models), of the training of experts, of mass education and, still further, of interpersonal relations and the participation of individuals in collective life. This 'cultural' transformation would not be a secondary, subordinate or quasi-superfluous aspect of development. Through this one could counter the 'bourgeois-ising' of the mode of life and thinking of the majority of dominant and privileged groups of the ex-colonised countries, which has greatly hindered up to now their development and chances of modernization and advancement on the way to economic independence. And finally, by conjoint action of a rediscovery of the interpersonal relations of their ancient civilisation and a new modern conception, one could ensure that their industrialisation can be carried out quite differently to what has been the case in Europe and the countries of North America.

5. CONCLUSIONS

One could remark that the considerations developed up to now represent an arbitrary displacement on other levels of the problems of growth poles, being essentially based on the level of the economic mechanisms.

We do not share this opinion, however, because the economic mechanisms cannot be disassociated from the institutional and social political variables. Like every theory, that of growth poles is also not ideologically neutral. We have seen that it implies general conceptions on the development of modern societies and normative values bearing on their 'should be'.

'All studies made on polarisation' states Jacques Boudeville in his final remarks, 'show that, far from being automatic, it depends on the effect of exogenous political variables, the effectiveness of which must be judged and from which a choice should be made'. At the conclusion of another study[7] Marc Penouil also supports the thesis that 'polarised development is a total phenomenon that has not only economic dimensions'. And finally Antoni Kuklinski rightly stresses that 'it is a dangerous mistake to reduce the problem of growth poles and growth centres to solely economic dimensions and to study it as a problem concerning the effectiveness of the investment policy'.[8] Whether it is a question of its application to the underdeveloped regions or to the ex-colonised countries, it would be blindness to consider the political, institutional, social and cultural variables as elements of simple differentiation of the process of polarisation. It is increasingly evident that they are determining and conditioning elements of it.

In an official document of the European Communities, *Une politique régionale pour la Communauté* (1969), we can read that 'The aim of regional policy is the creation, planning and administration of the conditions of location of economic and human activities, consideration given to the requirements of technique and the economy, to the needs and aspirations of the populations as well as to the characteristics of territories'. Even if such a formula represents a weak compromise between the priority of the aim of a constant growth of the community economy and the need to get all the regions and their populations to take part in obtaining the economic optimum, it is closely related to the formulation now given to the aim of the growth poles policy in the industrialised countries. But to conceive the aim of regional policy in these terms, does this not revert to putting in question at the same time the problems of the type of administration of the economic and human activities, the finalisation of the technique and economy, the priority of satisfying the needs and aspirations of the populations wherever they may be, the mechanisms of the decision making process, the functionability of the existing institutions, the relations of power between classes and social groups at various territorial levels?

For this reason, and in view of an adequate formulation and implementation of the growth poles policy in underdeveloped regions, we consider that research of a comparative nature at the all-European level should be made on the following themes:

a) study of trends in the strategy of investment at the *sectorial* level by private economic agents and public bodies;

b) study of trends in the strategy of investment at the *territorial* level;

c) comparison of these two strategies, analysis and redefinition by the public bodies of a global strategy responding to the interests of the community and the less privileged parts of the community. To this end definition and application of corrective instruments to existing mechanisms and of new instruments suitable for the pursuit of the strategic aims;

d) study of the role of the European, national, regional and local institutions in the formulation and implementation of public strategies and study of the necessary changes to be made so that these decision-making levels become functional, autonomous and flexible enough for the interdependence and collaboration to exercise their positive effects;

e) study of the conditions and transformations necessary to ensure, in the institutional, bureaucratic, social and cultural field, that the populations concerned, the economic groups, trade unions, political parties, take part in the working out of strategies, accepting the implicit orientations and obligations, change their behaviour and attitudes and do away with the obstacles they themselves raise in the application of public strategies.

With regard to the ex-colonised countries our thesis is that, to the extent in which the economies of the underdeveloped countries remain subordinated to the interests of the big industrial powers, the problem of their modernisation, their industrialisation and the strategies relating to it, which in the first place include the growth poles policy will always be hindered and conditioned by exogenous variables.

For this reason we consider also that new research should be carried out in the ex-colonised countries with the aim of achieving a theoretical and operational reevaluation of the growth poles policy. This research should above all entail:

a) study of the demographic, cultural, economic and political variables on which depend the problems of the free development of ex-colonised countries. To this end, study of the factors that act or can act both in its favour and against it;

b) study of the perspectives that will be offered in the field of their industrialisation by the pooling at the level of continental or subcontinental groupings of their resources and their efforts not only in the economic sectors but also in the civil infrastructures, education, mass education and the cultural policy. To this end analysis of the possibilities of the creation, within subcontinental groupings, of technological initiative centres of world importance that could act as a factor of polarisation of their autonomous development;

c) study of the common strategies of sectorial and territorial investment taking into account the restraints caused by the mechanisms of the world economy and the modifications to be made to the relations between ex-colonised countries and the big industrial powers. In this context, study of the conditions for the establishment of new forms of cooperation with the big industrial powers;

d) study of the transformations necessary to be made, inside each ex-colonised country, in social relations, interpersonal relations and in the awareness of the masses, so that they look without anxiety at the future perspectives of their economic liberation and civil development and that they feel directly involved in the work of economic reconversion to which we referred in the preceding paragraph;

e) and finally, more precisely, a study of the specific mechanisms that conditions their process of industrialisation by a balanced and adequate growth poles policy, freed from external negative restraints and internal hindrances.

NOTES

1. F. Perroux, 'Note sur la notion de pôle de croissance', *Economie Appliquée* 1955, p. 309.
2. See *supra*.
3. On this latter point see the report of I. Sachs in *Foreign Aid to Newly Independent Countries*, E. Boserup–I. Sachs (eds), European Coordination Centre for Research and Documentation in Social Sciences, Vol. 1. The Hague, Mouton, 1971.
4. See *supra*.
5. *Cf. Indirizzi strategici di assetto territoriale per l'inquadramento dei programmi di intervento nel Mezzogiorno*, document drawn up by the Bureau of Studies of the Ministry of Public Works, published in *Urbanistica '57*, March 1971.
6. A large part of the ideas put forward or mentioned on this subject can be ascribed to the works of S. Amin. *L'accumulation à l'échelle mondiale*, Dakar-Paris, IFAN-Anthropos, 1970; A. Gundar Franck. *Le développement du sous-développement*, Paris, Maspéro, 1970; P. Fougeyrollas, *Où va le Sénégal*, Dakar-Paris, IFAN-Anthropos, 1970; *Foreign Aid to Newly Independent Countries*, E. Boserup-I. Sachs (eds.), *op. cit.*
7. *Cf.* M. Penouil, 'Politique régionale et pôles de croissance', in *Le développement régional en Europe*, R. Petrella (ed.), European Coordination Centre for Research and Documentation in Social Sciences, Vol. 2. The Hague, Mouton, 1971, p. 119.
8. *Cf.* The collective work *Pôles de développement et centres de croissance dans le développement régional*. Paris, Dunod, 1970, pp. 12–13.

ANTONI KUKLINSKI 7 B

Macro regional planning in the developed countries
*Problems and issues**

I. INTRODUCTION

The term regional planning[1] is one of those concepts which is used by a broad range of professions in quite different situations. This produces a confusion in international discussions when the term has different meanings for different persons. Some of the confusion could be eliminated if we would consequently recognize in each situation the distinction between micro and macro regional planning. Micro regional planning emerges as a product from two intellectual, social and political traditions. The first is the tradition of city planning, transferring methods and approaches tested in the design of urban patterns to the solution of regional problems. This tradition is strongly promoted by some eminent members of the profession of architects, who, *per pacta and facta concludentia*, claim to have discovered the philosophers' stone of regional planning.

This claim is supported by training and market control systems, which create quite efficient barriers for other professions to invade the field of regional planning. It would be interesting to study the British and Australian experiences from this point of view.

The second is the tradition of community development which emerges as a sometimes spontaneous, sometimes guided popular movement, trying to improve the social and environmental conditions at the grass-root level. In the past, the ideology of community development was recognized as an important inducement to promote socially oriented regional planning. Now this initial enthusiasm has faded away and a balanced perspective has been achieved, indicating that community development has little value as a source of inspiration for regional planning. The traditions of city planning

* This article was written following an invitation from Professor Lucien Nizard. It is now printed in *Aménagement du territoire et développement régional*, Vol. 4, Grenoble, 1971. Professor Nizard kindly agreed to print in this place the English version of this article.

and community development have influenced in different ways in different countries the phenomenon, which I am calling micro regional planning. Nevertheless, some features can be indicated in the micro regional planning approach. For example, the concentration of attention of relatively small areas, and the implicit or explicit acceptance of the assumption that the regional plan for a given area can be prepared in an autonomous or semi-autonomous way. This means that micro regional planning is influenced very little – if at all – by the problems and solutions applied on a national scale.[2]

2. THE EMERGENCE OF MACRO REGIONAL PLANNING IN THE SOCIALIST COUNTRIES

In the history of macro regional planning, the experience of the Soviet Union is of primary importance. There are four chapters in this experience which deserve special attention.

1) The macro regional approach developed in the framework of the State Plan for the Electrification of Russia in the early twenties;

2) The macro regional disaggregation of five-year economic plans;

3) The Sownarchoz approach to management and planning;

4) The general scheme for the distribution of the productive forces in the Soviet Union.

The State Plan for the Electrification of Russia (GOELRO) was the first experience in the history of long-term planning.[3] The aim and scope of the plan was much broader and comprehensive than the title would suggest. In fact, this was a plan to start a large-scale and long-term process of revolutionary modernization of the Soviet economy. The process had an important regional dimension, and therefore the GOELRO studies were also the starting point in the Soviet theory of macro economic regionalization. This regionalization was the first attempt to develop a regional division of the country into areal units adapted to the needs of a centrally planned socialistic economy.[4]

Of particular interest is the experience of the Soviet Union in the field of macro regional disaggregation of the five-year economic plans. This experience started in the late twenties in the framework of the first five-year plan, and it is still being developed today, both from the theoretical and practical points of view. Probably the most important item of this experience is the interregional allocation of investments to promote economic and social development in the vast and deeply differentiated territory of the Soviet Union. The major difficulty in this field was the establishment of the proper interrelations between macro sectoral and macro regional planning. The model of macro regional planning developed in the framework of the Soviet five-year plans is a model in which the regional dimension of planning is, in most cases, subordinated to the sectoral dimension. The Sownarchoz approach developed and applied in the years 1958–1962 was an attempt to eliminate the sectoral bias in the planning and management of the Soviet economy. The failure of this approach indicates, however, that a regional bias in planning and management is also very detrimental for a modern economy, which needs to be guided by a strong sectoral planning, applied on a nation-wide scale.

The present state of macro regional planning in the Soviet Union can be described as an attempt to find an optimal solution for the regional dimension of the multi-level and multi-sectoral planning system applied to short-medium and long-term time horizons. The most interesting aspect of this experience is the planning studies developed by GOSPLAN and the Academy of Sciences in order to prepare a general scheme for the distribution of productive forces in the Soviet Union. The first version of this scheme has been developed for the years 1971–1980.[5] It is expected that the methodology and planning experience acquired during the preparation of the first scheme will be applied later in the process of preparing similar schemes for the years 1980–2000.

The similarity of the basic elements in the economic and social system is creating some common features in macro regional planning developed and applied in Eastern Europe. However, there are substantial differences between East European countries, because of their different economic, social, cultural and political traditions. Therefore, macro regional planning has some characteristic features in each East European country. In this respect, let us take the example of Poland which has three interesting chapters in the post-war history of macro regional planning: Primo, the experience in the field of macro regional physical planning developed in Poland in the years 1945–1949.[6] This was an attempt to integrate into a new approach the different elements developed in the framework of three streams of practical experience and theoretical discussion. The first stream was the central socialist planning in mixed economies. The second was the Polish regional planning experience in the thirties, and the third, the British experience in town and country planning in the forties.

The second chapter in the history of Polish macro regional planning was the adaptation and transformation of the Soviet experience in the field of regional disaggregation of national plans, expecially the medium-term five-year plans. The comparison of the Polish and Soviet experience in this context is indicating how important is a similarity in basic institutional solutions and how important is the difference in the size and the history of the countries.

The recent chapter in macro regional planning in Poland has been developed in the framework of the Polish experience in the field of long-term perspective planning and prognosis. In the years 1957–1970, an impressive number of valuable studies and preliminary versions[7] of different prognoses and plans have been prepared, concentrating on four time-horizons: 1960–1975, 1960–1980, 1965–1985 and 1970–2000. In this framework, the macro regional dimension of the future of the Polish society and economy was studied and discussed. The discussion will be continued in the coming years as an extremely interesting phenomenon, having as a background the broad stream of innovative thinking which was rejuvenated in Poland in December 1970.

In concluding these few remarks on the emergence of macro regional planning in the Soviet Union and in Poland, I would like to mention that this subject in Eastern Europe has been analyzed in a study by K. Mihailović.[8]

3. THE EMERGENCE OF MACRO REGIONAL PLANNING IN THE CAPITALIST COUNTRIES

The great depression of the early thirties has demonstrated that the traditional approach of physical and urban planning cannot be adapted to the solution of complicated economic and social problems which emerged in areas where the negative consequences of the depression were particularly acute and where the rate of regionally concentrated unemployment was particularly high. In this context one can explain the emergence of macro regional policies in the United Kingdom, which were started by the Special Area Act in 1934. This Act marked the acceptance by the Government of some responsibility for influencing the pattern of industrial location and regional development.

The objectives of this policy are described by B. J. Loasby[9] in the following way:

'The whole history of location policy in this country has been conditioned by its origins in the realization that acute problems of localized unemployment lay half-concealed beneath the general depression of the inter-war years. It was therefore, inevitable that location policy should be seen mainly as a means of alleviating such localized unemployment.'

The emergence of macro regional policies and plans in Italy is associated with the case of the regionally concentrated under-development in the Mezzogiorno. The Italian Government, via the activity of the Cassa per il M., has developed and implemented different economic policies and plans in order to diminish the gap between the North and the South and to eliminate duality in the regional structure of the country.

The comparison of the British and the Italian experience is indicating that the British have moved much earlier from a regional policy applied to selected areas to a regional policy applied to the whole of the country. This happened in Britain already in 1940 in the publication of the Barlow report.

The Italian regional policy was concentrated around the case of Mezzogiorno since it began in 1950. It was only in 1970 that a decision was reached to develop a regional policy for the whole country and to establish a regional government in all regions. As we know from the daily press, this has not been an easy process.

The case of France is similar to that of the United Kingdom and Italy in the sense that the French macro regional planning was also in the beginning applied only in a selective way to the most developed regions (Paris) and to the least developed region of the Southwest. However, the speciality of the French planning maison is a comprehensive attempt to develop a system of national planning in which the regional dimension is consequently incorporated.[10] From this point of view, France has probably the most advanced experience of the Western countries. The practical aspect of the French performance is somewhat weaker than the theoretical aspect. Of special importance in this respect was the rejection of the idea of regional governments by the famous Referendum of 1969.

The general direction of change in the Western countries is very clear. Macro regional policies and plans are introduced in the beginning in selected regions (underdeveloped, depressed or over-congested) and at a later stage extended to the national scale.[11] Of course, different countries are at different points along this route; in some cases even this process can be stopped or reversed for a few years.*

* From this point of view it would be interesting to study the most recent experiences of the United States.

4. THE ECONOMIC PROBLEMS OF MACRO REGIONAL PLANNING

There are three approaches to economic problems in macro regional planning: the regional approach, the sectoral approach and the national approach.

The first approach is represented by different institutions which are trying to improve the comparative advantages of the given area in the interregional competition for the location of new economic opportunities via the mechanisms of the market, via administrative decisions, via political pressures or via different amalgamations of those factors. One can propose different classifications of institutions involved in this activity, but the most important is the distinction between institutions representing the interests of strong regions and the institutions representing the interest of weak regions. The first group functions in a very selective way, promoting the development in a given region only the most attractive activities and discouraging, for example, the investment in ventures which, in consequence, could bring about the deterioration of environmental conditions. The main preoccupation of the institutions representing the weak regions is how to attract investments to create a sufficient amount of new jobs for the growing population. In this situation, the attitude is much less selective, sometimes trying to attract new industrial investments almost at any price.

The sectoral approach to macro regional planning is in most cases quite different. The main criterion is not the advantage of a given region but the efficiency of a sector or enterprise. The framework of macro regional planning is used in order to improve the quality of managerial and investment decisions in those sectors or enterprises.

In different countries, we will find different patterns of co-ordination, co-operation or collusion among different sectors and regions and among different amalgamations of strong and weak sectors and strong and weak regions. In the middle sixties, a very interesting discussion concerning this topic was started in Poland. It was W. Lissowski[12] who formulated the following question:

'In what way in the present conditions of regional planning in Poland can we find a joint sectoral and spatial optimum of the distribution of productive forces in the Polish perspective plan?'

According to W. Lissowski:

'the joint sectoral and spatial optimum does not develop spontaneously, because there exists a divergence between the techno-economic trends and tendencies of the modern production sectors, and the tendencies of the regions.'

W. Lissowski stresses:

'that this approach is quite different from the approach of the majority of Polish regional planners. Generally speaking, the opinion is accepted that the sectoral and regional pattern should "mutually supplement" themselves.'

'This unclear directive means more or less that the regional planners are supplementing the sectoral pattern by the introduction of spatial elements on the assumption that in good co-ordinated planning, both patterns represent the same tendencies (the over-all advantage of the national economy) and that the whole problem can be reduced to the proper organization of planning. In other words the divergencies in the trends of development of sectors and regions which are evident to me are interpreted as mistakes in the organization of planning.'

The validity of this problem was recognized by K. Secomski[13] in the following statement:

'In recent years there has been an important development of activity in the field of sectoral industrial programming. At the same time differences in opinion increased as to the future trends of development of regional economy and the influence of those trends on programming of industrial growth of a given region. Using the results of research activities, we have to find the proper way to reconcile those conflicts.

It seems to me that in the first stage of studies we should accept the guiding principle of maximization and optimization of the economic performance of each industrial sector.

Applying this principle, we will get the following results:

a) strong concentration of industry – ergo the construction and development in each industrial sector of optimum size plants ...

b) the establishment and growth of large inter-sectoral industrial agglomeration ...

In the second stage of studies we are confronted with the results of sectoral and inter-sectoral industrial programming and the criteria of optimal regional economic development.

These criteria are a tool to correct – sometimes basically – the sectoral point of view. In many cases the sums of optimal proposals of all industrial sectors create excessive concentration and agglomeration of industry with its negative consequences.

Therefore, starting from intra-sectoral and inter-sectoral optimisations we have to use an integrated sectoral and regional accounting method as a tool of short, medium and long-term evaluations of the advantages and disadvantages of industrial concentration and agglomeration.'

This is a problem that is discussed in many countries. In most cases, the national approach is accepted as the best framework for the reconciliation of the conflicts of sectoral and regional approaches and for the formulation of proper policies and plans. There are very few macro models which are trying to integrate central, sectoral and regional approaches to planning and decision-making. We have not yet arrived at a valid or satisfactory solution, but three examples of efforts which will probably contribute to a breakthrough in this field can be indicated. First, there is the long-term planning scheme for the regional development of the Soviet Union, prepared by the Council for Studying the Productive Forces of the USSR.[14] The second is an attempt of the Institute of Planning, Warsaw, to develop central, regional and sectoral models adapted to the needs of long-term planning.[15] The third is a research project which was carried out by the Netherlands Economic Institute, Rotterdam, with the cooperation of Resources for the Future, Inc., Washington.[16] These research projects analyse the regional problem in the framework of multi-level planning and decision-making.[17]

5. THE SOCIAL PROBLEMS IN MACRO REGIONAL PLANNING

There are three approaches to social problems in macro regional planning.[18] The social justice approach, the social services approach, and the social structure approach.

The social justice approach is in most cases expressed as a planning objective to diminish the per capita income differences among regions and among localities. This planning objective is accepted almost universally, and is the aim of most governments, if not in practical terms then at least in declarations. Nevertheless, this objective may be very harmful if it is driven too far. We have to remember that the main objective of our time is the equality among human beings and not among places. This problem is very closely related to the crucial question involved in the regional dimension of national employment policies. Should people move to the jobs or jobs to the people? In this context let us quote E. M. Hoover.[19]

'... Worshippers of the false god of Place Prosperity are of course convinced that jobs should always be moved to people rather than the other way round. But no one else has seriously suggested that either policy should be followed to the exclusion of the other. It is in fact hard to think of any sound and effective attack on regionalized unemployment that does not stimulate both people and job to move to one another.'

Until recently, social services and amenities were considered only at the national level and at the local and micro regional levels. Social services, such as health, education, culture and tourism were incorporated into the national budget or plans in global terms, and in local plans in physical terms. In most countries very few attempts were made to discuss or plan the social services and amenities in the framework of macro regional planning. The recent experiences of several countries, such as the Soviet Union, Canada, Poland and Sweden, indicate that modern macro regional planning has to take into account in a comprehensive way the social services and amenities which in turn cannot be planned effectively without the application of macro regional planning.

The socialist countries have an excellent experience of how to use the framework of macro regional planning as a tool to promote progressive changes in the social structure. In regional and locational planning in the Socialist countries, there are many examples of how this planning was applied to change the social structure of underdeveloped regions. Perhaps the Soviet and Yugoslav experiences are most interesting in this context. Naturally, here again, the social structure argument should not be driven too far. This was the case in the location of a steel mill in Warsaw which was definitely not the best decision in Polish national regional and urban planning.

6. THE ENVIRONMENTAL PROBLEMS IN MACRO REGIONAL PLANNING

The problem of the environment has recently become very fashionable in political, professional and academic discussions and at international meetings. This activity has one characteristic feature: in most cases the participants are trying to avoid the difficult and controversial side of the problem. The attention is concentrated on technology and institutions. There is no doubt that in recent years, many technological breakthroughs have been achieved and we can list very easily an impressive number of technological solutions which could be applied in order to diminish air pollution, water pollution, noise and other phenomena which destroy the quality of the environment. The technological progress in this field is very important, but still more important is the elimination of social economic barriers which, in different countries, in different ways, diminish or eliminate the possibility of applying the achievements of modern technology to the improvement of the human environment.

The social and economic barriers are very seldom mentioned in international discussions. At some international meetings, different delegations indicate that in country A, a Ministry for the Environment has been created; in country B, a Presidential Council; and country C, an Interministerial Committee. This shows that in many developed countries, importance is attached to the problem of the human environment. This is only the declaration of intentions and we know perfectly well that those ministeries, councils and committees can develop an impressive paper activity which will have very little effect on the real problems of the environment. Therefore, the new technological and institutional solutions have to face the crucial test of implementation. In each country, questions of the following type have to be answered:[20]

1. Who is interested in keeping the present *status quo*?
2. Who is interested in promoting substantial changes in the quality of the environment?
3. Who will bear the cost of the operation?
4. What kinds of political, social, economic and institutional innovations should be introduced in the country in order to create permanent conditions for the improvement of the human environment?

If in each country and at international meetings, questions along the above lines would be discussed, then there is a hope that the reality of the human environment would be substantially changed.

The activity cannot be restricted only to the national and local levels. At the national level we do not see the important issues involved in the interregional differentiation of environmental conditions within a country. On the local level, we are missing the advantages of scale which can be gained by regional solutions. Therefore a macro regional approach is a very effective framework for analysis and planning in the field of the human environment.[21]

7. THE TIME HORIZON IN MACRO REGIONAL PLANNING

The time horizon is a very important problem for macro regional planning. It is well known that different answers to questions will be given if different time horizons are applied. This point was demonstrated by T. Hermansen in a study on interregional allocation of investments.[22] I think there will be general agreement that an effort should not be made to find one optimal time horizon to apply to macro regional planning. In different conditions and situations, different time horizons should be applied to solve the leading regional problems of a country. Nevertheless, the aim of our discussion should be to try to find some common denominators and indicate the range of choices which would emerge in similar conditions and situations.

I think that it is necessary to distinguish the following four time horizons as applied in macro regional planning:

Primo, the time horizon of five years applied in medium-term planning. This is the best developed part of planning methodology both at the national and regionals levels. In the framework of five years, both in East European countries and in France, the basic current macro regional problems are solved.

Secundo, the time horizon of ten to fifteen years applied in long-term planning. This is a time horizon which is long enough to plan important structural changes, to anticipate less favourable phenomena, and to create more favourable conditions in a given macro region. It is short enough to correctly anticipate the basic elements of the plan, such as population, employment, investment, consumption, economic, social, technological and institutional innovations, land-use patterns etc. The most interesting example of a plan of this type is the general scheme of the distribution of the productive forces in the Soviet Union for the period 1971–1980. Experience to develop this scheme for the huge and interregionally differenciation territory of the Soviet Union should be examined separately in a comprehensive way.

Tertio, the time horizon of 20–25 years applied in long-term prognosis. In this case, the crucial difficulty is the correct anticipation of technological, economic, social, and cultural innovations which would have substantial validity for the conomy and society of a ecountry. From this point of view, one can compare the experience of France and Poland in their preparation of a long-term macro regional prognosis for the years 1965–1985.

Quarto, the time horizon of 30–40 years applied in futurological prognosis. This time horizon is very fashionable now in the futurology of the year 2000, in which a macro regional dimension is finding its proper place. Again we can refer to the interesting similarity of the French and Polish experience in this field.[23] Nevertheless, the most comprehensive example of futurological studies of this type are supplied by the United States, where Resources for the Future published in 1963 a study 'Resources in America's Future'.[24] In this study, the macro regional dimension for a time horizon of 40 years is well developed. This pioneering effort is indicating the basic difficulties of prognostical studies of this type. To my mind, a time horizon of 40 years is the upper limit in a rational anticipation of the future. Therefore I see little sense in mega regional prognoses as proposed by C.A. Doxiadis.[25] The discussion of the world-wide settlement network at the end of the 21st century can be accepted only as an exercise for the imagination and fantasy, but its operational value for decisions of our time is close to zero.

8. MACRO REGIONAL PROBLEMS AND THE REGIONAL DIVISION OF A COUNTRY

Macro regional planning in a given country has to apply not only a comprehensive set of time horizons but also a comprehensive set of regional divisions. Let us compare the French and Polish experience from this point of view.

The French regional planning machinery is using the division of the country into twenty-one programming regions, eight big socio-economic regions and three geographical zones. The smaller regions are applied in medium term planning, the bigger regions are applied in long-term prognosis.

It is an open question if the introduction of the twenty-one programming regions was a mistake. It might have been better to have used the eight big socio-economic regions in medium-term planning and in long-term prognosis. It can be argued that from the point of view of future oriented macro regional planning in France, the twenty-one programming regions are just too small. I would agree that, if the idea of regional governments could be accepted in France in the future, they should be built into the framework of the eight big regions and not (as it was proposed in 1969) into the framework of the twenty-one programming regions.[26] The establishment of eight strong regional governments in France would create a real countervailing power in relation to the central government and administration. From a political and social analysis, it would seem that this countervailing power would not be created by twenty-one weak regional governments.

In comparing the Polish and French experiences, there are interesting similarities and differences. The Polish regional planning machinery is using the division of the country into seventeen basic administrative units. Therefore, the planning regions are at the same time units of regional governments and administrations. The Polish theory and practice is stressing very firmly the necessity that regional planning must be incorporated not only into the institutions of the central government but also into institutions of regional governments and administrations.[27] If we compare the seventeen regions in Poland and the twenty-one regions in France, then we find that they are very similar and sometimes identical in size. In fact, I have been told that the idea of the programming regions in France was influenced by the Polish regional planning experience. This is an interesting example concerning the international transferability of the experience in regional planning. The size of the planning regions which was suitable for the conditions in Poland in the late forties was not suitable for France in the middle sixties.

In the field of long-term planning and prognosis, regional planning in Poland is using not only the division of the country into seventeen basic regions, but also into seven macro regions. Here again there are some similarities between the French and the Polish experience.

The comparison of the French and Polish experience is a good background to introduce the following general items:

1. How should a comprehensive multilevel division of a country into planning-regions be designed?
2. How can the different regional divisions be associated with different time horizons applied in regional planning and prognosis?
3. How can different regional divisions be associated with the administrative divisions of the country and with the geographic boundaries of the jurisdictions of the central, regional and local governments?

9. INFORMATION SYSTEMS FOR MACRO REGIONAL PLANNING

It is a general experience in most countries that macro regional planning in the first stages of its existence had to overcome fundamental difficulties generated by insufficient quantity and quality of regional statistics and other forms of information. Even in cases where regional information of a high quality was already available, it was adapted only to the needs of micro regional planning and there was little information which could be used in research policy and planning to determine in a comprehensive way the interrelations of economic and social development at the national and at the regional levels.

The first attempts to diminish this informational gap were performed by the institutions involved in national and macro regional planning. It would be interesting to study the time sequence of how, in different countries, the regional indexes were introduced into the national plans and the national indexes into the regional plans. In this way, the macro regional planning machinery started to produce internally new types of information which were necessary for the solutions of new problems and the application of new planning methods. This situation induced directly, or via the social sciences, the central statistical offices in different countries to develop a new approach to regional statistics and regional information. For example, the Central Statistical Office of Poland started to prepare and publish information on regional disaggregation of national income,[28] including its most important structural components, and the Central Statistical Office of The Netherlands, information on a nationally integrated system of input-output tables. An important item in this stream of change was introduced by the Swedish experience, which developed the grid method as a geographical basis for the national information system.[29] One could continue to indicate interesting examples from many countries under review. However, in this context, it would be perhaps sufficient to say that over the last ten years in Europe and in North America, many innovations in the field of regional information and statistics have been developed and applied. The following three types of innovations can be mentioned: 1. methodological, 2. technological, and 3. institutional. The idea of information systems for regional development and planning is the most important methodological innovation. The implications of this new approach were discussed at an international seminar, jointly organized by the University of Lund and UNRISD in 1969.[30]

The system approach to regional information is possible only if we could use the modern efficient technology in data collection processes, storage and distribution. The methodological and technological innovations open the way for new institutional solutions, one of which would be a national system of macro regional data banks.

These trends of change in regional information systems have important feedback effects for macro regional planning. It is possible now and even necessary to drop the practice of mono-alternative planning and develop a new practice of multi-alternative planning. In the past, the limited supply of information and the low level of information processing technology were a justification or an excuse to prepare one regional plan at a given time and present only one set of solutions. Now the situation can be different and it is possible to develop a multi-alternative and dynamic approach, presenting at a given time several sets of alternative solutions which have been tested in several time horizons.

The changes in the supply of information are opening up possibilities to consider in macro regional planning an increasing amount of valid choices and offering these choices as an input into the decision-making machinery functioning in a given country.

I am convinced that different national systems of macro regional planning have different levels of efficiency, but up to now, very little international research on regional development and planning has been undertaken in order to find an answer to the following question: Is a system of regional policies and plans better developed and more effective in country A than in country B?

To answer this question would be extremely difficult or even impossible because of the present limited international comparability of regional statistics and information. There are two basic limitations in this comparability:

1) the differences in the definitions and concepts applied in regional statistics in different countries, and

2) the difference in the patterns of areal units applied in regional statistics in different countries.

This problem was raised during a United Nations European seminar on regional statistics, which was held in Warsaw.[31] Three key areas were proposed for international study in the field of regional statistics:

a) interregional statistics on investments;

b) interregional statistics on the levels of living;

c) interregional statistics on flows of persons, commodities and information.[32]

In many countries, the investment process is the most important factor leading to economic growth and social change at the national and regional levels. Therefore, it is impossible to arrive at any comprehensive assessment of the efficiency of regional policies and plans without reliable investment statistics, and we know that very few countries collect and publish a comprehensive set of data on interregional differentiation of investment processes. It is an open question if the Polish experience in this field would be valid in other European countries. The following are the characteristic features of this experience:

1. The investment data are published for areal units of different sizes including the county level;
2. For each unit, a comprehensive set of data are provided on investments in the economic sectors, such as industry and agriculture, and in the social sectors, such as health, education and culture.

In evaluating regional policies, another set of statistical data is of significance, i.e. data on interregional differentiation in the level of living. One of the basic goals of regional policies is to diminish interregional differences in the level of living, but we know that regional statistics in this field are very weak.

The third key area for international studies is the improvement of statistics in the field of interregional flows of persons, commodities and information. As we know, we are much better equipped to answer questions regarding what is happening inside the different regions, or what the structural characteristics of the regions are than to answer the question on the interrelations between regions as manifested in the flows of persons, commodities and information.

The experience in this field is highly differentiated. In quite a few countries there are some studies on flows of persons and commodities but only in very few countries has research been done on information flows.[33] The Swedish experience indicates, however, that, in present conditions, the flows of information could be more important in analysis and planning than the flows of persons and commodities. According to G. Törnqvist,[34] a special role in the exchange of information is performed by direct personal contacts which are often more effective than contacts of other types. Let us quote G. Törnqvist[35] on the distinction between indirect contacts and direct personal contacts:

'Indirect contacts are best suited to the transmission of simple, well-structured, routine information. The more complicated or non-routine the information becomes, the greater the advantages of the direct personal contact.

'Direct personal contacts are greatly preferable in the following situations for example: when several people have to exchange information with one another at the same time; when the exchange of information contains an element of uncertainty; when it is difficult or impossible to foresee what situation will arise when the information given and received sparks off a chain of new situations demanding new exchanges of information; when the contacts contain essential elements of problem-solving, planning and intelligence work; when contacts are in the form of negotiations and discussions.'

I believe that the experience of the Swedish school of human geography in the field of information flow and contacts' systems could be tested with very good results in other countries. I think also that three key areas for international studies in the field of regional statistics, proposed at the Warsaw seminar, should now be supplemented by two additional items; the macro regional information system on the changes in the social structures, and the macro regional information systems on the changes of the human environment.

10. A PROPOSAL FOR AN INTERNATIONAL RESEARCH PROJECT

This review is indicating very clearly that in the developed countries of both the East and the West, the macro regional approach to national planning and decision-making systems is accepted in an almost universal way. This does not mean, however, that the fundamental, theoretical and practical problems involved in this approach are already solved.

In this review, several interesting and promising examples have been mentioned which could be used in the future in planning activities and in academic discussions.

It is clear that the performance of macro regional planning in each country is depending both on the internal experience and on the transfer of experience from other countries.

We have to look for more effective ways for this transfer. One way would be the implementation of an international research project which would compare the experiences of selected countries. In this paper, several comparisons of the Polish and French experiences have been presented. I think that this should be extended into a comprehensive comparative study of the Polish and French experiences in macro regional planning. Such a study should not be a parallel description of the two experiences, where the whole essence of comparison is the publication of two national pictures in one volume. The comparison should be problem oriented and could discuss, for example, the topics mentioned in this paper.

To my mind, a comparative study of this type would be very promising.[36] Perhaps the idea could be tested in an international research project, promoting studies on the following pairs of countries:

France	–	Poland	Sweden	–	Canada
Netherlands	–	Hungary	United States	–	Soviet Union
Spain	–	Romania	United Kingdom	–	Japan
Italy	–	Yugoslavia	Switzerland	–	German Democratic Republic
Austria	–	Czechoslovakia			

Naturally, the selection and the juxtaposition of countries has only the characteristics of an example to expose the main feature of my proposal.

II. CONCLUSIONS

The reader of this paper will agree with the author that this is only a very preliminary piece of research. It is highly possible that several value judgments expressed in the paper need clarification or change. The empirical scope of the paper is limited and the choice of examples is open to discussion. With these weaknesses and limitations in mind, the hope is expressed that nevertheless some new ideas for international studies can be found in the paper. If the answer to this question is in the affirmative, then the aim of the paper has been achieved.

NOTES

1. *Cf.* T. HERMANSEN, 'Spatial Organization and Economic Development – The Scope and Task of Spatial Planning', *Development Studies*, No. 1. The Institute of Development Studies, University of Mysore, India; H. PERLOFF, 'Key Features of Regional Planning', *Journal of American Institute of Planners*, May, Vol. 34, pp. 153–159; A. KUKLINSKI, 'Regional Development, Regional Policies and Regional Planning – Problems and Issues', *Regional Studies*, Vol. 4, Pergamon Press 1970, pp. 269–278.

Compare too the materials which are the result of a research project on 'Growth Poles Hypotheses and Policies – Comparative International Analysis'. Jointly sponsored by UNRISD and the Nueva Universidad Autonoma de Madrid. The results of the research will be published in 1972.

2. There is no doubt this is a simplification but a necessary one to create a clear starting point for discussion. A different appraisal is presented in the article written by L.S. BURNS, 'The Relationship Between Physical and Economic Planning', *The Town Planning Review* (Liverpool), January 1964.
3. Compare the extremely interesting remarks on the early days of Soviet history and planning by Academician S. STRUMILIN in *Socialisticzeskaja Industria*, No. 44, 1971.
4. Compare the discussion of this topic by G. CAIRE, *La Planification Régionale en Union Soviétique – Aménagement du territoire et développement régional*, Vol. III, Institut D'Etudes Politiques, Grenoble 1970;
   J.V. KOMAR, A.A. MINTS, *The Lenin principles of the distribution of productive forces and the development of economic regions of the* USSR, Proceedings of the USSR Academy of Sciences Geographical Series, No. 2, 1970;
   B. RYCHLWOSKI, *Regionalizacja Ekonomiczna (Zagadnienia Podstawowe)*, Instytut Geografii, Polskiej Akademii Nauk, Prace Geograficzne No. 64, Warsaw, 1967; pp. 96–118;
   A. WRÔBEL, *Projecie Regionu Ekonomicznego a Teoria Geografii*, Instytut Geografii, Polskiej Akademii Nauk, Prace Geograficzne No. 48, Warsaw, 1965, pp. 44–49.
5. N.N. NEKRASOV, Obshchaya metodika razrobotki generalnoj schemy razmeshchenya prozvoditelnych sil SSR na 1971–1980 gg. Sovet po Izuchenyu Priozvoditelnych sil pri Gosplanye USSR. Moskva, 1966.
6. See the Polish reports for the Congresses of the International Federation for Housing and Town Planning in Hastings 1946 and in Zurich in 1948: *Physical Planning and Housing in Poland*, Warsaw, 1946 and 1948.
7. *Cf.* K. SECOMSKI, 'On the Problems of the Perspective Plan of Development of Poland', *Ekonomista*, No. 2, 1962;
   M. KALECKI, 'Outline of a Method of Constructing a Perspective Plan', *Teaching Materials*, Vol, 8, Central School of Planning and Statistics, Warsaw, 1963;
   W. LISSOWSKI, 'The Perspective Plan – General Premises of Investment – General Premises of the Development of Regions', *Inwestycje i Budownictwo*, No. 5, 1963;
   S. M. ZAWADZKI, *Podstawy Planowania Regionalnego*, Panstwowe Wydawnictwo Ekonomiczne, Warsaw, 1969.
8. K. MILHAILOVIČ, *Regional Development – Experiences and Prospects in Eastern Europe*. The Hague, Mouton Publishers, (UNRISD Publications, Vol. 4), 1972.
9. B.J. LOASBY, *Location of Industry, Thirty Years of Planning*, District Bank Review, December 1965, p, 28.
10. P. VIOT, 'La régionalisation du Plan en France', *Pôles de développement et centres de croissance dans le développement régional*. Paris, Dunod, 1970.
11. A strong case for the growing role of the Federal Government in the regional development of the United States is made by J. CUMBERLAND in his study on *Regional Development – Experiences and Prospects in the United States*. The Hague, Mouton Publishers (UNRISD Publications, Vol. 2), 1971.

Compare the following conclusions of the study:

'In the history of the US experience in regional development, there has been a continuing tendency for the federal government to play a central, though far from an exclusive role, in determining policies and programs. The consistent logic behind this federal role has been the fact that regional development both requires and generates external economies and diseconomies. When the spatial distribution of these externalities extends beyond the geographic boundaries of the decision-making units involved, the possibility emerges for a higher level of decision-making to reduce the degree of suboptimisation and improve resource allocation processes.

During the era of internal improvements, Gallatin and others perceived that while transportation systems were a prerequisite to economic development of the nation's resources and its regions, adequate investment in transportation was unlikely to be undertaken either by private investors or local governments, because they would be unable to capture all of the profits. Spill over benefits would accrue over regions beyond the control of local agencies. Under these circumstances, the amount of investment made in transportation would be sub-optimal unless the federal government developed a national plan and provided financial subsidies, as it decided to do. This same logic was followed more or less successfully in the case of state and local subsidies for local systems. To the extent that these systems were well-designed with respect to relationships between urban centers, resource supply areas, market areas, and transport linkages, and were efficiently implemented, they resulted in major advances in regional development.

However, in more recent times, external diseconomies of economic development have become increasingly recognized as causing requirements for federal intervention of a different nature. Large scale external diseconomies resulting from pollution, congestion, and environmental deterioration have been intensified, and accelerated urban and regional development are generating wastes and residuals which producers and consumers discharge into common property resources of air and water. The divergence between private cost and social cost is resulting in excessive exploitation of resources and waste of output in those industries and activities which do not bear the full social cost of proper waste management. The US is now faced with the urgent need to design national, regional, and urban development programs which can generate the growing production needed to meet urgent social priorities while restoring and protecting the quality of life and environment. This will not be an easy task, but it is one which will require at least as much imagination, innovation, and effort which was devoted to earlier programs for economic development.

Finally, regional economic development in the US, despite its major successes, and despite efforts to justify it on the basis of poverty alleviation, has benefitted primarily the affluent and the established, leaving behind too many victims of discrimination, members of minority groups, alienated sub-cultures, and young persons who assign social justice, human values, and the quality of life priority over economic development. The major future challenge of regional and urban development will be to relate economic development more effectively to improvements in the quality of life for man in his environment.'

12. W. LISSOWSKI presented his point of view during several meetings in the Polish Academy of Sciences in 1964. In this paper, reference is to his article published in 1965 in the *Bulletin of the Committee of Space Economy and Regional Planning*, No. 34, Warsaw, 1965. Quoted from 'Criteria for Location of Industrial Plants (Changes and Problems)', United Nations, New York, 1967., p. 70.
13. K. SECOMSKI, 'Some Problems of the Theory of the Distribution of Productive Forces' in the volume *Theoretical Problem of the Distribution of Productive Forces*, Warsaw, 1965, p. 60. Quoted from 'Criteria for Location of Industrial Plants (Changes and Problems) ', *op. cit.* pp. 70–71.
14. N.N. NEKRASOV, *op. cit.*
15. K. PORWIT, *Metody Planowania Dlugookresowego.* Warsaw, Polish Academy of Sciences, 1969.
16. L.B.M. MENNES, J. TINBERGEN and J.G. WAARENBURG, *The Elements of Space in Development Planning*, Netherlands Economic Institute. Amsterdam, North-Holland Publishing Company, 1969.
17. Report of Informal Meeting on Regional Disaggregation of National Plans, UNRISD/69/C.76.
18. *Cf.* J. ZIÓLKOWSKI, *Methodological Problems in the Sociology of Regional Development*, UNRISD/69/C.2; also published in: *Regional Sociology, Environment and Regional Planning*, edited by A. KUKLINSKI. The Hague, Mouton Publishers (UNRISD Publications, Vol. 7), 1972.
    H.J.A. MORSINK, *Sociological Aspects of Regional Development and of Planning for Regional Development – Some issues and areas for further exploration*, MSOA/6/71;
    P.DREWE, *Sociology and Regional Policy*, UNRISD/71/C.23;
    L.H. KLAASSEN, *Social Amenities in Area Economic Growth – an analysis of methods of defining needs*, Organisation for Economic Co-operation and Development, Paris 1968;
    B.K. PRANDECKA, *Wzrost Gospodarczy Polski Wukladzie Przestrzennym*, Warsaw, Panstwowe Wydawnictwo Ekonomiczne, 1969.
19. E.M. HOOVER, 'Some Old and New Issues in Regional Development', in E.A.G. ROBINSON (ed.), *Backward Areas in Advanced Countries*. London, Macmillan, 1969.
20. *Cf.* the following statement by J. CUMBERLAND, *op. cit.*, pp. 119–120:
    'The future economic development of Alaska will provide a critical testing ground for US regional development theory and practice. It is here that the demands of the future for fuel and economic expansion will confront all of the traditional issues in regional development. But in addition, more recent conflicts in contemporary US values are emerging in Alaska on a very large scale.

    In many ways, Alaska combines all of the important characteristics of the historical frontier in America. Its vast expanses (586,000 square miles) are dominated by a harsh environment with which its native Eskimos and Indians had worked out a viable ecological balance. However, the attraction of the wilderniss and of great potential wealth from resource exploitation has attracted a half million white settlers, most of whom are eager to get on with the business of conquering this environment and modifying it in order to exploit its resources. As on earlier frontiers, they view their priorities as utilizing public sector financial support to provide the transportation and other infrastructure systems needed to facilitate private sector development. As in the case of the western frontier, the rights of the native inhabitants have largely been ignored and are in serious jeopardy. The federal government retains nominal ownership of most of the Alaskan lands and monumental power struggle for possession are being fought between federal, state, and private interests. As in the case of Appalachia, the private developers are to a large extent absentee corporate giants.

But the most critical issue in the development of Alaska is the basic conflict which has characterized all recent US regional development, namely the imposition of massive systems of technological exploitation upon a thin and fragile environment. Traditional US assignment of highest priorities to use of technology to conquer nature in order to meet national and regional economic development goals poses a major threat to the future of one of the last major expanses of wilderness left in the nation.

The discovery of the new oil fields in Alaska and the rush to develop them have emphasized the harsh fact that neither at the federal level nor at the state level does there exist the planning and management capabilities essential to the development of these resources without irreversible damage to this vast region. The history of US regional development, especially in Appalachia, offers critical lessons in the large scale mismanagement of resources systems, but it is questionable whether these lessons will be applied in time in Alaska to avoid repetition of the tragic Appalachian experience.'

21. *Cf.* J.P. GERASIMOV, *Man and environment. Modern aspects of the problem, Proceedings of the* USSR *Academy of Sciences*, Geographical Series, No. 1, 1971;
J. GOTTMAN. *The Renewal of the Geographic Environment*, Oxford, 1969;
M. DROBIL, 'Der Lärmschutz in der Raumplanung , *Mitteilungen des Osterreichischen Institutes für Raumplanung*, Nr. 143/144;
The Quality of the Urban Environment, edited by H.S. PERLOFF, Resources for the Future, Inc., The John Hopkins Press, Baltimore, Maryland, 1969;
A.V. KNEESE, R.U. AYRES, R.C. D'ARGE, *Economics and the Environment – A Materials Balance Approach*, Resources for the Future, Inc., The John Hopkins Press, 1970.
22. T. HERMANSEN, *Interregional Allocation of Investments for Social and Economic Development. An elementary model approach to analysis.* UNRISD Report No. 70.4, 1970. Also published in: *Regional Disaggregation of National Policies and Plans*, edited by A.R. KUKLINSKI. The Hague, Mouton Publishers (UNRISD Publications, Vol. 8), 1972.
23. *Cf.* the journal *2000 Avenir Aménagement du Territoire*, and the publications of the Committee of the Year 2000 of the Polish Academy of Sciences.
24. H.H. LANDSBERG, L.L. FISHMAN, J.L. FISHER, *Resources in America's Future*, RFF, John Hopkins Press, 1963. The evaluation of RFF activities is given by V.M. GOKHMAN, L.N. KARPOV, V.P. KOVALEVSKY in: 'Latest Works on the Prognostication of Providing Productive Forces Development with Natural Resources in Canada and the USA , *Izviestia Akademii Nauk* SSR, Seria Geograficheskaja 1964, No. 2.
25. A. DOXIADIS, 'L'Ecumenopolis', *2000 Avenir Aménagement du Territoire*, No. 12, Mars 1969.

26. I am in complete agreement with the following conclusion of Y. DURRIEU, *Régionaliser la France – Capitalisme ou socialisme*, Paris, Mercure de France, 1969:
    Les cadres traditionnels de l'administration française (meme rénovés) sont insuffisants pour satisfaire les besoins de la vie économique moderne sauf en ce qui concerne la gestion courante.
    La création de huit régions à l'échelle européenne, donc plus étendues que les vingt et une régions programmes actuelles est indispensable; celles-ci comprendraient une region 'Bassin parisien' incluant la Région parisienne actuelle et huit autres départements, mais aussi une région 'Centre'; elles seraient toutes dotées d'une capitale régionale.
    Les pouvoirs concerneraient essentiellement l'élaboration et le contrôle de la *planification*, avec les attributs financiers nécessaires; ces plans régionaux s'inséreraient dans le plan national qui les coordonnerait.
    Les régions seraint dotées *d'assemblées élues démocratiquement*, mais leur exécutif serait nommé hors du cadre préfectoral par le pouvoir central (à moins que l'on ne s'oriente vers le fédéralisme).
    Elles devraient jouir de toute *l'information décentralisée* indispensable à la prise des décisions.'
27. *Cf.* the special issue of the Polish journal *Regional Economy and Administration*, July 1969, Warsaw.
28. W. KAWALEC, *Perspective Development of Regional Statistics in the Light of Polish Experience*, UNRISD/70/C. 30.
29. *Case Studies on Information Systems for Regional Development – Sweden*, UNRISD Report No. 70.8, Geneva, 1970.
30. *Information Systems for Regional Development*. Proceedings of an UNRISD/University of Lund Seminar, Lund Studies in Geography, 1971. Edited by T. HAGERSTRAND and A. KUKLINSKI.
31. A. KUKLINSKI, 'International Research on Regional Development and Implications for Regional Statistics', *Problems and Methods of Compiling Regional Statistics*, Conference of European Statisticians, Statistical Standards and Studies, No. 20, United Nations, New York, 1971.
32. 'Głowny Urza Statystyczny Polskiej Rzeczypospolitej Ludowej', *Naklady Inwestycyjne Welug Powiatów 1961–1965*, Warsaw, 1966.
33. W. WÄRNERYD, 'Urban Regions as Spatial Systems', *Proceedings of the Second Poland-Norden Regional Science Seminar*, Warsaw, Polish Scientific Publishers, 1970;
    B. THORNGREN, 'Regional Economic Interaction and Flows of Information', *Proceedings of the Second Poland-Norden Regional Science Seminar*, *op. cit.*
34. G. TÖRNQVIST, *Contact Systems and Regional Development*, Lund Studies in Geography, Series B. Human Geography, No. 35. Lund C.W.K. Gleerup Publishers 1970. Also published in: *Regional Information and Regional Planning*, edited by A. KUKLINSKI. The Hague, Mouton Publishers (UNRISD Publications, Vol. 6), 1972.
35. *Ibid.*
36. Some elements of my proposal can be seen in the study of V. DUSAN, *Analyse Comparative du Développement Economique Régional en Pays de Structure Differente. Comparaison France – Yougoslavie*, Paris, Université de Paris, Febr., 1971.

Appendix

ANTONI KUKLINSKI* A

UNRISD research programme on regional development

I. INTRODUCTION

A programme of research on regional development was implemented during the years 1967 to 1971 in UNRISD. This programme was closely related to the United Nations Research-Training Programme in Regional Development (Economic and Social Council Resolution 1086 C).

The aim of the programme was to promote a new approach to the strategy of regional development designed to integrate social, economic and administrative aspects within the framework of multi-level (national – regional – local) planning. The programme consisted mainly of the following projects:

- A worldwide study of regional development: experiences and prospects
- The role of growth poles and growth centres in regional development
- Information systems for regional development
- Regional sociology
- Regional disaggregation of national policies and plans

* The author was from 1967 to 1971, the Programme Director of Regional Development at the United Nations Research Institute for Social Development. Now, Dr. Kuklinski acts as Editor of the UNRISD/MOUTON Regional Planning Publication Series. This note is a corrected and extennded version of a short paper which was published by the author in the *Bulletin* of the International Geographical Union No. 1, 1971. The partial reproduction of this paper was kindly permitted by Professor Chauney D. Harris, Secretary General of the International Geographical Union.

** The United Nations Research Institute for Social Development started work in 1964 as an autonomous United Nations activity, with the purpose of conducting research into 'problems and policies of social development and relationships between various types of social development and economic development during phases of economic growth.' UNRISD *Research Notes* No. 1, Geneva, June, 1968.

2. REGIONAL DEVELOPMENT: EXPERIENCES AND PROSPECTS A WORLDWIDE STUDY

The aim of this project was to fill in a major gap in both international reports and academic publications. Up to now, publications on regional development have been concerned mainly with two types of study:

a) general studies,
b) case studies.

The first type of study usually contains sweeping generalizations of presumed universal validity; basic differences in regional activities in countries of different economic and social systems, levels of development, size and density of population are overlooked.

In the second type, the generalizations are restricted to one country or one region, reducing the comparative perspective.

It was therefore felt that a third type of study was necessary which would be sufficiently general and, at the same time, sufficiently specific to serve research-training and planning purposes. This task could be performed by continental or sub-continental studies of regional development which would give a worldwide assessment and yet take account of differential conditions. The proposal for such a study was approved and supported by an Advisory Meeting which took place in Geneva in December 1967. This project was implemented in the years 1968 to 1970 and the following studies have been prepared:

1. South and Southeast Asia, by L. Lefeber and M. Datta-Chaudhuri;
2. Southwest Asia, under the auspices of the UN Economic and Social Office in Beirut;
3. Africa, by R. Von Gersdorff (Senior Regional Adviser at the Economic Commission for Africa);
4. Latin America, by W. Stöhr, with the assistance of the Ford Foundation;
5. United States, by John H. Cumberland, under the auspices of Resources for the Future, Inc., Washington, D.C.;
6. Canada, by T. N. Brewis, under the auspices of Resources for the Future, Inc., Washington, D.C.;
7. Eastern Europe, by K. Mihailović;
8. Western Europe, under the auspices of Mens en Ruimte V.Z.W., Brussels.

The publication programme for these studies is implemented in the following way:

a) Items 1 and 5 were published in 1971 as Volumes I and II in the UNRISD/MOUTON Regional Planning Series;

b) Items 4 and 7 will be published in 1972 as Volumes III and IV of the UNRISD/MOUTON Regional Planning Series;

c) Item 3 was published in 1968 as a mimeographed document of UNRISD;

d) Items 6 and 8 will be issued in 1972 as blue cover publications of UNRISD;

e) Item 2 was published as 'Regional Planning and Development in Selected Countries in the Middle East' in: *Studies on Selected Development Problems in Various Countries in the Middle Eeast*, United Nations, New York, 1969.

3. GROWTH POLES AND GROWTH CENTRES IN REGIONAL PLANNING

The Institute's approach to the study of growth poles and growth centres is to view them as instruments for comprehensive (multi-sectoral) development in a spatial setting. The effective integration of industry, agriculture and social services, as well as of urban and rural aspects of development, can usually be conceived in more concrete and manageable terms at the regional than at the national level, and growth poles and growth centres are major instruments of such concerted development at that level.

This has been the second major project in the Institute's Regional Development Programme. A comprehensive set of theoretical and empirical studies in this field was initiated. The results of these studies were discussed at two International Seminars: the first, organized jointly with the European Coordination Centre for Research and Documentation in the Social Sciences, took place in Geneva in 1969; the second was organized in Madrid in 1970 in the framework of a Joint Research Project on Growth Pole, Hypotheses and Policies, carried out during 1970 and 1971 by UNRISD and the Nueva Universidad Autonoma de Madrid. As a result of these activities the following four publications will be printed:

1. *Growth Poles and Growth Centres in Regional Planning*, as Volume V in the UNRISD/MOUTON Regional Planning Series;
2. *Growth Poles and Growth Centres as Instruments of Modernization in*

Developing Countries, as Volume IX in the UNRISD/MOUTON Regional Planning Series;
3. *Growth Poles and Regional Policies*, papers of a seminar jointly sponsored by UNRISD and the European Coordination Centre, as Volume III in the CEUCORS/MOUTON Publication Series;
4. *Growth Poles Hypothesis and Policies in the Developed Countries*, a volume jointly sponsored by UNRISD and the Nueva Universidad Autonoma de Madrid.

4. REGIONAL INFORMATION AND REGIONAL PLANNING

One of the basic obstacles to the development and implementation of regional policies is the inadequacy of regional statistics and other types of regional information, not only in the developing countries but also in many developed countries. There are two aspects of this situation:
(i) the quantitative aspect: the limited amount of regional data; and
(ii) the qualitative aspect: the scatter and haphazard nature of existing information, and the absence of a well-designed system of regional information suitable for development policies and research.
In view of the above, UNRISD has considered it necessary to establish in 1967 a research project on information systems for regional development. The first steps in the project have been a) the preparation of a general paper of a methodological character which sets out the framework for the project (by T. Hermansen), and b) the preparation of four case studies (Chile by S. Boisier, India by M. Pal, Poland by W. Kawalec, and Sweden by T. Hermansen).

These four case studies supplemented by other materials will be published in 1972 under the title *Regional Information and Regional Planning* as Volume VI of the UNRISD/MOUTON Regional Planning Series.

A seminar on information systems for regional development took place in Lund, Sweden, in October 1969, jointly sponsored by the Institute and the University of Lund. The fifty participants of the seminar represented a broad range of professional and geographical backgrounds. Twenty-five papers were discussed at the seminar, covering major theoretical problems and practical experiences in the development of regional information systems. The topics discussed included: operational models for regional analysis, the question of regional data banks, problems of integrating land data and socio-economic data within the context of a unified information system, the role of diffusion of information and innovations in regional development and planning. The proceedings of the seminar were printed in 1971 as a joint publication of UNRISD and the University of Lund (Department of Economic and Social Geography). The volume was edited by T. Hägerstrand and A. Kuklinski.

As a follow-up of the Lund Seminar, a second volume on 'Information systems for regional development – case studies' is planned.

5. REGIONAL SOCIOLOGY AND REGIONAL PLANNING

The Institute organized a workshop on this subject which was held in Geneva in November 1968, with the cooperation of the Economic Commission for Latin America. The main purpose of the meeting and of the papers presented was to draw the attention of sociologists, social planners and social geographers to the pressing social problems in regional development, which have hitherto received relatively little attention from them, and to discuss the substance of some of these problems and the related policies. The meeting sought to define those practical questions in which sociologists could play a role, and to specify the fields and instruments within existing sociological knowledge which are relevant to regional development problems and policies.

Following on the workshop, the Economic Commission for Latin America organized a seminar in Santiago in November 1969 on 'Social aspects of regional development'.

The papers of these two meetings will be published in 1972 under the title *Regional Sociology, Environment and Regional Planning* as Volume VII of the UNRISD/MOUTON Regional Planning Series.

6. REGIONAL DISAGGREGATION OF NATIONAL POLICIES AND PLANS

It was decided in 1968 that the Institute should introduce a new project on 'Regional disaggregation' of national policies and plans. This would deal with such problems as: reconciliation of conflicting national, sectoral and regional targets in policies and planning; problems of designing a plan that takes into account the regional disaggregation of economic and social policies; assessment of the minimum size of a region to be included in national plans; applicability at the regional level of concepts, methods and indices used in national planning.

As an introcution to this project, two papers have been prepared by T. Hermansen:

a) 'Interregional allocation of investments for social and economic development – An elementary model approach', December 1968;

b) 'Regional disaggregation of national plans within the context of national, sectorial and regional planning', May 1969.

An informal meeting of experts convened in Geneva in May 1969 to advise the Institute on research in the field of regional disaggregation of national plans and policies urged a widening of the concept to include study of the problems of regionalization of national plans within the context of multi-level planning and decision-making; it was considered that an international comparative study on this subject would be particularly useful.

Financial resources were not available to develop this project as originally planned. However, a comprehensive set of original or reprinted papers will be published in Volume VIII of the UNRISD/MOUTON Series. This Volume will include:

a) Reviews of concepts and models which are relevant to regional aspects of multi-level planning systems;

b) Empirical studies analyzing the practical and theoretical problems involved in regional disaggregation of national plans in selected countries.

A feature of this volume is the juxta-position of theoretical approaches, models and data reflecting the experiences of both developed and developing countries and with centrally-planned and market economy.

7 CONCLUSION

It is too early for a comprehensive evaluation of the UNRISD Regional Development Programme. The majority of these studies have yet to be presented in printed form to the competent judgment of planners and scholars around the world. The final evaluation will depend on answers to questions like the following:

1. Whether the leading projects were correctly related to the leading issues of Regional Development and Planning today in the Developed and Developing Countries?

2. To what extent the programme generated or promoted new ideas and approaches which could be applied in practical regional planning operations and theoretical studies.
3. Whether by its empirical studies it effectively increased the knowledge of regional development and planning as practised in different parts of the world.
4. Whether the programme served as an efficient channel of communication among regional planners and scholars and was thereby instrumental in the promotion of regional planning in countries or regions where communications barriers have been an obstacle to the application of regional planning.

ALEXEY KUPRIANOV*

B

UNIDO activities in the field of industrial location and regional development

I INTRODUCTION

1. The United Nations Industrial Development Organization (UNIDO), was established in 1967 with Headquarters in Vienna (Austria).

One of UNIDO's areas of work is that of industrial location and regional development which constitutes an integral part of a set of problems connected with industrial programming. The problems concerned with the choice of industrial location are second in importance only to the problems of choosing the industries themselves. Profitability of industrial investment will vary considerably from both the commercial and national points of view according to the geographic allocation of such investment. Incorrect spatial distribution of industrial activity may, under any economic system, seriously retard the economic development of a country. The problem of planning industrial location at the regional level is particularly relevant in developing countries. Most of them are not yet settled with major mislocations of industries and therefore have the possibility of avoiding the serious negative consequences of such mislocations.

Within the context of industrial location the problem of industrial growth poles (following the work of François Perroux[1]) was touched upon during some of UNIDO's workshops and seminars, and was highlighted in a number of studies prepared for the gatherings held by UNIDO in recent years.[2] The issue, however, was rarely expressed in terms of growth poles but was mostly hidden within the discussions over the problems of industrial complexes, depressed areas, dispersion of industry, locational aspects of industrial project evaluation, and urbanization. To a great extent these discussions and materials reflected the recent growth of economic literature in the field

* The author is Industrial Development Officer, Industrial Policies and Programming Division, UNIDO.

of industrial location planning, and the new ideas elaborated in developed and developing countries.

At the same time, in all these works and discussions, the emphasis has been placed on the problem of practical applicability of modern achievements in regional science to the needs of the developing countries.

Among other topics which have been discussed are the following two which are of a general character:

a) The problem of the principal applicability of the means and methods elaborated in developed countries to the needs of the developing countries.

b) Industrial location and national economic growth.

In the debates of each of these problems the issue of industrial growth poles was touched upon in one way or another. This paper will try to amalgamate some of these scattered ideas and give them in a more or less systematic way. Two other topics of a more specific character, namely the structure and mechanism of industrial complexes and the possibilities of creating poles of industrial growth in developing countries were also considered.

Alongside the problems mentioned above, which may be called 'traditional' now, some new facets of UNIDO's activities should be mentioned. Among them are the following:

- Planning for regional co-operation
- Social aspects of regional development
- Environmental aspects of location of industry.

In dealing with these problems UNIDO is still at a very initial stage of work, but the fact that these new aspects are likely to gain more importance in the near future justifies their brief mentioning.

In addition a certain amount of UNIDO's activities was focused on the problem of industrial estates. However, the issue of concrete siting of the industrial establishment and physical layout of the industrial estates is less relevant to the subject concerned and is beyond the scope of this report.[3]

2. APPLICABILITY OF INDUSTRIAL LOCATION THEORIES TO DEVELOPING COUNTRIES

It is common knowledge that the convential theories on industrial location developed in countries with advanced economies are obviously based on conditions prevailing there at the time when economic development had reached a relatively high degree of maturity and when the economic structure had become rather complex. Furthermore, the political, social and economic conditions were, to speak very generally, rather similar in these industrialized countries and exhibited some extent of homogeneity. Thus, the situation was quite favourable to the evolution of refined location theories pertaining to economic activities. Except in a few cases the present condition in the developing countries is quite different. Not only is there a picture of great economic contrast and heterogeneity among the countries but also the pace of development differs sharply from one country to another, and political, social and economic conditions have but little similarity. The only common criterion is the concerted effort towards rapid industrialization.

The above-mentioned peculiarities make well known the achievements of regional sciences but have limited use for the practical needs of developing countries. According to W. Alonso, 'classical location theory is ill-suited to the conditions of developing countries. It is based on perfect knowledge, predictable mobility of factors, inexhaustible entrepreneurship and, to a large extent, a fully developed transportation network. None of these conditions obtain in developing countries.'[4] Two main aspects of this problem were stressed at UNIDO meetings. They are:

a) Limitations in applying location criteria to the developing countries' own situations and existence of non-economic considerations.

b) Adaptation of location theory to the conditions of developing countries.

Speaking of the first aspect, the Report of the Minsk Seminar stressed that 'it is necessary to exercise great caution when making broad generalization. Any conclusion must be viewed in light of the structural characteristics of the economy of the individual country, its stage of development and the institutional and *political conditions*.'[5]

In another UNIDO document[6] it has been stated that 'there will be times when location decisions are made on the basis of motivations other than economic optimization' (a situation which is usually neglected by the classical theory) and 'several criteria which are legitimate in the context of their own assumptions and of the goals they designed to pursue can be applied to the problems of location planning.' Among others, they are:

a) National integration (location decisions are evaluated on the basis of their effect on bringing various regions of the economy into closer touch)

b) Political stability (pleasing of dissatisfied population)

c) National defence, etc.

Most of these factors were not considered by the classical location theory but they constitute an important part of the locational considerations in developing countries.

In stressing the importance of analysis of the so-called non-economic criteria, it was stated at the same time that, in any case (some times even in spite of the fact that the so-called non-economic considerations prevail in that particular country) proper consideration should be given to the criteria of economic efficiency. For example, for political reasons and perhaps in order to foster national unity, a new plant may be built in a particular region even though it is economically not the best place for it – i.e. where it would yield a smaller return than if located elsewhere. The country, however, should at least be aware of the economic costs involved and exercise extreme care that the location decision does not seriously retard its economic development as otherwise neither economic nor political aims will be realized.

At the same time (and this is the second aspect of the problem) there are basic factors such as transportation and processing costs, supply of raw materials, demand for the finished product, marketing considerations, labour and others which have retained, and will continue to retain, a marked significance in choosing the correct location after a decision which, generally speaking, might contribute to the economic growth of the country. But all these factors and methods of their analysis cannot be given in the 'pure' forms elaborated in advanced economies. It has been stated that 'traditional criteria could provide only some broadly acceptable guidelines for location and regional planning in developing countries.'[7] In other words, 'the criteria and methods set forth in economic works on industrial location must be interpreted and revised if they are to be applicable to industrial location planning in developing countries.'[8] However, full adaptation of location theory to the conditions prevailing in developing countries is still a task for the future. The following illustrates the situation.

During discussions at the Minsk seminar the consensus was that some types of infrastructure projects in developing countries were bulky and required large absolute amounts of expenditure. Unless such infrastructure facilities were constructed in conjunction with a number of directly productive projects in the region their rate of utilization would be low and the infrastructure cost per unit of final output high. The attention of the participants was drawn in this context to the importance of industrial complex building. It was pointed out that 'development of infrastructure system should be based on the construction of productive complexes in regional centres which would serve as growth poles for the development of the entire region'.[9] The experience of Turkey is indicative of how the above issue might be approached. Investment in transport in eastern Turkey was made in combination with the planned creation of growth poles in that area. The principal conclusion was that expenditure on a newly-created transport network should be related not only to the demand generated by extractive industries but also to the anticipated demand of mineral producing industries created in the region. Having come to this principal conclusion one could easily calculate the amount of investment required. But in the case of developing countries this issue might show only one certain (but not sufficient) feature, i.e. the high cost of investment to which a certain amount of uncertainty has to be added. Among these uncertainties are the following: local customs, the cost and timing of operations, the quality and seasonal patterns of water, etc., all of which make the calculation more complex, and the more remote the region the less is known about it.

According to W. Alonso, 'the uncertainties add to the risks and the certainties to the cost, and both lead to a need for a large and clear advantage to justify locations outside of the developed centres'.[10]

Another important factor in the location of industry in developing countries, which is normally neglected in the classical theory, is that of entrepreneurship and technical skills. In accordance with the classical theory when the situation of perfect competition exists in its pure state, it would mean that the entrepreneurs, workers and capital should be completely mobile within the region. Even in developed countries the actual solution diverges from this condition and in developing countries, in fact, this is not the case at all. Needless to say, especially in developing countries, the quality of management and the competence of technicians is likely to be the most important factor for an enterprise. But entrepeneurs like to remain tied to the places which offer amenities and they exhibit great reluctance to move from major urban areas. Furthermore, for various historic economic and cultural reasons, one area may produce better entrepreneurs and generate more capital to be used intra-regional than another which produces only second-raters or nothing at all.

Despite the shortcomings of existing locational criteria when applied to developing countries, they do provide a first approximation towards solutions of locational problems. Certainly it is inconceivable that planning for economic growth in developing countries can take place without careful attention being paid to the question of location. Decisions as to where to place new projects can be as crucial as the decisions to undertake them at all. Through location analysis one can judge the economic soundness of plans to engage in particular activities at particular places.

3. INDUSTRIAL LOCATION AND ECONOMIC GROWTH

It is well known that completely different solutions may emerge if the location criteria are based on national objectives rather than on regional ones. In UNIDO's work a long-run national economic growth point of view was adopted. Economic efficiency expressed in terms of national economic growth and often measured in terms of per capita national product was recognized as a principle of correct industrial location.

It has been stated that 'the most relevant economic criteria for developing countries is that of economic growth, i.e. the contribution of location decisions to the economic growth of the nation' and 'regional location decisions are merely instruments to achieve the national objective'.[11] At the same time it was recognized that the efficiency goal is frequently opposed to the equity goal by which is meant a more equal distribution of income. The point is that the efficiency and equity were two different commonly-held goals which were very often in conflict.

The two main approaches to the development strategy are recognized as being the 'balanced growth' and the 'unbalanced growth' approaches. In one version the 'balanced growth' approach maintains that simultaneous investment in a large number of different industries is required to create an effective demand capable of absorbing the production of each industry. 'Therefore, it is argued, to make development possible it is necessary to start at one and the same time a large number of new industries which will be each other's clients through the purchases of their workers, employees and owners'.[12] The second version of the 'balanced growth' approach stresses the existence of external economies which tend to be incorrectly estimated by private investors working on the principle of maximizing the commercial profitability of their own firm individually concerned. 'If 10 projects could be undertaken jointly any one of them would be more profitable than the same project undertaken in isolation'.[13]

The conclusion reached is that a 'big push' must be made and the investment must be planned in a centralized and 'balanced' fashion over a large number of projects of varying sizes that dovetail with each other. It is quite clear that whether one stresses technical interdependence of projects or demand interdependence the balanced growth notion does not at all imply balanced regional growth. On the contrary, the greater the potential interrelationship of the new projects is, the closer together these projects should be located and the greater the geographic concentration of industrial investment should be.

The 'unbalanced growth' approach to economic development recognizes the interdependence of economic activities but adds the all important qualification that since decision-making capability is the principal scarce resource in developing countries, a balanced growth path is likely to be unfeasible and utopian. It is therefore proposed to take advantage of the stimuli provided by sequential investment decisions and to follow an unbalanced growth path, thus maximizing induced investment and economizing on decision-making capabilities. In brief, the view adopted in a number of UNIDO documents indicates that the efficiency goal is best served by a policy which permits concentration at least in the short run.

Another fundamental question which remains to be answered is that of determining at what level of industrialization an attempt to decentralize industry becomes beneficial in order to achieve further national growth.

It was stated in the conclusions of the UNIDO Ad Hoc Advisory Expert Group Meeting, held in Geneva in 1967, that 'at early stages of development there is a very strong economic and technological tendency for industry to concentrate geographically. Decreasing inequality of regional incomes may occur only at high levels of industrialization. Policies directed to counter-react the tendency towards geographic concentration of industry in developing countries for whatever national objectives, should take into account the possible detrimental effects of industrial decentralization attempts upon the achievement of other national objectives'.[14]

During the Minsk seminar it was stressed that 'the decision of the stage at which it becomes possible to follow industrial decentralization policies without impairing national economic growth brought forth the view that there must be some balance reached among conflicting national goals. Sustained economic growth is one of the main objectives of national planning. It is important therefore to recognize that at least in the early stages of development national growth is fostered by geographic industrial concentration and that a policy of industrial dispersal involves a 'trade-off' between reduction of interregional inequality and national economic growth'.[15]

The view was expressed that some notion of 'balanced regional growth' was necessary for industrial planning. It was also remarked, however, that the notion of balanced regional growth was subject to different interpretations. Among such interpretations might be:

a) equalization of growth rates of different regions;

b) narrowing of the absolute income gap between regions;

c) progressive equalization of per capita of consumption levels.

The last interpretation was preferred provided that it was understood that it did not rule out changes in the distribution of population across regions of a country, i.e. interregional migration. In this connexion it was also generally agreed that the proper concern of regional development policies should be people and not land per se. A country needed to industrialize but not necessarily in each administrative region. Interregional migration could, therefore, permit both exploitation of optimal location patterns and the progressive reduction of per capita income differentials. This clearly suggests that concentration is typical of the take-off stage of development and it leads to the increasing disparity among developed and underdeveloped regions. Or, following W. Alonso, 'polarization, regional inequality or primacy are normally aspects of the early stages of development but there will be a tendency towards 'concentrated decentralization' and equalization as the economy reaches maturity'.[16]

4. STRUCTURE AND MECHANISM OF INDUSTRIAL COMPLEXES

The concept of industrial complexes as a form of implementation of regional plans of industrial development was considered and classified at the UNIDO seminar held in Tashkent in 1964.[17] The following definitions of industrial complexes were adopted:

a) an industrial complex is an ensemble of technologically and economically interconnected industrial units located on a given territory; and

b) an industrial complex may be of a different scale or size depending on the type, number and size of its component industrial units.

Normally an industrial complex ought to be planned and should be developed around one major industry which may compose the core of the complex. This core in most cases would be a heavy industry. Although industrial complexes may form the core of industrial development of an 'economic region' or an 'industrial centre' the notion of industrial complexes is different from that of the territorial concepts of economic regions or industrial districts or centres. The latter may have several industrial complexes and other industries without the interconnexion necessary to form industrial complexes. Basically the two concepts are different and should not be confused. The concept of an economic region or industrial centre remains territorial or spatial in character. It shares, therefore, the unique characteristics of the particular region to which it refers. The notion of an industrial complex is based on the techno-economic characteristics which establish the interconnexion between the industries concerned and, as such, permits the occurrence of similar complexes in different countries or regions.

The concept of an industrial complex has also to be distinguished from that of an industrial estate. The two concepts are different. The industrial complex refers to a group of technologically interconnected industries. The industries on an industrial estate may not be so related. They may only share the common facilities of water, electricity, transportation or factory buildings.

By branches of industry, industrial complexes may tentatively be classified as follows: a) complexes of extracting industry; b) energy complexes; c) building materials complexes; d) metallurgical complexes; e) machine-building complexes; f) chemical complexes; g) food and light industry complexes.

The establishment of industrial complexes requires detailed central planning irrespective of whether they are to be implemented in the public or private sector of the economy. Successive steps have to be taken in the proper order. The first stage is to investigate the needs and possibilities of the key industry, followed by determining the economic effectiveness of the industrial complex.

In planning an industrial complex attention should be given to industrial enterprises which are intended for servicing the population. The next step is to determine the location of the complex, i.e. to define the general area for the establishment of the complex. The location would depend upon the type of industrial complex to be established: a) raw material oriented complexes; b) fuel and power oriented complexes; c) transportation oriented complexes; d) labour force oriented industry complexes; e) market oriented industrial complexes. The next step is the siting of the industrial complex, i.e. fixing a specific site for each of the industrial units. The final stage is the actual construction of the industrial units.

The concept of industrial complexes, usually considered as a means of industrial development within a centrally-planned economy, has at the same time some features in common with the concept of industrial growth poles.

5. POSSIBILITIES OF CREATING POLES OF INDUSTRIAL GROWTH IN DEVELOPING COUNTRIES

An attempt to outline the application of the EEC-Italconsult concept in developing countries has been given in one of the papers to UNIDO's recent seminar on industrial location and regional development. The main findings of this study may be summarized as follows:[18]

According to the EEC-Italconsult concept, the most interesting application for developing countries for the determination and promotion of poles of industrial growth concerns that of a pole based on a given sector or subsector of metal working industries with a system of auxiliary industries and industrial services. This type of pole has the advantage of focusing on one of the main targets of the industrialization of these countries, namely the expansion of the metal working industries, to which is added the expansion of other manufacturing industries with ample markets, with direct and indirect effects on demand concerning the output of important basic industries. In establishing industrial poles in developing countries a distinction must be made between the design of a pole in countries where a) engineering industry is still at an initial stage, and b) in countries where agglomerations of metal working industries already exist on a reasonable scale even though with considerable structural deficiencies.

The creation of industrial poles must be examined in relation to problems of spatial coordination of industrial and urban growth and problems of spatial coordination of economic activities. The latter should be viewed in its dual aspects.

The achievement of an equilibrium of product and income among the various regions of a country and the adequate distribution of industrial activity among developing countries form a common market. In countries with engineering production at an initial stage, industrial policy should be directed towards the determination and direct promotion in an adequately equipped area of an integrated ensemble of main metal working projects together with auxiliary units and the most necessary services. In substance it would mean setting up a nucleus to become the prime modern industrial centre in the country. The nucleus which, from the very outset, offers a modern industrial environment and therefore constitutes a pole of attraction for successive investments in metal working industries and related activities. The ensemble of pole projects, including the existing industries, should be adequate to justify economically the creation of the most essential auxiliary units. For example, a tool shop for medium-small specific tools, a repair and maintenance unit based on a number of sections. These auxiliary units should offer more efficient services than those provided by general repair workshops operating in such developing countries.

The natural growth process of the pole should be sustained by a well-defined industrial policy which, among other measures if necessary, envisages direct promotion of important industrial projects whose delayed creation or non-realization could eventually create a bottleneck in this process.

In developing countries where metal working industries with diversified production lines already exist, the prime objective in creating a pole is to rationalize and modernize the productive structures of the existing industries. Therefore, the pole area coincides with the country's main industrial centre or industrial agglomeration.

On the basis of the industrial development, policy targets of sectoral orientation of the pole are fixed in terms of specific metal working sectors or subsectors. The modernization and re-sizing of the principal industries in the area in set sectors or subsectors should be studied and a selection made of new main plans to be promoted. At the same time, the types and sizes should be determined of the auxiliary industries and other essential intermediate units which will be required according to the new structure of production and its degree of technological specialization.

The new auxiliary industries should, right from the beginning, show a trend towards relatively advanced specialization and cover, with adequate types of units, the whole range of sectoral services.

Also in the field of production, the promotion of a pole in an existing agglomeration of a certain size is a far more complex operation than the creation of a first nucleus in a newly-established pole. This is due both to the amount of investigations, studies and designs collected for, and to the existence of inertial factors in the productive organization of existing industries. To the extent to which the slow insertion of these industries into the new system is envisaged, there must be a corresponding increase in the number of new plants to be created in order to ensure the requisite overall level of intermediate demand to operate the modern new auxiliary industries.

The creation of poles in developing countries implies considerable efforts both in implementing the programme properly and with reference to general industrial policy measures. Especially concerning the simultaneous carrying out of an ensemble of projects, the inherent difficulties are undoubtedly greater in market economy countries than in planned economy countries where the government provides the necessary direct investments.

The creation of industrial poles of growth can assume an important role in regional policies of especially intermediate and larger sized developing countries. In general, however, during the first stage of a country's development, the limited human and economic resources make it necessary to concentrate spatially on industrialization efforts in contrast to aims of balanced regional industrialization.

Judging from the experience of European backward peripheral regions there would be no wishful thinking about future processes of spatial self-equilibrium of production and income. A conflict of sectoral and regional approaches in developing countries has to be faced. This conflict can be settled only by a policy of territorial specialization of industry. The inclusion of spatial planning in policies of industrial development is not a new idea but the poles of industrial growth, as defined in the present report, do represent a new instrument to arrive at such objectives in line with criteria of techno-economic efficiency. The productive specialization and the operational nature of a pole makes it possible to distribute geographically sectoral programmes on metal working and other industrial activities.

6. PLANNING FOR REGIONAL COOPERATION

During the Interregional Seminar on Industrial Location, UNIDO's approach to the problem of regional development was tested and further direct technical assistance was based on its recommendations. This Seminar concentrated on the problem of integrative development among regions within a national economy. The guiding idea of this Seminar and some of the previous meetings was that each region must be developed to its maximum potential. This idea was naturally associated with the problem of choosing the optimum location for industrial enterprises inside a national economy.

Another important point that emerged from the discussion was that in smaller developing countries an economic definition of region might very often result in geographic divisions that overlap national boundaries and that sometimes would be larger than the country itself. It was emphasized that in such cases the need for multi-national co-operation resulting in joint industrial undertakings will arise.

Later on, in response to various requests by regional groupings, UNIDO began to concentrate its effort on supporting technical assistance projects concerned with problems which arise in relation to regional industrial co-operation. In dealing with this problem, UNIDO efforts were focussed on establishing criteria for macro-location of industries in the member countries and studying the mechanism and suitable organizational structure for co-operative arrangements. In the course of this work the social value added (the direct and indirect value-added of projects calculated by means of the shadow prices) and transportation costs were taken as a main criterion for allocating projects. It was recognized that the projects should be located in that country where they accrue the highest social value added for the region as a whole, under the condition that each country receives benefits on an equitable basis, and also that eventually the mutual flow of goods is almost equal. This distribution of benefits must take into account the capital contribution of each participating country. In principle, that allocation should be preferred which, besides satisfying the two restraints, maximizes the social value added for the region. These are the principal positions accepted by UNIDO in its work for regional co-operation.

7. SOCIAL AND ENVIRONMENTAL ASPECTS OF REGIONAL DEVELOPMENT AND LOCATION OF INDUSTRY

Although this subject has manifold dimensions, it was considered appropriate for UNIDO to focus on the areas of interaction between economic and non-economic considerations in industrial locational decisions.

It was recognized that in practice the region becomes the principal setting for the social processes of development. Regional inequalities become apparent in social problems. It was felt, therefore, that the location of new industries is of prime importance for securing a harmonious development, both social and economical.

It was recognized that at the regional level comprehensive approach to planning is needed. It means that economic analysis could not limit itself to pure economic and technical factors as was the case in the classical analysis, but also has to involve social factors.

The most recent UNIDO undertaking of a very preliminary character is connected with an effort to appraise the influence of a number of environmental factors on the location of new industries in developing countries. The first steps are being taken towards elaborating criteria for minimizing environmental disturbances in locating new industrial projects, in making an assessment of total costs and benefits to the community of any particular industrial location choice.

NOTES

1. F. PERROUX, *L'économie du XXe siècle*, Paris, PUF, 1961, pp. 123–245.
2. Among others, the most important were: Seminar on Industrial Complexes (Tashkent, USSR, 1964); Ad Hoc Advisory Expert Group Meeting on Regional Industrial Planning (Geneva, 1967); International Symposium on Industrial Development (Athens, 1967); Seminar on Industrial Location and Regional Development (Minsk, BSSR, 1968).
3. See *Criteria for Location of Industrial Plants (Changes and Problems)*, ID/Conf. 1/B.3.
4. W. ALONSO, *Urban and Regional Imbalances in Economic Development*, Economic Development and Cultural Change, Vol. XVIII, No. 1, October 1968, p. 5.
5. *Report of the Interregional Seminar on Industrial Location and Regional Development*, Minsk, 14–26 August 1968, ID/19, New York, 1969, p. 23.
6. *Industrial Location Planning*, ID/Conf. 1/12, p. 4.
7. Minsk seminar report, *op. cit.*, p. 15.
8. *Industrial Location Planning*, *op. cit.*, p. 22.
9. Minsk seminar report, *op. cit.*, p. 31.
10. W. Alonso, *op. cit.*, p. 5.
11. *Industrial Location Planning*, *op. cit.*, p. 5.
12. A. HIRSCHMAN, *The Strategy of Economic Development*, New Haven, Yale University Press, 1958, p. 185.
13. A. HIRSCHMAN, *op. cit.*, p. 55.
14. *Report of the Ad Hoc Advisory Expert Group Meeting on Regional Industrial Planning*, ID/WG. 9/16, p 5.
15. Minsk seminar report, *op. cit.*, p. 23.
16. W. ALONSO, *op. cit.*, p. 9.
17. *Report of the Interregional Seminar on the Role of Industrial Complexes in Economic Development*, E/C. 5/67.
18. The text of this part of the report has been taken from E.S. Tosco's paper on *The Relevance of Intermediate Industries and Industrial Services for Correct Location Planning*, ID/WG. 9/12, suitable condensed and modified for this particular purpose.

RICCARDO PETRELLA*

C

Vienna Centre activities in the field of regional development and industrial location problems

1. GENERAL AIMS OF THE VIENNA CENTRE

Created in 1963, following a resolution adopted at the twelfth session of the General Assembly of UNESCO, as an autonomous organisation of the International Social Science Council, the Vienna Centre has two main purposes: to promote contacts and cooperation between researchers and institutes in the social sciences of East and West European countries; to launch and coordinate multinational comparative research in the field of human and social disciplines.

One of the major problems on which the Vienna Centre started its research activity in 1964 was the 'Development' problem, in particular the problem of the 'Backward Areas' in the various European countries.

2. BACKWARD REGIONS IN INDUSTRIALISED COUNTRIES

The objective of this project, launched at the end of 1964 under the direction of Professor S. Groenman (University of Utrecht) and Professor P. Turčan (Institute of Economic Research, Bratislava) was to compare, on the basis of material and information provided by the different countries, the concepts relating to the problem of backward regions in industrialized countries as well as the methods employed and the solutions adopted to ensure the development of such regions.

Despite the difficulties existing in view of ensuring a minimum of comparability of the data relating to different countries, for the disparities that exist between the socio-economic systems of the participating countries,

* The author is Director of the European Coordination Centre for Research and Documentation in Social Sciences, Vienna.

the different degrees of industrialization, the differences in the size and the character of the backward regions as well as the variety of economic, social and political measures, *a unified questionnaire* was decided upon, on the basis of which the national reports were to be composed.

Three lines of research were prepared in the questionnaire for the *first stage* of the project:

1. *Typology of the backward regions*: this item was to collate the general concepts of 'region' and 'backward region', the causes and factors of the backwardness and the effects of the backwardness of a region on both the regional and national levels,
2. *Ideas and conceptions concerning the development of these regions*: under this item it was a question of a systematic collation of the various theoretical concepts of the development of backward regions and of the methods of integrating it into the development of the national economy,
3. *Measures intended to ensure the development of the regions concerned*: this item was intended to compare the elaboration of the development objectives of these regions, the character of the institutions concerned, the plans implemented, the concrete measures taken, the role of the agencies responsible for the regional economic policy (respective roles of central and regional agencies), the resources utilised and the investments aiming at development.

The research was carried out during the years 1965–1966 in twelve European countries including Austria, Belgium, Bulgaria, Czechoslovakia, the Federal Republic of Germany, France, Italy, the Netherlands, Poland, Switzerland, the United Kingdom, Yugoslavia. The country reports, as well as four general reports aiming at drawing some comparisons from sociological, institutional and economic points of view, were published in the book *Regional Disequilibria in Europe*, edited by the Vienna Centre in 1968, by the Editions de l'Institut de Sociologie, Brussels.

By 1967 two initiatives had been taken by the European research group in view of pursuing fruitful cooperation and enlarging the platform of the international discussions and exchanges of ideas on regional development problems.

On the one side the aim was to continue the common research focussing the analysis of the *second stage* of the project on some concrete cases of backward regions within the participating countries; on the other, to hold, in cooperation with the International Economic Association, a conference for a detailed confrontation of the experiences in almost all industrialized countries of Western Europe, United States, Socialist Republics of Eastern Europe, in the backward areas policy.

The conference was held in Varenna (Italy) in September, 1967, and its results were published in *Backward Areas in Advanced Countries*, edited by E.A.G. Robinson, MacMillan, London, 1969.

The objectives of the *second stage* (1967–68) were to carry out the following analyses in the participating countries:

a) to study the socio-economic development of a given backward region during the period 1950–1965 on the basis of the greatest amount of available regional statistics and to confront its development with that of another developed region in the country. To this end a common questionnaire was formulated, to be applied by all the participants;

b) the results of the descriptive analysis were to be used for studying:
1. the methods, institutions and measures by which the problems of the backwardness of the chosen region have been integrated into the national economic plan or national economic policy,
2. the relationships and interdependencies between the national sectoral policy and the regional policy implemented in the given region by national and local authorities,
3. the growth pole policy and its eventual application to the development of the investigated region,
4. the consequences on the given region of the processes of economic supranational integration in Western (EEC) and Eastern Europe (COMECON), as well as the policies and countermeasures adopted by these supranational institutions in favour of the backward region.

The backward regions chosen were Southeastern Styria and Southern Burgenland (Austria), Liège (Belgium), Southeast Rhodopes (Bulgaria), Eastern Slovakia (Czechoslovakia), Catalonia (Spain, only in relation to the backward internal areas of the region), Aquitania (France), Apulia (Italy), Noorden des Lands (Netherlands), Legnica-Glogow, Konin, Turoszow (Poland), Eifel (Federal Republic of Germany), Västerbotten (Sweden), Fribourg (Switzerland), Montenegro (Yugoslavia).

Thirteen case studies and eight general reports eleborated in view of some general conclusions were presented and discussed in the course of 1968 and finally published by the Vienna Centre in 1971 in *Le développement régional en Europe*, edited by R. Petrella, by Mouton Publishers, The Hague.

During the discussions the importance and role played in the development policies in favour of the investigated regions by the idea of growth poles and the polarised development policy could be clearly seen. Consequently, the participants decided to devote the analysis of *the third stage* of the project to this important topic. Similar research being carried out in 1967 and 1968 on a world level by the United Nations Research Institute for Social Development, an agreement was reached between this Institute and the Vienna Centre to prepare jointly an expert conference on growth poles and regional policies. The purpose of the meeting, held in Geneva in May, 1969, was, in fact, to assess and evaluate the respective roles of growth poles and growth centres in regional development and planning. The experts group was demanded to pay particular attention to the feasibility of transfer of theories and concept developed and experiences gained in practical planning in industrialized countries to the underdeveloped countries. Finally, the meeting was intended to consider the concept of growth poles within the context of the general theory of polarised development in its various dimensions on the economic, sociological, geographical and urban, institutional and political level in order to ensure a most intensive as possible real inter-disciplinary approach to the problem. The present book presents the updated results of the Geneva Conference with the hope that it will constitute a useful contribution to international discussion of regional policies and planning.

Finally, the Vienna Centre research group pursued in 1969 and 1970 its own programme at a European level, the object of which *(fourth and conclusion stage of the project)* was the investigation of the relationships between the sectoral economic structures and the regional development. A set of research papers was commissioned by the group to some participants who proceeded in their work in close contact with the other members of the group in the participating countries. The items chosen were as follows:

- Agricultural Sector and Regional Development,
- Secondary Activities and Regional Development
- Tertiary Sector and Regional Development
- Transport System and Regional Development
- 'Quartenary' Sector and Regional Development
- Urban Structures and Regional Development
- Regional Development and Optimal Combination of Sectors and Regions.

The reports, as well as the results of discussion at the *final conference* of the project, held in Bonn in 1970, are published in 1972, under the title '*Le développement régional et les secteurs économiques*', edited by R. Pötsch–F. Voigt, by Mouton Publishers, The Hague.

3. THE COST OF URBAN GROWTH

The participants in the *Backward Regions in Industrialized Countries Project* decided, at their concluding conference in Bonn, to maintain the Vienna Centre Research Group and to continue their cooperation in launching a new comparative research on the urbanisation problems.

A draft research proposal was submitted by G. Gaudard and J. Valarché on behalf of the group at the end of 1970 on the problem 'The social and economic cost of urban growth'. In the meantime, the Institute of Town Planning and Architecture, Warsaw, submitted to the Vienna Centre a proposal for a comparative research on the theme: 'Changeability of man's environment and limits of the adaptability of the human organism under the impact of the economic and physical development of towns.'

The Board of Directors of the Vienna Centre approved in April 1971 the two proposals and charged the Secretariat with taking the necessary steps in view of elaborating and implementing a common research programme on the line of the two research proposals. Consequently an exchange of views, notes and proposals took place in 1971 among various interested scientists from Austria, Belgium, Bulgaria, Czechoslovakia, France, Hungary, Italy, the Netherlands, the Federal Republic of Germany, Poland, Romania, Soviet Union, Sweden, Switzerland and Yugoslavia. A first working meeting of representatives of these countries will be organised by the Vienna Centre in February, 1972, in view of discussing, elaborating and approving a definitive common research programme which will probably engage more than 15 research institutes in Eastern and Western Europe for a period of 5 years.

4. THE SOCIO-ECONOMIC FACTORS AFFECTING THE LOCATION OF NEW INDUSTRIES

Launched in 1969, following a preparatory meeting in Belgrade, the aim of this project was to investigate the main factors which have influenced the location of new industries in the various European countries during the fifties and sixties.

Several theoretical disputes among participants in the course of the years 1969 and 1970 on the fundamental problems related to the research design, basic definitions, methods to be used for the common investigations, have finally led the group to limit the area of research to the study of the location factors of some selected growth industries according to the following common research sequency:

1. *Determination of growth industries in each country.* Being impossible to adopt the same criteria in all participating countries, the last but not the least being the diversity of available national and regional statistics, participants were free to use the elements or criteria they wished in order to select the growth industries in each country, as well as the techniques of manipulation of the chosen criteria. However it was demanded that at least use be made of the annual growth rate of the production (or alternatively gross value added), employment and investment.

The period to take into consideration was 10 years, at least divided into 2–3 sub-periods in order to consider the development of the selected growth industries.

2. *Analysis of the territorial distribution of the selected growth industries,* over all regional or provincial administrative units of the country, or if this was impossible, in some particular regions characterised by different levels of development.

3. *Analysis in each country of the interindustrial relations between growth industries and the other activities.* Taking into account the fact that some members of the group have been applying in their previous researches on this problem the input-output techniques, the regression analysis and the interindustrial attraction model, it was agreed, under this point of the programme, to try, according to the statistical facilities provided in each country, to test the hypothesis that interindustrial relations explain the location pattern of growth industries.

4. *Analysis of other location factors at regional level.* Participants were asked to analyse at least in the selected regions characterised by different levels of development (see point 2) the effective role on the location of the chosen growth industry of the following elements:

- wages and salaries
- employment (available labour force, skilled labour, professional training)
- economic policy (governmental subsidies, legislation, facilities)
- financial variable (deposits in regional banks and credits granted in the given region by the bank system)
- political variable (importance and role of local associationist leaders and groups, of trade unions and chambers of commerce, national priorities, strategic resources and so on).

Furthermore, participants were free to investigate all other additional elements which have played a specific role as location factors in the particular country.

The abovementioned research were in the course of execution in 1970 and 1971 in eleven European countries: Belgium, Czechoslovakia, France, Great Britain, Italy, the Netherlands, Poland, Romania, Soviet Union, Sweden and Yugoslavia.

The results of the national studies will be presented and discussed at a general conference in Bordeaux in March, 1972. On that occasion the further steps of the research will also be examined and elaborated.

Bei Fragen zur Produktsicherheit wenden Sie sich bitte an:
If you have any questions regarding product safety,
please contact:

Walter de Gruyter GmbH
Genthiner Straße 13
10785 Berlin
productsafety@degruyterbrill.com